THE HISTORY OF NEW ZEALAND

THE HISTORY OF NEW ZEALAND

Tom Brooking

The Greenwood Histories of the Modern Nations
Frank W. Thackeray and John E. Findling, Series Editors

Greenwood Press
Westport, Connecticut • London

Library of Congress Catalog Cataloging-in-Publication Data

Brooking, Tom, 1949–
The history of New Zealand / Tom Brooking.
p. cm. — (The Greenwood histories of the modern nations, ISSN 1096–2905)
Includes bibliographical references and index.
ISBN 0–313–32356–9
1. New Zealand—History. I. Title. II. Series.
DU420.B745 2004
993—dc22 2004004720

British Library Cataloguing in Publication Data is available.

Library of Congress Catalog Card Number: 2004004720
ISBN: 0–313–32356–9
ISSN: 1096–2905

First published in 2004

Greenwood Press, 88 Post Road West, Westport, CT 06881
An imprint of Greenwood Publishing Group, Inc.
www.greenwood.com

Printed in the United States of America

The paper used in this book complies with the Permanent Paper Standard issued by the National Information Standards Organization (Z39.48–1984).

10 9 8 7 6 5 4 3 2 1

Contents

Series Foreword

The *Greenwood Histories of the Modern Nations* series is intended to provide students and interested laypeople with up-to-date, concise, and analytical histories of many of the nations of the contemporary world. Not since the 1960s has there been a systematic attempt to publish a series of national histories, and, as editors, we believe that this series will prove to be a valuable contribution to our understanding of other countries in our increasingly interdependent world.

Over thirty years ago, at the end of the 1960s, the Cold War was an accepted reality of global politics, the process of decolonization was still in progress, the idea of a unified Europe with a single currency was unheard of, the United States was mired in a war in Vietnam, and the economic boom of Asia was still years in the future. Richard Nixon was president of the United States, Mao Tse-tung (not yet Mao Zedong) ruled China, Leonid Brezhnev guided the Soviet Union, and Harold Wilson was prime minister of the United Kingdom. Authoritarian dictators still ruled most of Latin America, the Middle East was reeling in the wake of the Six-Day War, and Shah Reza Pahlavi was at the height of his power in Iran. Clearly, the past 30 years have been witness to a great deal of historical change, and it is to this change that this series is primarily addressed.

With the help of a distinguished advisory board, we have selected nations whose political, economic, and social affairs mark them as among the most important in the waning years of the twentieth century, and for each nation we have found an author who is recognized as a specialist in the history of that nation. These authors have worked most cooperatively with us and with Greenwood Press to produce volumes that reflect current research on their nations and that are interesting and informative to their prospective readers.

The importance of a series such as this cannot be underestimated. As a superpower whose influence is felt all over the world, the United States can claim a "special" relationship with almost every other nation. Yet many Americans know very little about the histories of the nations with which the United States relates. How did they get to be the way they are? What kind of political systems have evolved there? What kind of influence do they have in their own region? What are the dominant political, religious, and cultural forces that move their leaders? These and many other questions are answered in the volumes of this series.

The authors who have contributed to this series have written comprehensive histories of their nations, dating back to prehistoric times in some cases. Each of them, however, has devoted a significant portion of the book to events of the last thirty years, because the modern era has contributed the most to contemporary issues that have an impact on U.S. policy. Authors have made an effort to be as up-to-date as possible so that readers can benefit from the most recent scholarship and a narrative that includes very recent events.

In addition to the historical narrative, each volume in this series contains an introductory overview of the country's geography, political institutions, economic structure, and cultural attributes. This is designed to give readers a picture of the nation as it exists in the contemporary world. Each volume also contains additional chapters that add interesting and useful detail to the historical narrative. One chapter is a thorough chronology of important historical events, making it easy for readers to follow the flow of a particular nation's history. Another chapter features biographical sketches of the nation's most important figures in order to humanize some of the individuals who have contributed to the historical development of their nation. Each volume also contains a comprehensive bibliography, so that those readers whose interest has been sparked may find out more about the nation and its history. Finally, there is a carefully prepared topic and person index.

Readers of these volumes will find them fascinating to read and useful in understanding the contemporary world and the nations that comprise it. As series editors, it is our hope that this series will contribute to a heightened sense of global understanding as we embark on a new century.

Frank W. Thackeray and John E. Findling
Indiana University Southeast

Preface

Most American students probably know New Zealand as the spectacular backdrop to Peter Jackson's sumptuous movie version of *The Lord of the Rings.* Yet there is really very little in common between Middle Earth and what our best-known pop group once labeled the "Enz of the Earth." New Zealand is ancient geologically, which gives it an unspoiled and undeveloped appearance ideally suited to epic movies of long ago, but in fact it is the last significant landmass to be settled by humans. Even the eastern Polynesians who later became Maori arrived less than a thousand years ago. European, that is, largely British, settlers constituted the second major wave from less than 200 years ago. The very recent influx of Asian migrants and a rapidly growing Maori population mean that the country is still very much in the flux of formation. It remains, in consequence, a country in a hurry. The absence of any human structures of long duration make for an uncertain national identity other than a decided propensity to experiment with social organization, political systems, and the environment. This desire to experiment characterizes every era of New Zealand history and became dominant after the arrival of the Europeans. Yet, while this obsession with change creates unease amongst most New Zealanders, it also makes for a history that is much more exciting, dynamic, and complex than the small size of the population would suggest. This long, thin country's wide range of climates and environments adds to that complexity.

The many American exchange students whom I teach confess that they know little of this remote and small democracy, but they soon express surprise at the range and variety of what is a very short history by global standards. Race relations have worked out in quite distinctive ways, and historical investigation of this subject has produced much innovative scholarship of international importance. Similarly, gender relations have worked rather differently in New Zealand than in neighboring Australia, and this development has also stimulated much excellent scholarship. New Zealand's early experiments with democracy have similarly attracted scholarly investigation, and New Zealand historians have produced a surprisingly large number of political biographies of a high standard. Overseas scholars have been long interested in New Zealand as kind of test case for rapid environmental transformation. New Zealand scholars have been slower to investigate this area, but a new wave of research is now underway. Consequently, New Zealand has produced a surprisingly rich historiography. Naturally, it is not as sophisticated as that of Britain and the United States, where there are massed battalions of historians at work. Nevertheless, New Zealand's modest-sized company has managed to produce scholarship of international standard and interest. Part of the reason for this is the high level of book purchasing and the widespread habit of reading that goes back to the very beginnings of European settlement. Books have been and still are of importance to New Zealanders. Another key factor is the vigorous reassertion of the indigenous people, which has stimulated a mass of scholarship in relation to land claims.

It gives me great pleasure to share this interesting but little known history with the students of another land. I would like to thank Greenwood Press and Kevin Ohe for this opportunity. Marcia Goldstein of Greenwood and Paul Sorrell here in one of the world's most southerly cities smoothed my prose and edited this work with commendable efficiency and skill. I would also like to thank Bill Mooney of the Geography Department at the University of Otago for drawing the maps, which should at least give Americans an idea where we are! Thanks too to several generations of hard-working New Zealand historians, postgraduate researchers, and history teachers without whose labors such a book could never have been written. Thanks also go to those thousands of undergraduate students on whom I have tried out my ideas for the last quarter of a century. Teaching several hundred American exchange students has forced me to make comparisons with American historical examples where possible, and I have tried to continue this practice in the book. Special mention must also be made of our wonderful research libraries, whose underpaid and overworked staff make carrying out research such a pleasure. These libraries deserve the attention of more international scholars, and the creation of Web sites should help in raising their profile. No country has had its history recorded more fully on paper, canvas, audiotape, and still and moving film.

Mention must be made of the help, courtesy, and hospitality I have always received from American historians such as Tom Isern and David Danbohm at North Dakota State; John Findlay at the University of Washington; Richard White at Stanford; Elvin Hatch at Santa Barbara; William Cronon at the University of Wisconsin, Madison; Jim Fleming at Colby College; Sherry Smith at the University of Montana; George Herring and Theda Purdue at the University of Kentucky; Larry Foster at Georgia Tech; John Gates at the College of Worcester; Robert Weir of Bay College; John McNeill at Georgetown; and David Hackett Fischer at Brandeis. I hope that they all can use this book somewhere in their teaching.

Finally, I would just like to mention that my maternal grandfather, an American citizen from New York, and my father, who was always very proud that his French grandmother had been born in Dubuque, Iowa, would both be delighted that I have written a book for such an audience.

Timeline of Historical Events

Ca. 1180	Eastern Polynesians discover and settle New Zealand.
1400	Mini ice age ends return voyaging to Polynesia.
1500	Extinction of the Moa and depletion of seals.
1500–1769	Maori become more warlike as competition for resources intensifies.
1642	Abel Tasman rediscovers New Zealand for Europe.
1769	James Cook rediscovers New Zealand for Britain.
1772	Cook returns and disproves the existence of the Great South Land.
1792	Beginning of sealing.
1793	The flax trade begins.
1794	Beginning of timber trade.
1807	Battle of Te Kai-a-te-Karore in which Ngati Whatua inflict a heavy defeat on Nga Puhi.
1814	Establishment of the CMS mission at Rangihoua in the Bay of Islands.

1820	December 22, Hongi Hika sails for England.
1820–1839	Main period of deep-sea whaling.
1821	October, Hongi begins musket wars.
1821–1823	Te Rauparaha leads a migration of Ngati Toa from Kawhia to the southern North Island.
1823	Arrival of Henry Williams at CMS mission and establishment of Wesleyan Methodist Mission Society mission at Whangaroa.
1828	March 6, death of Hongi.
1829–1844	Main period of onshore whaling.
1830	Te Rauparaha kidnaps and kills Te Maiharanui of Ngai Tahu.
1832	Te Rauparaha takes Kaiapoia pa and decimates Ngai Tahu.
1833	Appointment of James Busby as British resident.
1834	Busby designs Maori flag.
1835	Busby signs Declaration of Independence with Bay of Islands and Hokianga chiefs.
1837	Aborigines Protection Society formed along with report of parliamentary committee on treatment of aboriginal peoples. Captain Hobson recommends the factory system. Baron de Thiery arrives in the Hokianga. December, New Zealand Association formed in London.
1838	Arrival of Bishop Pompallier and the Roman Catholic mission.
1839	New Zealand Association reformed as the New Zealand Company. August 14, Captain Hobson dispatched with final instructions. September-December, Colonel William Wakefield purchases 20 million acres.
1840	January 22, first settlers arrive in Wellington. January 29, Hobson arrives in Bay of Islands. February 6, Treaty of Waitangi signed. May 21, all of New Zealand proclaimed a British colony. September, capital moved to Auckland. First settlers arrive at Wanganui. November 16, New Zealand becomes a Crown colony separate from New South Wales.
1841	March 30, first settlers arrive at New Plymouth.

1842 February 1, first settlers arrive at Nelson. September 10, death of Governor Hobson. First merino sheep arrive in Nelson.

1843 Captain William Cargill and the Reverend Tom Burns take control of the Otago settlement scheme. June 17, Wairau affray in which 22 settlers and 6 Maori are killed. December 23, arrival of Governor Robert FitzRoy.

1844 March 26, abolition of Crown preemption over land sales. July 8, Hone Heke cuts down the flagpole at Kororareka. July 31, sale of Otago block by Ngai Tahu to the New Zealand Company.

1845 The Papahurihia adjustment cult emerges in the Bay of Islands. January 10, Hone Heke cuts down the flagpole at Kororarareka again. March 11, Heke and Kawiti sack Kororareka. May 8, Heke and Kawiti defeat Colonel Hulme at Puketutu. July 1, Heke and Kawiti defeat Colonel Despard at Ohaewai. November 14, arrival of Governor George Grey. Wairarapa opened for sheep farming.

1846 January 11, Despard takes Ruapekapeka pa for Grey. July 23, Grey kidnaps Te Rauparaha. New Zealand Constitution Act passed in the British Parliament to create provinces of New Ulster in the north and New Munster in the south. Marlborough opened for sheep farming.

1847 Grey overcomes Maori resistance at Wanganui and suspends Constitution Act for seven years.

1848 March 23, first setters arrive at Otago. The Crown acquires 20 million acres of South Island land from Ngai Tahu under the Kemp purchase on June 12. September, Grey makes peace with Te Rangihaeata.

1850 December 16, first settlers arrive in Canterbury.

1851 Gold discoveries in Victoria, Australia, stimulate Maori farming as well as pastoral farming by British settlers. Governor Grey introduces cheap rentals for large sheep runs.

1852 Grey's constitution grants virtual self-government under a federal system of provincial councils, introduces a restricted franchise, and largely excludes Maori from political participation.

1853	Grey departs for South Africa, having bought up most of the South Island.
1854	Maori opposition to land sales gathers momentum. May 24, first parliament meets in Auckland.
1855	Provinces win the proceeds of land sales. September 6, Governor Gore-Browne arrives. European population moves ahead of Maori.
1856	Otago drops the sufficient price for land sales. Responsible government and dual control of native affairs (by governor and parliament) introduced on April 18, when Henry Sewell establishes the first responsible ministry.
1858	Te Wherowhero of Ngati Mahuta crowned as Potatau, the first Maori king.
1859	Governor Gore-Browne accepts Teira's offer of land at Waitara and incenses Wiremu Kingi. Hawke's Bay and Marlborough established as separate provinces.
1860	March 17, hostilities break out in Taranaki. June 27, Colonel C. E. Gold defeated at Puketakauere. November 6, Ngati Haua defeated at Mahoetahi by Major General T. S. Pratt. Tawhiao becomes Maori king on the death of his father Potatau.
1861	April 8, Wiremu Tamihana and Governor Browne secure a peace. September, George Grey recalled as governor. June, gold discovered in Otago. Southland breaks away from Otago. Bank of New Zealand founded along with Wright, Roberston and Stephenson and Co. Ltd., stock and station agents.
1863	April 4, Grey occupies Tataraimaka block. May 4, Rewi Maniapoto orders ambush of blockade at Tataraimaka. May 11, Grey declares in favor of Wiremu Kingi's claim to land at Waitara. June 4, Grey retakes Tataraimaka. July 12, General Cameron invades the Waikato with 4,000 troops. October, habeas corpus removed for Maori rebels and land confiscation proposed. November 21, Maori defeated at Rangiriri. Bank of Otago established.
1864	February 1, burning of supply village at Rangiowhia. March 30 to April 2, Cameron defeats Rewi Maniapoto at Orakau.

	April 24, Ngai Te Rangi defeat the British at Gate Pa near Tauranga. June 21, British avenge Gate Pa at Te Ranga. December, confiscation authorized.
1865	March 2, the missionary Carl Sylvius Volkner killed by Hauhaus at Opotiki as a spy. Native Land Court established. Capital moved from Auckland to Wellington.
1866	Scorched-earth policy implemented in Taranaki by General Trevor Chute.
1867	First four Maori parliamentary seats established. Maori schools set up to amalgamate Maori children.
1868	Titokowaru begins successful resistance in South Taranaki until November. November 10, Te Kooti raids Matawhero and kills 70. November 13, Europeans and Ropata Wahawaha avenge Te Kooti at Ngatata hill near Gisborne by executing 120.
1869	Te Kooti's raids continue in the central and eastern North Island. Julius Vogel becomes colonial treasurer.
1870	June 28, Vogel introduces the idea of taking a large loan in his public works budget. Large-scale public works and immigration begins. Secret ballot introduced.
1871	Otago Girls' High School established as one of the first half-dozen public girls' secondary schools in the world.
1872	Cessation of hostilities as Te Kooti escapes to the King Country. National Bank established.
1873	Repudiation movement in the Hawke's Bay wins the appointment of a commission of inquiry into alienation of Maori lands in the area. Dalgety's Stock and Station Agency commences operations. New Zealand Shipping Company established in Christchurch. Mosgiel Woollen Mills begins production.
1874	Union Steamship Company founded at Port Chalmers near Dunedin.
1875	Women ratepayers entitled to vote in local body elections.
1876	Abolition of the provincial system. New Zealand connected to the international telegraph cable.

1877 Establishment of county and borough councils. Introduction of compulsory, free, and secular primary education. October 9, George Grey elected premier. Kate Edger first women to graduate B.A. New Zealand and Australian Land Company formed.

1878 Grey ministry introduces women's franchise bill. Collapse of City of Glasgow Bank.

1879 Collapse of British grain farming; long depression ensues. New Zealand secures another £10 million loan. October 8, Hall ministry defeats Grey government. Hall introduces women's franchise bill.

1880 New Zealand Seamen's Union founded. James Pope appointed director of native schools.

1881 November 5, Parihaka invaded and Te Whiti arrested. December 9, a country quota of 28 percent weighting introduced to protect rural voters being swamped by more populous city electorates.

1882 February 15 to May 24, first successful shipment of refrigerated meat to London. First cooperative dairy factories established at Edendale in Southland and on the Otago Peninsula. Male franchise broadened and secret ballot introduced. William Rolleston introduces a perpetual lease with right of purchase. Women empowered to vote for licensing committees.

1884 Married Women's Property Act passed and Women's Christian Temperance Union branch formed in Invercargill. August 19, Stout-Vogel ministry wins in an endeavor to save the beleaguered New Zealand Agricultural Company. King Tawhiao visits London.

1885 Women's Christian Temperance Union founded on a colonial basis. Kotahitanga (unity) movement appoints a committee of 30 to check the progress of legislation in Wellington.

1886 John Ballance introduces village settlement scheme for part-time farmers.

1887 John Ballance introduces small grazing runs for struggling sheep farmers. August 29, Women's Suffrage Bill almost passes the House of Representatives. October 11, Harry Atkinson defeats the Stout-Vogel ministry in an election where colonywide sectoral organizations make their first appearance.

1888 Atkinson introduces a modest tariff. September to December, the sweating scandal breaks in Dunedin.

1889 July 11, formation of the Tailoresses' Union. September 2, introduction of universal male suffrage and abolition of plural voting. October 28, Maritime Council formed to unite new unions of the unskilled. Free kindergartens established in Dunedin.

1890 August to November, maritime strike. December 5, confused election result, which persuades Premier Atkinson to stack the Legislative Council.

1891 A definite Liberal government emerges by March. Factories Act passed to limit employment of women and children, labor bureau set up to find work for the unemployed, and Truck Act passed to ensure payment in wages. Mild land tax introduced to encourage subdivision of the great estates. Ballance and Seddon appeal to the Privy Council in London to break the power of the Legislative Council.

1892 Ballance falls ill, and Seddon takes over as leader. Employers' Liability Act passed to provide compensation for employees, and Labor Bureau becomes Department of Labor. October 8, McKenzie introduces lease-in-perpetuity after establishing the Department of Agriculture. Women's Franchise League founded. Kotahitanga formally constituted at Waitangi and forms own parliament.

1893 McKenzie purchase Cheviot estate. May 1, Seddon becomes leader on death of Ballance. Joe Ward secures £3 million loan. 30,000 signature presented by New Zealand women demanding the vote. Women win the vote on September 19. November 28, Liberals win big mandate of 51 to 20 seats. Colonial Bank in trouble. McKenzie increases Crown monopoly over Maori land sales, and King Tawhiao bans Europeans from New Zealand.

1894 McKenzie passes Land for Settlements Act, and Ward establishes Advances to Settlers' Office. Reeves introduces the industrial conciliation and arbitration system. King movement establishes its own parliament. King Tawhiao dies. Native

Rights Bill rejected, and McKenzie reintroduces virtually full Crown preemption over Maori land sales.

1895 Liberals rescue the Bank of New Zealand, which absorbs the troubled Colonial Bank. Grace Neill becomes first woman inspector of factories, and *Daybreak,* the journal of the National Council of Women, begins publication.

1896 Upturn for agricultural commodity prices begins heralding a virtually unbroken period of economic prosperity down to 1921. Reeves promoted to agent-general in London. Emily Siedeberg becomes first women doctor in New Zealand. Native Rights Bill thrown out by parliament again. December 4, Liberals win 40 of 70 seats.

1897 Seddon attends Queen Victoria's golden jubilee in London. Ethel Benjamin becomes the first woman lawyer in New Zealand. Te Aute Students' Association formed.

1898 Old age pensions introduced. April 15, Seddon established Lib-Lab Association. Divorce Act makes it possible for women to divorce violent, drunken, and unfaithful husbands.

1899 September 28, New Zealand joins Boer War effort and sends troops on October 21. December 6, Liberals win 52 of 70 seats and restore their parliamentary dominance.

1900 September 28, New Zealand annexes Cook Islands. Testators' Family Maintenance Act passed to force maintenance payments and protect women in inheritance cases. Incest also moved out of canon law and into civil law. Seddon passes Maori Councils Act with Apirana Ngata as organizing secretary to increase Maori participation in local government and land sales.

1901 New Zealand rejects federation with Australia. Registration of nurses made compulsory.

1902 August, formation of New Zealand Farmers' Union and Employers' Federation. The Maori king Mahuta appointed to Legislative Council. November 25, Liberals win 52 of 80 seats.

1903 Free places introduced in secondary schools for academically able children. September 9, William Massey takes over as leader of the opposition.

1904 Registration of midwives made compulsory.

1905 Massey establishes reform leagues at local level. Seddon introduces St. Helen's hospitals for working-class mothers. Apirana Ngata elected for the northern Maori seat. December 6, Liberals win 61 of 80 seats.

1906 June 10, death of Seddon. August 8, Joe Ward becomes premier. June, the Maori prophet Rua Kenana waits for King Edward VII in Gisborne.

1907–1909 Brief recession.

1907 Stout-Ngata Commission into Maori land appointed, and Tohunga Suppression Act passes. September 26, New Zealand granted Dominion status. Ward drops lease-in-perpetuity. Plunket Society founded in Dunedin to promote more scientific methods of child raising. Dental school opened in Dunedin.

1908 June 23, Rua meets Premier Ward at Whakatane. August 4, Blackball strike results in formation of the New Zealand Federations of Miners in October. Quackery Prevention Act passed to stop sale of fraudulent medicines. November 24, North Island small farmers challenge Liberal dominance, but Liberals win 51 of 80 seats.

1909 February, Reform adopted as name of the opposition. October, creation of the Federation of Labor or Red Feds. Te Rangi Hiroa (Peter Buck) elected MP for Northern Maori. Home Science School opened at the University of Otago.

1910 Formation of the New Zealand Sheep Owners' Federation. 1909 Defence Act passed into law to introduce compulsory military training. One million population mark passed.

1911 Census shows that a majority of New Zealanders now live in towns. Widows' pensions introduced. December 7 and 14, close election result and New Zealand nearly goes dry. Maui Pomare elected MP for western Maori.

1912 May to November, bitter gold miners' strike in Waihi. District nurses introduced. Cost of Living Commission reveals rising expectations of the population. July, Massey wins power after the Liberal government of Thomas Mackenzie loses a vote of confidence. Massey immediately introduces the right to freehold leasehold properties at original valuation.

1913 January 21, United Federation of Labor formed. October 22 to November 28, Watersiders' strike.

1914–1918 Over 100,00 men serve in First World War, with 17,000 deaths and 41,000 serious casualties.

1914 August 5, New Zealand declares war on Germany. October 16, 8,574 men sail as first Expeditionary Force. December 10, Massey retains office by 41 seats to 39.

1915 April 25, Gallipoli landing. August 8–9, New Zealanders take, then lose Chunak Bair. Commandeer introduced for frozen meat. August 12, coalition government formed.

1916 April 15, New Zealanders enter western front at Armentières and the Maori Pioneer Battalion formed. July 7–8, Labor Party formed. August 1, introduction of conscription. Commandeer introduced for wool and cheese. September 15, New Zealanders join the battle of the Somme.

1917 July 11, Protestant Political Association formed. Six o'clock closing of hotels introduced. Early June, New Zealanders win some gains at Messines. Commandeer introduced for butter. October 9–18, disaster at Passchendaele. Ngata recruits Maori while Princess Te Puea opposes enlistment.

1918 March 25–30, New Zealanders help halt the German spring offensive. August to November 5, New Zealanders advance with Allied troops. November 4–5, New Zealanders take the walled city of le Quesnoy. Influenza epidemic spreads rapidly from Armistice Day on November 11. Ratana has visions during the flu outbreak, which ravages the Maori population, and a new Maori leader emerges.

1919 April 10, New Zealand votes to go dry, but returning soldiers reverse the result. June 28, New Zealand signs the peace treaty and becomes a founding member of the League of Nations. Country Women's Institute arrives in New Zealand from Canada. Te Rangi Hiroa appointed medical officer for Maori health. December 17, Massey's government returned by 46 of 80 seats; formation of the Alliance of Labor; and women given the right to stand for parliament.

1921	Recession arrives in New Zealand, and civil service salaries cut by 7 percent. Introduction of the dental nurse service. Princess Te Puea builds Turangawaewae model pa at Ngaruawahia, and Gordon Coates becomes minister of native affairs.
1922	Establishment of the Meat Board and formation of the Country Party. December 7, Labor wins central city seats and threatens the Liberals as official opposition. Reform win 39 seats, Liberals 22, Labor 17, and Independent 3.
1924–1926	A time of recovery and considerable public works.
1924	The borstal system introduced for young offenders.
1925	May 10, Massey dies. May 30, Gordon Coates takes over as the first New Zealand-born prime minister (Francis Dillon Bell only held the post temporarily until Coates's appointment). November 4, Coates and Reform easily win the election by 25 seats to 25 for all opposition parties. Child welfare system and children's courts introduced. Women's Division of the Farmers' Union established.
1926	Dairy Board established. September 9, family allowance introduced. Establishment of the Department of Scientific and Industrial Research, the Dairy Research Institute, and Massey Agricultural College. Ngata sets up carving school in Rotorua. Sim Commission recommends compensation for Waikato and Taranaki tribes.
1927	Economic prosperity recedes as debt climbs. Late March, Labor abandons usehold policy. United Party established under Joe Ward, made up of the remnants of the old Liberals and the business wing of Reform.
1928	December, Joe Ward narrowly wins the election with Labor's support. Ratana turns his attention to politics; Ngata becomes native minister in the United government and F. A. Bennett appointed first Maori Bishop of Aotearoa.
1929	Ward tries 1890s land settlement solutions and increase the land tax, but fails to head off economic depression. Te Puea opens Mahinarangi meeting house, and Ngata wins state funding for Maori farming.

1930 Arrival of the Great Depression. May 28, Ward resigns and George Forbes takes over as prime minister. June Ward dies July 8.

1931 February 2, Hawke's Bay earthquake kills 256 people. February, hated No. 5 scheme of public works introduced to ease unemployment. March, 10 percent salary cuts introduced for civil servants. September 18, coalition government of United and Reform Parties formed. Agreement secured between Ratana and Labor before the election. December, the coalition wins the election by 51 seats to Labor's 25.

1932 Unemployment rises to record levels of 80,000 or more. April 8 and 11, riots in Dunedin. April 15 and 16, riots in Auckland. May 10, riots in Wellington. Eruera Tirakatene wins the southern Maori seat.

1933 Coates establishes the Reserve Bank and devalues the pound. William Downie Stewart resigns as minister of finance in protest.

1933 January, New Zealand pound devalued and taken off parity with Sterling. Reserve Bank established. February 8, the quasi-fascist New Zealand Legion formed. October 12, Savage takes over as Labor leader after death of Harry Holland.

1934 Election delayed for a year as an economy measure. July, dole introduced. September, right-wing Democrat Party formed. Dairy Commission presents a bleak report. Ngata resigns as native minister.

1935 November 24, coalition government jams Uncle Scrim's broadcast. November 27, Labor wins the election by 55 to 19 seats and restores pensions for Christmas.

1936 Primary Products Marketing Act passed, and guaranteed prices for butter introduced. Compulsory unionism introduced. May 13–14, National Party formed with Adam Hamilton as leader. Ngata calls *hui* of all Maori tribes.

1937 Education conference. April, Federation of Labor reformed. John A. Lee establishes Housing Construction Department.

1938 February to April, serious land slips and flooding in the east coast of the North Island. April 2, Savage promises welfare state based around social security. October 15, Labor wins election by 53 to 25 seats with 56 percent of the vote. Paraire Piakea wins northern Maori for Ratana. December, Labor introduces exchange controls and import licensing.

1939 September 3, New Zealand declares war on Germany. October, Maori Battalion formed under its own command.

1940 January 5, First Echelon sails. Centenary celebrations in February. March 25, John A. Lee expelled from Labor Party. March 27, death of Savage; Fraser takes over as prime minister. July 16, war cabinet of three government and two opposition members created.

1941 March to early May, defeat in Greece. May 20–27, defense of and evacuation from Crete. December 8, New Zealand declares war on Japan.

1942 May 27–28, United States wins battle of the Coral Sea. June, New Zealand troops fight their way out of Axis ambush at Minqar Quaim. October 23 to November 11, battle of El Alamein. American marines arrive in New Zealand. Maori War Effort Organization established.

1943 May, Afrika Corps surrender. November, Italian campaign begins. September, National MPs withdraw from war cabinet. November, Labor wins election by 45 to 35 seats, and Ratana win all 4 Maori seats.

1944 January 21, Canberra pact signed with Australia. February-March, battle for Cassino and withdrawal from Pacific begins. Introduction of compulsory secondary education.

1945 May 2, New Zealand troops take Trieste. May 8, end of war in Europe. September 2, end of war against Japan. New Zealand pushes for a role for small nations in the UN, and government passes Maori Social and Economic Advancement Act and nationalizes Bank of New Zealand in December.

1946 November 27, Labor wins election with support of four Maori MPs.

1947 New Zealand reluctantly gives up its Dominion status for full nationhood. *Maori* replaces *Native* in official usage. *Landfall* begins publication.

1949 August 3, Fraser introduces peacetime conscription. November 30, National wins government by 46 seats to 34, with Sidney Holland as the new prime minister.

1950 July 26, New Zealand enters Korean War. August 18, Legislative Council abolished.

1951 February, waterfront strike crushed by the Holland government. September 1, snap election won by National 50 seats to 30, and ANZUS Pact signed. Maori Women's Welfare League established.

1952 New Zealand's population passes the 2 million mark.

1953 The new British Queen Elizabeth II visits New Zealand and meets the Maori king, Koroki. December 24, Tangiwai railway disaster in which 151 people die.

1954 Social Credit League formed. Marzengarb inquiry into juvenile delinquency. November 13, National wins the election 45 seats to 35.

1956 January 23, New Zealand forces begin operations in Malaysia. New Zealand beats the Springboks (South African rugby team) in home series.

1957 September 20, Keith Holyoake becomes prime minister on death of Sid Holland. November 30, Walter Nash leads Labor to election victory by one seat. Janet Frame's *Owls Do Cry* published.

1958 June 26, black budget introduced to cope with exchange crisis.

1960 Introduction of television. Equal pay for women employed in the public sector introduced. New Zealand. Maori Council established, and small opposition to rugby tour of South Africa. November 26, Keith Holyoake leads National to victory by 12 seats.

1961 Hunn report on Maori assimilation published, and Maori Education Foundation set up.

1963 April 1, Arnold Nordmeyer elected leader of the Labor party. November 30, National wins election by 10 seats.

1964	June, New Zealand engineers arrive in Vietnam. Massey Agricultural College expanded into a full university. Downstage Theater opens in Wellington.
1965	July, New Zealand artillery arrives in Vietnam. December 16, Norman Kirk elected leader of the Labor Party.
1966	November 26, National win election by nine seats. Vernon Cracknell takes Hobson for Social Credit.
1967	Serious trade deficit for the first time since the early 1930s. Robert Muldoon becomes minister of finance. Abolition of six o'clock closing for hotels. Lloyd Geering, Presbyterian theologian, faces heresy charge. *New Zealand Journal of History* begins publication. Maori Affairs Amendment Act accelerates alienation of Maori land.
1968	Waikato University opened. Mercury Theater opens in Auckland. April 10, *Wahine* disaster costs 51 lives as the inter-island ferry sinks in a massive storm.
1969	November 29, National wins election by six seats and wins Hobson back from Social Credit.
1970	*Up from Under* published as the first periodical of the second-wave feminist movement. Nga Tamatoa (Young Warriors) founded in Auckland to express dissatisfaction of Maori youth.
1971	Vietnam protests reach their height. Census shows 60 percent of Maori are living in cities.
1972	February 7, Holyoake retires and John Marshall takes over as prime minister. New Zealand Film Commission established. Court Theater opens in Christchurch. November 25, Norm Kirk leads labor to election victory by 23 seats. December, equal pay for women in the private sector introduced; no-fault accident compensation recommended; compulsory military training ended; and troops brought home from Vietnam. *Broadsheet* begins publication as a voice of radical feminism, and Witi Ihimaera's *Pounamu, Pounamu* is the first set of short stories published by a Maori writer.
1973	Labor sends a frigate to Muroroa to protest French nuclear testing in the Pacific. Britain joins the European Economic Community. Overseas debt reaches $1 billion. New Zealand's

population passes the 3 million mark, and New Zealand Author's Fund established.

1974 First oil shock. British people mandate their membership of the EEC. Accident compensation scheme enacted. Second television channel and color television introduced. Maori Affairs Amendment Act tries to promote biculturalism. July 9, Muldoon becomes leader of the National Party. August 31, Norm Kirk dies. Wallace (Bill) Rowling takes over as prime minister. September 21, franchise extended to 18 year olds.

1975 September to October, massive Maori land march to Wellington. Waitangi Tribunal and Women's Electoral Lobby established. November 29, Muldoon wins election for National by 23 seats.

1976 July 23, national superannuation scheme introduced at age 60. Significant unemployment appears for the first time since 1938.

1977 February 19, Bruce Beethan wins a by-election for Social Credit. Ngati Whatua protest development of tribal land at Bastion Point in Auckland.

1978 May 25, massed police and army remove protestors from Bastion Point. Eva Rickard occupies Raglan golf course. Sonja Davies is the first women elected to the federation of labor executive. Muldoon releases Think Big strategy for economic development. Closer Economic Relations agreement proposed with Australia. November 25, National's electoral majority reduced to 11 seats.

1979 September 6, Gary Knapp wins for Social Credit in by-election. Matui Rata forms the Mana Motuhake (Maori Sovereignty) Party and breaks from Labor.

1980 Working Women's Charter passed by the Federation of Labor.

1981 Springbok rugby tour divides the nation. November 28, Muldoon hangs on because of the support of provincial seats by 46 to Labor's 44 and Social Credit's 2. Mana Motuhake second to Labor in the Maori electorates.

1982 Sue Wood becomes the first woman president of the National or any other political party in New Zealand.

1983 February 3, David Lange replaces Rowling as leader of the Labor Party.

1984 Unemployment soars toward 100,000. Entrepreneur Robert Jones forms a free market New Zealand Party. July 14, Lange leads Labor to victory by 19 seats at snap election. Exchange and constitutional crisis follows immediately after the election. Antinuclear policy implemented despite stiff American and British opposition. Ann Hercus becomes the first minister of women's affairs. Margaret Wilson becomes the first woman president of the Labor Party. Donna Awatere publishes *Maori Sovereignty*. Te Maori exhibition opens in New York.

1985 Labor moves to the right as the dollar is floated. Roger Douglas launches a program of corporatization of the civil service, winds up tariffs, and opens the economy to the world. A goods and services tax (GST) on all transactions introduced, and the progressive rates lowered. July 10, bombing of the *Rainbow Warrior* by French frogmen in Auckland harbor. Waitangi Tribunal given power to make recommendations on land dealings back to 1840. Keri Hulme's *The Bone People* wins the Booker (English literary) Prize.

1986 Free market reforms accelerated. August 16, Te Maori Exhibition opens in Wellington. December, the Homosexual Law Reform Bill makes homosexuality legal.

1987 The Maori Council wins the right to stop Crown land being transferred to the new state owned enterprises and Treaty of Waitangi to apply to any such lands. This decision unleashes an avalanche of new treaty claims over land grievances. August-September, All Blacks win inaugural Rugby World Cup. October, share market crash. Lange lead Labor to electoral victory over National's Jim McLay by 19 seats.

1988 Royal Commission on Social Policy reports arguing for targeting of welfare. Gibb Report recommends more business-like approach to running the health system. Picot Report recommends greater parent input into school governance.

1989 Reserve Bank Act passed to secure price stability by empowering an independent governor to hold annual inflation under 2 percent. GST raised from 10 to 12.5 percent. Post Bank sold to the Australia New Zealand Bank. New Zealand Steel, Coal Corp, and State Insurance privatized. School boards of trustees meet for the first time. Sunday trading begins, and third television channel begins broadcasting. Jim Anderton leaves Labor to form the more left-leaning New Labor Party. August 8, David Lange resigns as prime minister. Labor moves right under Geoffrey Palmer. Bastion Point returned to Ngati Whatua. Maori Fisheries Act grants 10 percent of the fishery to Maori, and the Department of Maori Affairs abolished. Its responsibilities devolved to Te Tira Ahu Iwi or Iwi Transition Agency and new Manuta Maori (Ministry of Maori Affairs) takes over policy advisory role.

1990 February, both Queen Elizabeth II and the Maori Bishop Wharehuia Vercoe criticize New Zealand race relations at the Sesquecentennial (150th) celebrations. Telecom sold to an American-dominated overseas consortium. Limited Bill of Rights passed. First volume of *Dictionary of New Zealand Biography* published. Palmer deposed and replaced by Mike Moore as prime minister on September 4. Successful Commonwealth Games held in Auckland. National win a landslide election under new leader Jim Bolger by 37 seats. New National government introduces welfare cuts in December. National Congress of Tribes established.

1991 Welfare benefits cut further by over $1 billion. Unemployment passes 200,000, and inflation falls under 2 percent. March, Winston Peters launches Ka Awatea (the new dawn) and announces establishment of a Ministry of Maori Development (Te Puni Kokiri). May, Employment Contracts Act passed, abolishing compulsory unionism. August, Gilbert Miles and Hamish McIntyre leave National to form a new Liberal Party, and New Zealand troops serve with the United States in the Gulf War in Iraq. October, Winston Peters sacked as minister of Maori affairs. December, New Labor, Mana Motuhake, the Greens, and Democrats (old Social Credit) coalesce into the Alliance Party.

1992 January 1, Te Puni Kokiri commences operations, and Iwi Transition Agency phased out two years early. New Zealand wins seat on United Nations Security Council. August, Sealord fisheries deal secured under Maori Fisheries Treaty of

Waitangi Act. October, Peters dismissed from National party. Regional Health Authorities and Crown Health Authorities established to provide a funder/provider split in health administration. University fees raised substantially, and loans scheme at market rate of interest introduced. Fran Wild becomes the first woman to be elected mayor of a major metropolitan center (Wellington).

1993 April, Peters wins by-election against his own party and launches the New Zealand First Party in July. New Zealand Rail sold to the Wisconsin Central Transport Company. Centenary of women's suffrage celebrated, and Dame Silvia Cartwright becomes the first woman judge of the high court. October, National hangs onto power once Labor's Peter Tapsell accepts the job of speaker of the house. The electorate votes 53 to 47 percent in favor of a change of electoral system from the old British first past the post to the West German mixed member proportional representation (MMP). Jane Campion's film *The Piano* wins international acclaim.

1994 May, New Zealand troops sent to Bosnia as peacekeepers. Roger Douglas and Richard Prebble found the ACT (Association of Consumers and Taxpayers) Party. Treasury tries to set a limit of $1 billion on treaty land grievance claims (the so-called fiscal envelope). Unemployment starts to fall. Alan Duff's novel *Once Were Warriors* is made into a movie, which wins critical acclaim

1995 February, Waitangi Day celebrations canceled, and Ken Mair occupies Motua Gardens in Wanganui. March Prime Minister Bolger meets President Bill Clinton in the White House, the first such meeting since 1984. May, New Zealand wins America's Cup from American yachtsmen in San Diego. June, United Party formed by seven breakaway MPs, four National, and three Labor, led by Clive Matthewson. Christian Heritage Party launched by Graham Lee. Broadcasting Corporation of New Zealand private radio stations sold off. All Maori reject fiscal envelope proposal, and in November Waikato Raupatu Claims Settlement Act provides $187 million and a government apology as reparations for the Tainui tribes. November, Commonwealth heads of government meet in Auckland, and Nelson Mandela visits New Zealand.

1996 April, Te Runanaga o Ngai Tahu Act establishes this *iwi* as a full legal entity and $170 million pay in reparations by October. July, Danyon Loader wins New Zealand's first two gold medals for swimming at the Olympics. August, Taranaki settlement condemns genocide practiced against Taranaki tribes and pays $145 million in reparations. Some 271 farms held on lease-in-perpetuity by Pakeha used as part of the compensation. September, $40 million settlement offered to Whakatohea tribe, but rejected. October, the first MMP election produces a hung parliament with powerbroker Winston Peters eventually siding with a National-led coalition government.

1997 The National/New Zealand First Coalition wobbles under pressure of the Asian financial crisis. December 8, Jenny Shipley replaces Bolger as National's leader after a bloodless coup and become New Zealand's first woman prime minister.

1998 Shipley breaks up the coalition and hangs on with the support of United's Peter Dunne and the votes of the maverick Alamein Kopu. A successful visit by President Clinton in late 1998 does little to shore up the coalition's declining fortunes.

1999 The Greens break from the Alliance, and Labor under Helen Clark's leadership soars in popularity. Ongoing scandals and declining economic indicators ensure that Labor wins comfortably and forms a coalition with the Alliance (Jim Anderton serving as deputy prime minister) and general support from the Greens, who won seven seats. This guarantees the government 66 out of 120 votes within parliament. New Zealand retains the America's Cup.

2000 Millennium celebrations fail to produce a tourist boom, but the steady as she goes policies of the new centrist government are helped by high commodity prices. Despite constant initial criticism by big business, the economy picks up. Dairying, especially, booms down to 2002, and growth climbs to 4 percent per annum.

2001 Unemployment drops to under 6 percent of the workforce, and some New Zealanders begin to return from overseas. September 11 hurts the New Zealand tourist industry, and the government is forced to bail out Air New Zealand in

October. The crack SAS unit is sent to Afghanistan. December, first of Peter Jackson's film trilogy of *The Lord of the Rings* launched to international critical acclaim and big audiences.

2002 The Alliance Party disintegrates, and Jim Anderton forms a Progressive Coalition Party. Helen Clark decides to call an early election in September and wins relatively easily with 41 percent of the vote, despite an emotional fallout with the Greens over genetic engineering The socially conservative United Futures Party does as well as the Greens, winning 8 seats, and forms a coalition with Labor and Anderton's 2-seat party. The Greens with 9 seats generally support the Labor coalition, giving it 62 safe votes and usually 71 votes in parliament. National slumps to an all-time low of 21 percent of the vote and 27 seats despite the best efforts of new leader Bill English.

2003 The Iraq war and the SARS scare hurt the New Zealand economy, but the small nation remains relatively prosperous. New Zealand refrains from supporting Australia, the United States, and Britain in Iraq, but sends engineers to help with reconstruction as it had done in East Timor and Afghanistan. English and National continue to languish in the polls despite several government mistakes. The electorate awaits the end of the GMO moratorium in October with interest.

1

Geography, Environment, Peoples, and Government

ISOLATION

To the outsider, New Zealand's most distinctive feature is the country's extraordinary isolation, or what the nineteenth-century English novelist Anthony Trollope called "the feeling of awful distance." No other major place of human settlement is situated so far from other large centers of population. New Zealand's closest large neighbor is Australia some 1,200 miles away—farther than the distance from Los Angeles to Chicago, or from New York to the Grand Canyon. The nearest continent is South America, over 4,000 miles to the east, while Asia lies 5,000 miles to the north, or over 10 hours' flying time away. Americans living in Alaska, the remotest parts of the Midwest, or the Deep South are still much closer to major centers of population. The role of distance is accentuated by the fact that the largest group of settlers came from Britain, over 12,000 miles away.

This extreme geographical isolation, coupled with a relatively small population of 4 million, has made New Zealand particularly vulnerable in terms of both economic development and defense. New Zealand has had no option but to trade and has always been dependent on one of two major world powers—Britain and the United States—to defend its long

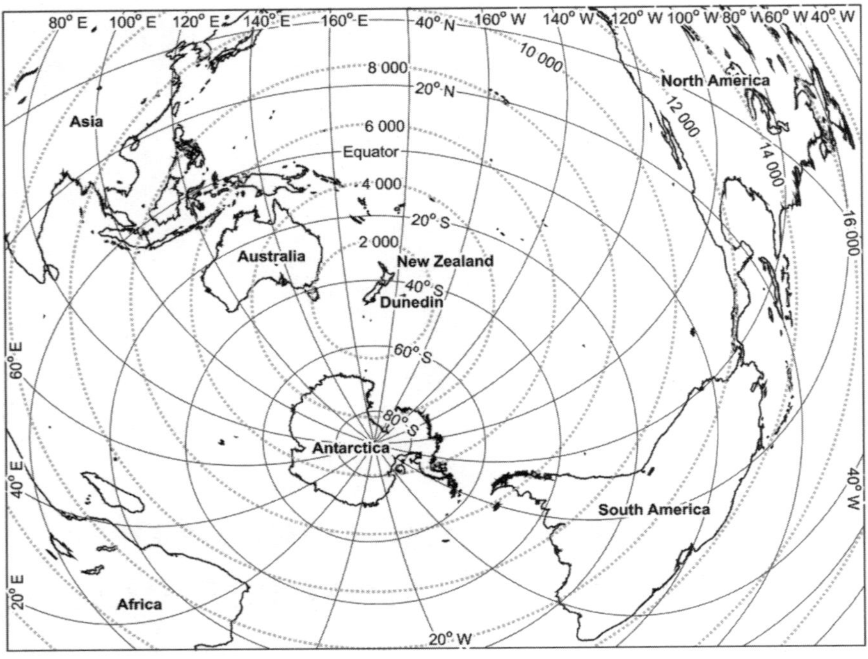

New Zealand's isolated place in the world.

coastline of over 6,000 miles. (The numerous indentations of bays and inlets make New Zealand's coastline more extensive than that of the United States.)

PEOPLING

Yet the impact of isolation should not deflect attention from the second major feature that strikes outsiders: New Zealand is the last major settlement in human history, partly *because* of its sheer remoteness. Even the eastern Polynesian people who became Maori have occupied the country for less than a thousand years. This is late indeed, even when compared with the First Nation peoples of North America who trudged across the ice bridges of the Bering Strait some 13,000 years ago, let alone with the Aborigines of neighboring Australia who began to settle perhaps 60,000 years ago. Europeans began arriving in numbers only in the nineteenth century, by which time the Industrial Revolution was well underway and the forces of modernity were marching forward relentlessly.

New Zealand as a political entity came into being only in 1840 and was born modern. From its beginnings, industries such as sealing, whaling, and timber milling locked it into the networks of global capitalism. Sailing ships, followed by steam ships, then airplanes, and from the 1960s jet airliners have broken down what the Australian historian Geoffrey Blainey has called the "tyranny of distance." Connection to the international cable system from 1876, the expansion of telephone services soon after, the popularity of radio from the 1920s, then television after 1960, and the widespread use of the fax machine and Internet in the 1990s have enabled New Zealand to enjoy full and active membership in the global village. As a result, today's visitor to New Zealand finds a country apparently little different from many others in the developed world. Yet the distinctive environment and history of this group of large and mountainous islands covering 103,000 square miles (about the same area as Colorado) and stretching over 1,000 miles from north to south (from subtropical 34 degrees to subarctic 47.5 degrees south) make any similarities rather superficial.

ENVIRONMENT AND GEOGRAPHY

Less than a quarter of the New Zealand landmass lies below 650 feet, and there are 253 named peaks over 7,000 feet tall. The Dutch explorer Abel Tasman accurately labeled it "a land uplifted high." Extensive mountain ranges drag down precipitation from the surrounding oceans to create an unpredictable climate. In general terms, it is temperate (especially compared with Britain or the northern United States) and lacks the freezing winters and scorching summers of continental countries. But the weather never locks into predictable patterns like those of southern California or the Mediterranean, creating headaches for meteorologists. The country is subject to bouts of severe flooding, while the so-called El Niño and La Nina oscillation produces frequent droughts on the east coast and snowstorms in the mountains—as featured so vividly in Peter Jackson's movie version of *The Lord of the Rings.*

These climatic hazards are amplified by geological instability. New Zealand straddles the large Pacific and Indian-Australian tectonic plates, which are moving in opposite directions. Consequently, earthquakes occur regularly. Among the most destructive were those that leveled Wellington in 1855 (now the capital city, but still a village when the earthquake struck) and flattened the small cities of Napier and Hastings in 1931. Strict building codes and clever engineering initiatives have helped reduce the risks of earthquake damage, but a large event is inevitable, especially in Wellington, which like San Francisco is sited on a fault line. Three large volcanoes in the central North Island are still active, and spectacular eruptions of steam and ash are seen from time to time. New Zealand's largest city, Auckland in the north, is largely free of earthquake risk—although Rangitoto, the volcanic island in the city's Waitemata harbor, erupted as recently as 1500.

Geological instability and frequent floods have not, however, bequeathed great natural wealth to New Zealand. Unlike Australia it is not mineral-

Location of places, rivers, mountains, and lakes mentioned in the text.

rich. Enough gold lay buried to sustain a small gold rush in the nineteenth century, and there is ample coal, but the vital industrial ingredient of iron ore is missing. New Zealand does make steel today, but only by extracting ore from the black sands of beaches on the west coast of the North Island. Bauxite, used in the manufacture of aluminum, and uranium, which is of such importance to the nuclear industry, are abundant in Australia but absent from New Zealand. This dearth of mineral resources is compounded by soils that are rather infertile. Native grasses that evolved over countless millennia through interaction with large flightless birds failed to provide adequate pasture for the cloven-hoofed grazing animals introduced by European settlers. Consequently, they were replaced with English grasses once the extensive rain forests had been removed by chopping and burning. Although nineteenth-century migrants were lured by promises of rich soils, these exist only in pockets, and New Zealand is not ideally suited to European-style stock and crop farming. The large flocks of sheep and herds of dairy cows and domesticated deer that the tourist views today all graze on soils whose fertility is enhanced with vast amounts of artificial fertilizers and chemicals.

In short, New Zealand is a hard land transformed by massive human effort—so that today it presents the appearance of a neo-Europe rather than an ancient piece of the old supercontinent of Gondwanaland. While the southwestern corner of the country still looks much as it did in the time of the dinosaurs 65 million years ago (which is why the BBC filmed much of its *Walking with Dinosaurs* series there), most of the north and east has been transformed more substantially and rapidly than any comparable country. Changes that took two millennia in Europe and four centuries in North America have occurred in New Zealand in little over a hundred years. The most extreme example is seen in the draining of wetlands. New Zealand has removed some 85 percent of these areas, as against 60 percent in Great Britain and the Netherlands, 53 percent in the United States, and 10 percent in France. These swamplands were important places of food-gathering for Maori and were often appropriated by force, or the application of law, before conversion to dairy and sheep farms.

IMMIGRANT MIX

American visitors also notice that New Zealanders are much less ethnically diverse than the population of the United States. In appearance and cultural style, New Zealanders are either Polynesian or British. Maori now make up over 15 percent of the population, and Pacific Islanders, mainly from Western Samoa, over 5 percent. By 2020 these two groups will constitute over a quarter and 10 percent of the population respectively. Asians represent a third major non-European grouping—as in, say, the Pacific northwest of the United States—and in 2020 are predicted to make up about 15 percent of the population.

European New Zealanders, who will become a minority before 2040, are still largely Anglo-Celtic in origin. Indeed, New Zealand is the most Anglo-Celtic of any of the New World countries. In the nineteenth century settlers from Britain made up 96 percent of white migrants. Other Europeans, largely Scandinavians, Germans, and Croatians, made up the rest. This resembled settlement patterns in Australia, except that Scots were more important in New Zealand and the Irish less important. Scots made up about 21 percent of nineteenth-century immigrants compared with 12 percent of Australia's migrants before 1900. The Irish made up 18 percent—although the 4 percent of total immigrants who were Presbyterians from Northern Ireland could be regarded as more akin to the Scots. The southern Irish, who made up around a quarter of Australia's migrants, only represented a conspicuous Catholic minority of 14 percent in her smaller neighbor. The remainder of the European population was English—but if we separate the 9 percent of migrants from Cornwall, there is a good case for labeling the nineteenth-century New Zealand migrant mix Celtic–Anglo. Nevertheless, the English, predominantly from the south and west, still constituted the single biggest group. New Zealand diverged from Australia after the Second World War when it continued this essentially British pattern (with the addition of a few Dutch), while Australia opened its borders to a large inflow of southern Europeans. It is easy, therefore, to detect American students taking courses in New Zealand because so many of their names are German, Scandinavian, Polish, Italian, and Ukrainian—rather than English, Scots, Irish, or Polynesian.

CONSTITUTIONAL AND POLITICAL SYSTEMS

New Zealand is not a republic but a member of the British Commonwealth. American history students studying in New Zealand are often surprised that, until relatively recently, New Zealanders were enthusiastic members of the Commonwealth and, before 1947, the British Empire. Should New Zealand ever become a republic, its Maori "rebels" could be reinvented as heroes—but this should not disguise the fact that before the 1970s the new nation maintained a staunchly pro-British stance. However, it was more an unshakeable belief in representative and responsible government by early colonists in the 1850s, similar to their counterparts in the 13 American colonies some 80 years earlier, that helped to bring about a parliamentary democracy in New Zealand only 12 years into the colony's existence.

The original Crown Colony Government, bestowed on New Zealand once sovereignty had been acquired from the reigning Maori chiefs through the Treaty of Waitangi in 1840, gave the governor, appointed by the British monarch, full control. Settlers were dismayed that in this new country they had no say in the laws passed by the governor and his nominated legislative council. By 1852, after considerable agitation for change, the young colony was granted representative government through an act passed by the British Parliament, which is still the basis of government in the country today, albeit with several important changes. The original Constitution Act created a bicameral arrangement similar to some of the constitutions adopted by the 13 states of America in the 1770s and 1780s. The executive power rested with a governor, and the legislative council was nominated by him. This upper house was abolished almost a century later. However, the lower house was elected and remains today, still known as the House of Representatives. A relatively wide franchise enabled men over 21 years of age who owned land worth £50 or who leased land at an annual rental of £10 or more to vote. This limitation fell short of the full manhood suffrage of Victoria in Australia but was still much broader than most places at the time, including Britain. Maori males were effectively excluded by the property-owning requirement, since land remaining in Maori hands was traditionally owned collectively by tribes or subtribes. However, after 1853 more and more Maori males had their shares in communally-owned property transferred to private ownership and became eligible to vote. The white settler government was able to limit their potential influence by granting all Maori men over 21 years of age the right to vote, but only for four Maori seats. This was grossly disproportionate to the number of Maori people in the colony. At the same rate of representation enjoyed by non-Maori people, Maori people would have been entitled to 16 seats. The measure was supposed to have lasted only five years, but it was extended, and made indefinite in 1876. Today the same four seats exist although, since 1975, Maori voters have had the option of voting either for these seats or for the general electorates. Maori were also disadvantaged in other constitutional ways. The secret ballot was introduced in 1870, but not for Maori voters, who had to wait until 1937 for the same reform. Enrollment for voting became compulsory for non-Maori, or Pakeha, voters in 1927 but not for Maori voters until 1956.

An electoral roll had existed for Pakeha voters since 1854 but there was no provision for a Maori roll until 1942, and the first one was not completed until 1949.

Such inequities were able to happen because in the 1860s the British Colonial Office had handed control of "native affairs" over to the settler government. At this time the members of parliament were mostly wealthier farmers or businessmen who had an agenda to shift as much land in the North Island from Maori ownership to settler ownership (virtually the entire South Island had already been "purchased" by fair means or foul by 1860) and the North Island offered areas that were amongst the most fertile land in the world, particularly in Taranaki on the western coast, the Waikato south of Auckland, and the aptly named Bay of Plenty to the east. Not surprisingly, these were the three areas where war broke about between Maori people, reluctant to sell, and settlers on a mission to buy or acquire at all costs. The guerrilla phase of this conflict dragged on until 1872.

In the original 1852 Constitution Act there was a provision for six provincial governments, in addition to the bicameral parliament based in Auckland. These were seen as necessary because of the geographical spread of the country. However, improvements in communications, particularly the rapid growth of railways, made the provincial councils unnecessary, and they were abolished in 1876. Their demise meant that central government and its state bureaucracy came to play a greater part in New Zealand's development than in most New World societies, but the relatively small population in New Zealand was never going to support a "state" government system as that in Australia and the United States.

The fledgling unitary government entrenched its hold by deciding against federal union with Australia in 1890 and 1901—the electorate accepted the politicians' argument that the great distances involved would make it impractical of New Zealand to become the seventh state of Australia. Both in 1890 and 1901 New Zealand ranked as the third-biggest Australasian colony (after New South Wales and Victoria), and its capital, Wellington, lay closer to the eastern Australian coast than did Perth in Western Australia. Regardless, successive New Zealand governments decided that the nation was big enough and sufficiently different culturally and historically to go it alone. Some historians see this decision as a mistake, but the experience of smaller states within the Australian union, such as Tasmania, suggests that the country would have struggled to secure its fair share of expenditure. More importantly, the decision to stay separate pushed new Zealand towards a different historical trajectory and cemented its independent character.

In 1889, all adult males were granted the vote; and all women won the franchise in 1893, although Maori women were, like their male counterparts, limited to voting for only four representatives. New Zealand beat South Australia by one year as the first largely self-governing colony to give women the vote. As a result it can lay claim to be the world's oldest full democracy, albeit an imperfect one due to the differences in participation remaining between the Maori and Pakeha. Full statehood was finally secured under the Statute of Westminster in 1947 after New Zealand had played a key role in securing small nations a voice within the new United Nations organization. The Upper House was abolished soon after, in 1951 by a supposedly conservative government on the grounds of cost. As a result the executive branch—the cabinet of the government in office—assumed even greater powers than before. The New Zealand Supreme Court had never assumed the role of counterweight to the power of the executive branch as in the United States, and a very limited Bill of Rights was enacted only as recently as 1990.

Much to the surprise of older citizens in New Zealand and the rest of the world, in a referendum held in 1993 New Zealand abandoned the "first past the post" system inherited from Westminster and used in all general elections. As a result, since 1996 New Zealand has employed the West German system of Mixed Member Proportional representation (MMP). Under this system only half of the 120-strong House of Representatives is selected by the electorate, with the other 60 members elected as "list" MPs depending on the size of party votes. To be represented in parliament, a party must score at least 5 percent of the total party vote—a safeguard designed to avoid the chronic instability of countries like Italy and Israel. It is too soon to say how well the change has worked, or to predict whether it will survive. But it clearly reflects an attempt by the electorate to reduce executive power and secure a parliament that is more representative of the total electorate than parliaments elected under the old two-party system—Labor and National being the New Zealand equivalents of Democrats and Republicans in the United States.

GENDER AND RACE RELATIONS

The shape of both gender and race relations developed differently in New Zealand than in other comparable countries. Paradoxically, the early achievement of full female suffrage may have slowed the struggle for greater equality for women by removing the need for ongoing campaigning as occurred in both the United States and Great Britain. Nevertheless, feminists in New Zealand have been determinedly active since the 1880s.

Second-wave feminism added new impetus to reform in the 1970s, and today women occupy a more prominent place in New Zealand public life than anywhere else in the New World outside the United States. Scandinavian countries may have granted more rights to women, but in 2003 New Zealand has a woman prime minister (our second in succession), governor-general, and chief justice—and, perhaps most remarkably, the nation's second biggest corporation (Telecom) is headed by a woman. Women have also made huge inroads into the medical and legal professions and now outnumber men in all university courses outside commerce and engineering. Despite these advances, women are still economically more vulnerable than men, suffer unacceptable levels of physical violence and abuse, and have a low profile in big business; yet there is no doubt that they hold a stronger position in New Zealand society than do their Australian sisters.

Race relations in New Zealand are even more complex than gender relations. Although Maori have made tangible gains over the last century, their advances have proved much more modest than those enjoyed by women. Nevertheless, along with their Pacific Island cousins, the cultural contribution of Maori in the twentieth century has prevented New Zealand from becoming a kind of southern Britain—as tourists discover on arrival in Auckland, the world's biggest Polynesian city. Maori subverted and resisted the British imperial project from the beginning of contact, initially by offering stiff military resistance and later by passive resistance. More recently, the vibrancy of Maori culture has helped force legal recognition of grievances, especially through the Waitangi Tribunal process discussed in chapter 9.

Although New Zealand has experienced high levels of intermarriage, this has failed to resolve major health problems experienced by Maori or close the gap in economic and educational achievement. Although Maori fare better than indigenous Australians, New Zealanders must still deal with alarming statistics that point to areas of severe disadvantage. Maori women, for example, suffer the highest level of lung cancer in the world. Gross overrepresentation in prisons, high crime levels, and unacceptable school dropout rates all suggest trouble ahead unless the underlying issues are addressed promptly. Maori and Pacific Islanders, who urbanized very fast over little more than a generation after the Second World War, still form something of an underclass in the larger cities. Even when allowance is made for outstanding contributions in sports, music, and art and the visibility of Maori protocol and ceremony on major public occasions, a great deal of effort and reconciliation is required if New Zealand is to overcome the negative legacies of its colonial past.

2

Eastern Polynesians become Maori

ARRIVAL

The consensus among prehistorians is that Maori arrived in New Zealand about 800 years ago, around 1180 A.D. A few scholars still opt for an earlier date of arrival, but claims of longer occupation are increasingly dismissed as eccentric. There is much less agreement about where Maori migrated from, and Maori traditions about their origins were unhelpfully couched in mythological terms. When British explorer Captain James Cook visited New Zealand in 1769, Maori replied to questions about their origins by pointing to the sky and tracing their *whakapapa,* or genealogy, from Rangi, the sky father, and Papatuanuku, the earth mother. Scholars agree that groups of migrants from Southeast Asia began long sea voyages around the Pacific as long as 3,000 years ago. Although New Zealand was the last major settlement made by east Polynesians, their jumping-off point remains unclear. Some scholars, particularly linguists, argue for the Marquesas, while others suggest the Society Islands. The closer Cook Islands, however, seem a much more logical place of embarkation because of the hardships involved in long sea voyages in chilly waters. The case remains open.

We do know, however, that Maori voyaged to New Zealand quite deliberately in large, double-hulled, oceangoing *waka*, or canoes. The suggestion made by historian Andrew Sharp that they arrived by accidental voyaging was disproved by explorer David Lewis, who undertook a voyage of his own using traditional Polynesian methods involving long-range and accurate navigation against prevailing winds. Maori seafarers were expert at reading the stars, following the flight paths of birds, and tracing currents and wave patterns. They truly deserved the title, bestowed by eminent Maori scholar Sir Peter Buck, of Vikings of the Sunrise. Polynesian settlers voyaged to New Zealand deliberately, probably to escape war and famine, like immigrants everywhere.

Several names for New Zealand survive in Maori tradition. The name given to the land as a whole, Aotearoa, is often translated as land of the long white cloud—but this reflects a romantic nineteenth-century construction. Some scholars argue rather that Aotearoa means the land of long daylight because tradition is consistent that Maori arrived in the summer, and New Zealand has much longer evenings than tropical Polynesia. Te Ika a Maui (the fish of Maui—a mythological demigod and mischief-maker with supernatural powers) and Te Wai Pounamu or Wahi Pounamau (the waters or place of greenstone, a type of jade) are probably much older names for the North and South Islands respectively. When considering these names for New Zealand as a whole, we should remember that Maori took a very tribal view of a country several times larger than the whole of Polynesia put together.

The ancestors of Maori did not arrive in one great fleet in 1350—an influential theory suggested by the late nineteenth-century ethnographer Percy Smith. By reexamining Maori canoe traditions, scholars such as David Simmons and Janet Davidson have shown that the immigrants arrived intermittently, drifting south from the top of the North Island as earlier arrivals took their pick of food resources in the mild climate of the far north. These settlers were all eastern Polynesian; there is no evidence that their arrival was preceded by pacifist peoples from elsewhere in the Pacific, as Smith, Edward Tregear, and other early investigators suggested. These so-called Mori-ori were, in fact, nothing more than a myth invented by these British-born ethnographers to justify British colonization of New Zealand. Stories of great fleets and conquest of earlier peoples offered remarkable similarities to the Norman conquest of England in 1066. Little wonder that this parallel history remained widely accepted within the broader New Zealand community down to the 1990s. The Moriori did in fact exist, but they were simply a group of eastern Polynesians who migrated early (around 1350) to the Chatham Islands, about 500 miles east of the South Island mainland. There, in a food-rich environment, a rela-

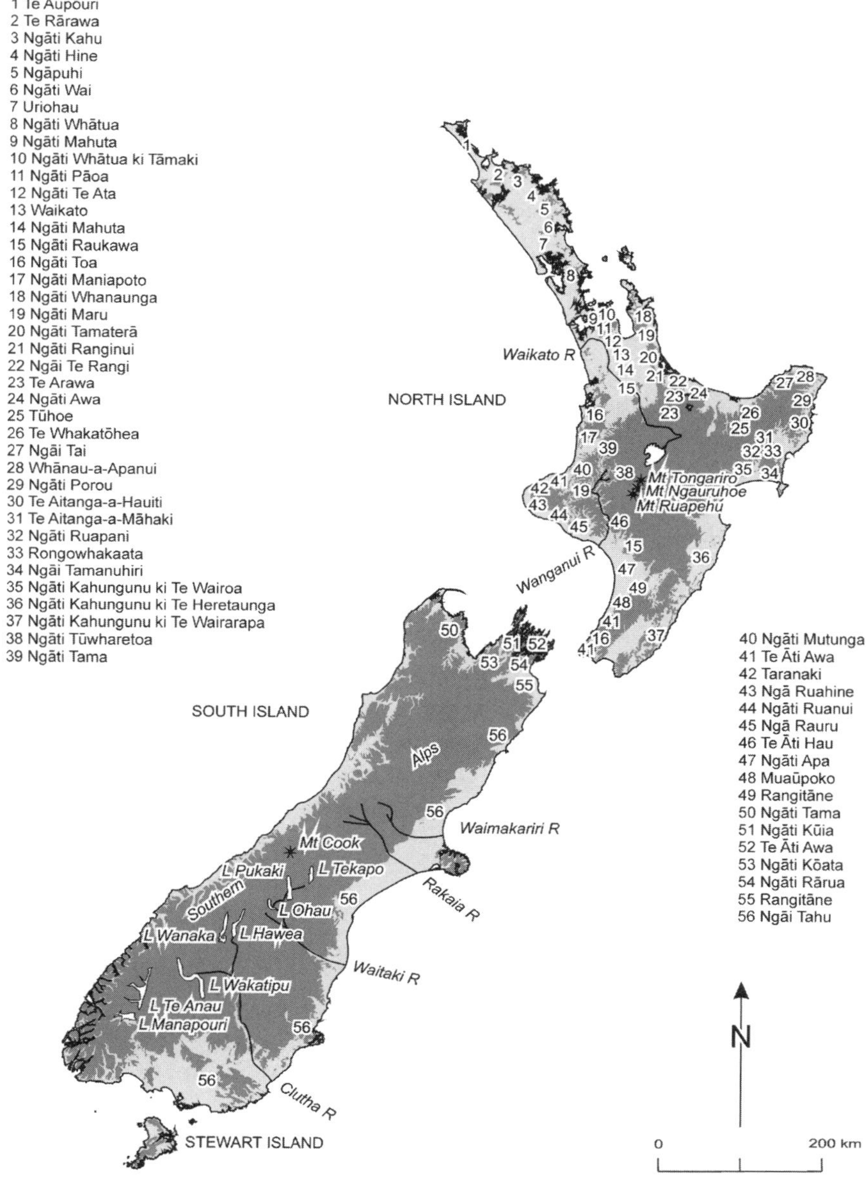

Location of Maori tribal areas.

tively pacifist society developed in isolation until overrun by invading Maori (Ngati Tama and Ngati Mutunga of northern Taranaki) in the 1830s.

Having established themselves in New Zealand, Maori experienced little contact with their Polynesian homeland. The so-called mini ice age of the fourteenth century produced rough seas and adverse wind patterns, which made return voyaging to Polynesia impossible. Maori society developed in isolation for over 300 years before Europeans made sustained contact from 1769. (The Dutch explorer Abel Tasman made fleeting contact in 1642, but this produced little impact, and the *iwi* or tribe he encountered seemed to have disappeared by the time of Cook's arrival in 1769.) Time apart from the rest of humanity enabled a distinctive Maori culture to emerge. This is reflected in the terms Maori used to name themselves. The word *Maori* means normal, but came into common use only in the nineteenth century as a means of distinguishing Maori from Pakeha. Before that, New Zealand's indigenous people identified themselves by their tribal or clan *(hapu)* affiliations. Although Maori retained a language very close to that of Tahiti and the Cook Islands, they became much more warlike than the rest of Polynesia, partly as a result of the much harsher environmental conditions encountered in their new land.

ENVIRONMENTAL IMPACT

The colder New Zealand climate in which coconut, bananas, and breadfruit would not grow, and where taro *(Colocasia esculenta)* could only be grown in milder northerly areas, forced the newcomers to become very competitive as their population grew to around 100,000. Yam (probably *Dioscora alata*) and gourd (ahure or *Lagenaria siceraria*), used for storing water and food, could also be grown only in the north. It took every bit of 4,000 years of accumulated gardening skills to get them to grow at all. Little wonder, therefore, that Maori society rapidly became based on competing and hostile clans, or *hapu,* rather than larger tribes, or *iwi.* Scholars such as Angela Ballara have made it clear that these larger units became much more important after the European intrusion. A very rough comparison is to the highlands of Scotland, where fealty to clan determined political allegiances down to the eighteenth century. Before European arrival a tribe could often be made up of relatively few *hapu,* but by the 1800s as many as 150 *hapu* could support the war campaigns organized by the larger tribal groupings. *Hapu,* which could be as large as 2,000 persons, were in turn usually based on a few dozen extended families or *whanau.*

In this kin-based, tight-knit, and warlike society, genealogy provided the very essence of life. Knowledge of the ancestors and ancestral lands bound the individual and larger groups to particular stretches of jealously guarded territory. Land could be claimed by discovery or conquest, but occupation had to follow for at least three generations to sustain the claim. This usufructuary system, known as *ahi ka* (literally, my smoke rises, or my fires burn over the land), encouraged constant skirmishing in the summer months. Claims to territory were further strengthened through frequent intermarriage between clans.

The most prized land was rich in seafood *(kai moana),* eels *(tuna),* and fish *(ika)* and was capable of growing the sweet potato or *kumara.* The *kumara* could be grown only through sophisticated agricultural practices that involved warming the ground and stowing seeds in special bell-shaped chambers. But even Polynesian inventiveness could not cope with the chilly winters experienced south of Christchurch, halfway down the South Island. As a result, the Maori population became concentrated in the North Island.

Despite its huge size relative to the rest of Polynesia, New Zealand's environment provided, in the words of prehistorian Atholl Anderson, "a fragile plenty." New Zealand could sustain a population of about 100,000 preindustrial people, but only if they managed their food resources with skill and care. The Australian paleontologist Tim Flannery has shown that initially Maori, like new settlers everywhere, behaved as "future eaters," consuming resources at will. By 1500 they had hunted to extinction all 12 species of the easily caught moa, a giant, flightless bird up to 10 feet tall, which provided easy feasting for hungry clans. The Polynesian rat *(kiore* or *Rattus exulans)* and dog *(kuri)* also wreaked havoc with flightless birds, of which the new land had many species. Maori worsened these impacts by reducing seal populations to very low levels and exterminating nearly 40 bird species (about half those known before human arrival), including the giant, brightly colored Haast's eagle. They also accounted for three to five species of frogs, one bat, and an unknown number of lizard species. More importantly, they removed about half the original forest cover of New Zealand. Debate continues on the extent of the Maori impact on forest destruction, as natural fires, especially those resulting from regular volcanic activity, also played a part. But there is little doubt that using fire to hunt moa and to clear forest for swidden agriculture (that is, taking advantage of the initial soil fertility induced by burning before moving to new garden sites within three or so years) helped shrink one of the world's great rain forests to more manageable proportions.

As Atholl Anderson points out, Maori behaved little differently from any other colonists on first discovering a new land. This interpretation runs counter to the popular romantic portrayal of indigenous peoples as innately conservationist. Work on the First Nation peoples of North America by contemporary prehistorians like Flannery reveals similar patterns. But as it became clear that the wealth offered by the land was not limitless, Maori learnt environmental lessons quite rapidly and from the 1500s developed elaborate rules concerning resource management. By the time Europeans had arrived, therefore, they were living in relative harmony with the natural environment and were applying *rahui,* or sanctions, to the harvesting of crops, wild plants, and seafood in an effort to conserve those resources. Unfortunately, European settlers generally ignored the environmental lessons learned so carefully by Maori and repeated the same mistakes all over again. The results were much more destructive because of the new settlers' greater numbers and their access to more sophisticated technology—although fire would, once again, act as the great destroyer.

BELIEFS, LORE, AND SOCIAL ORGANIZATION

Like everything else in their world, Maori response to the natural environment was shaped by a widely shared set of values and beliefs. The details of traditional stories concerning creation and settlement differed between *iwi.* Southern Maori, especially the Ngai Tahu and Waitaha peoples of the South Island, explained their dramatic, mountainous landscape in terms of wrecked canoes and wandering giants. North Island Maori, on the other hand, attributed the creation of the land to the forest god Tane, who separated the sky father Rangi and the earth mother Papatuanuku and so let light into the world. Coastal *iwi* tended to revere Tangaroa, god of the sea, above Tane, who held first place among inland tribes. Otherwise mythology is characterized by similarity rather than difference. A single language that could be understood by all (despite dialectal differences) helps explain why Maori shared common cultural and social concepts such as the limits to warfare and obligations to *whanau, hapu,* and *iwi.*

Like many preliterate cultures, Maori society organized itself along hierarchical lines, although even the high-born had to earn *mana* or prestige to retain their standing. In a society where status was ascribed on the basis of family, clan, and tribal affiliation, rather than individual achievement, genealogy or *whakapapa* was a key concept. Even today the central question of identification in the Maori world is "who are you?" rather than "what do you do for a living?" The highest rank in traditional society was that of *ariki* or chief of a large tribe or alliance of tribes. The chief's position depended on his ability to trace his descent via the most senior patriarchal and matriarchal lines back to the eponymous (or founding) ancestor of the tribe. As a chief often took more than one wife, descent was counted through the first wife. Yet an element of meritocracy also operated within the Maori world, and a leading *ariki* would have some outstanding achievement to his credit, most probably a major military success, that enabled him to win his preeminent rank. Some scholars argue that Maori society was the most egalitarian in Polynesia, which would explain why the institution of kingship failed to develop as in Fiji, Tonga, Tahiti, and Hawaii. The same principles applied to *rangatira,* or chiefs, who led *hapu.* Senior chiefs could be supplanted by chiefs from junior lines who succeeded in battle or possessed outstanding ability as poets, historians, or composers of *waiata* (song). And because Maori rated seniority ahead of gender difference, women could also hold chiefly rank. In modern parlance, Maori culture was ageist rather than sexist.

The rung immediately below the *rangatira* was occupied by *tohunga*—specialists such as priests, canoe-builders, carvers, poets, and storytellers. Sometimes these people became more influential than *rangatira,* especially if they possessed the gift of foresight and could act as seers or could practice *makutu* or sorcery. Yet it would be wrong to dismiss them as witch doctors, as they performed a much wider role within Maori society. These highly ranked individuals worked with the elders or *kaumatua* to run the everyday affairs of the clan or tribe. One of their responsibilities involved distributing resources to the heads of *whanau* for their lifetimes. When the latter died, these resources, including land, were returned to the community for redistribution. Persons from junior or *teina* lines filled the role of commoners. They constituted the mass of the people, as *rangatira* made up only about 1 percent of the population. The bottom rung of society was occupied by *taurekareka* or slaves, usually war captives.

Conquering tribes humiliated their slaves by forcing men to undertake women's work in the *kumara* gardens. Captured warriors also suffered enormous psychological anguish at being removed from their home territories and preferred death to capture. Yet the main fear arising from battle was the possibility of being cannibalized by one's enemies. Cannibalism was a rare practice throughout Polynesia, but in Aotearoa/New Zealand chiefs gained great *mana* from devouring the eyes and hearts of their victims: the stars in the night sky were seen as the eyes of slain chieftains. Acquisition of *mana* by such extreme methods underscores the competitive nature of Maori society, far and away the most warlike within Polynesia. No other Polynesians developed defensive villages or *pa* to such a high level, or engaged in warfare on such a grand scale. Kings or any other kind of pan-tribal leaders had little chance of emerging in such a highly competitive culture. Yet there were limits to aggression and, before European military technology disrupted the balance of power, military activity was constrained by the complex lore governing every aspect of Maori life.

Two key concepts underpinned the worldview held by traditional Maori: complementarity and reciprocity. These notions have bemused Pakeha ever since first contact. Whereas Europeans tend to think in opposites such as male and female, or sacred and profane, ancient Maori believed that each part of our world is interconnected with and dependent upon every other part. Consequently, while women were classed as *noa* (of the earth) and men as *tapu* (sacred), women were by no means regarded as inferior. On the contrary, they were equally as important as men because without them the human race would not exist. Maori also believed that everything in the world, including inanimate objects such as stones, possessed a *mauri* or life force and deserved, therefore, to be treated with respect. Such understanding also had a practical side. In a society without maps, fishing grounds, eel weirs, and other food resources such as fern-root and berry-bearing trees could be declared *tapu*—placing them out of bounds to anyone not connected with a particular clan or tribe. As a result, movement around the Maori world often became rather convoluted and rarely followed straight lines.

This belief in the complementarity and interconnectedness of all things gave rise to a whole series of complex obligations. For example, one action must be complemented by an appropriate counteraction. The key Maori institution of *utu,* often mistakenly translated as revenge, bears out this point. The demands of *utu* meant that an act of hospitality—such as offering a visitor a feast—must be followed by another, preferably grander, feast. Hospitality was regarded as an obligation to be rendered without question; little wonder that the Maori language has no word for *thank you.* A darker aspect of *utu* required that an act of ill will or insult, even if unintended, must be countered by a stronger response. At the mildest level, this could involve *muru* or the appropriation and/or vandalizing of property—coincidentally a means of redistributing resources. More serious insults or breaches of accepted codes of behavior required some form of physical punishment and even the offender's death. Breach of custom, such as infidelity after marriage, could also be punished by death—although women below chiefly rank adopted a fairly relaxed attitude toward premarital sex. The most serious form of *utu,* known as *uto,* involved full-scale warfare. This might take years to organize through the building of alliances and intermarriage, and it culminated in the unleashing of large *taua*, or war parties, on the hapless *iwi* or *hapu* who had given offence.

COSMOLOGY AND RELIGION

Aotearoa/New Zealand lacked the elaborate temples and large priestly castes of other places in Polynesia. Yet this does not mean that Maori were not religious. Rather, they internalized their religion and possessed an elaborate mythology that explained everything about the life of the spirit as well as human existence. When some British colonists dismissed Maori as basically superstitious, they failed to understand the holistic nature of their cosmology. Everything in the material world held links to the spiritual world *(wairua)*. This linking of the mundane and the supernatural is not so different from preindustrial views within the European world, or those of First Nation peoples in the United States.

Theologians such as Michael Shiras argue that Maori held a profound sense of the sacred and knew exactly what the gods expected of them. Any breach of this relationship could bring disaster, known as *hara*. The capsizing of a canoe, drowning, or loss in battle, for example, all reflected the anger of the gods. Debate continues as to whether Maori believed in a supreme being sometimes referred to as Io, but there is no doubt that they believed that the nature gods of the forest, sea, wind, agriculture, and earthquakes determined the fate of every tribe, clan, and individual. While students of institutions of higher learning known as *whare wananga* may have contemplated the existence of Io, all Maori paid close attention to avoiding angering a host of lesser deities as well as committing dangerous breaches of *tapu*.

MATERIAL CULTURE AND HEALTH

Despite the admiration expressed by Captain Cook for Maori health and physical strength and stature (the men averaged about five feet, seven inches, when the European average was more like five feet, four inches), life was harsh for early Maori. Soft kumara proved so difficult to grow that *iwi* restricted its use to ceremonial occasions. Tough fern root served as a kind of chewing gum for warriors on long marches. This limited, hard, and fibrous diet, made more tedious by the lack of moa and seal meat through overhunting, wore teeth to the gums by age 30. Anatomist Phillip Houghton estimates that few Maori lived past 30 as result, much as in preindustrial Europe. On the positive side, after 1600 Maori suffered little from tooth decay, whereas earlier arrivals who feasted on seal and moa suffered extensive dental caries. Houghton and Atholl Anderson also suggest that the rigors of long sea voyages triggered the selection in the Polynesian gene pool of individuals who were bigger, more muscular, and more athletic than their forebears.

Within their short life span Maori lived relatively healthy lives. Infant mortality appears to have been quite low, and the average woman gave birth to about four children. At least three usually made it to adulthood, a much higher proportion than in preindustrial Europe. Geographical isolation also meant that Maori suffered from relatively few diseases. Colds, flu, and measles were unknown, as were other great killers such as smallpox, cholera, and typhoid. Maori did not suffer from any venereal diseases, and yaws, the great scourge of other Pacific communities, never found its way to New Zealand. Most Maori died, therefore, in battle or more commonly from accident or simply from wear and tear. As Alfred W. Crosby points out in his book *Ecological Imperialism*, such a pathogen-free environment made Maori particularly vulnerable to contact with groups carrying unfamiliar diseases.

On balance, Maori lived as well as their essentially stone-age technology allowed. Their canoes could capsize in rough weather, but this did not stop them from traveling long distances to trade, especially for jade or *pounamu*. They worked the inshore fishery with considerable skill, using large, woven nets and bone fishhooks. Their carving was as elaborate as their stone adzes allowed, and women developed weaving to high levels of intricacy. Houses built on pole supports and covered with closely woven flax provided adequate shelter, even if Europeans found them rather too smoky for comfort. The elaborate ceremonial meeting places, or *marae*, that are found throughout Polynesia may have developed in Aotearoa only after European contact. Although the *kiore* or Polynesian rat thrived in the thatch-style housing, Maori maintained high levels of hygiene and paid particular attention to ensuring clean water supplies. Drinking water could be taken only from upstream sources, with cleaning restricted to areas downstream of settlements. Human waste was always kept separate from cooking areas, and Maori buried their dead in distant caves or clearly demarcated graveyards *(urupa)*.

In short, this adaptable and highly competitive society possessed the flexibility and capacity for change to cope reasonably well with the large-scale contact with completely different societies that took place from the late eighteenth century. They were certainly far better equipped to cope with the European intrusion than the Aborigines of Australia, who had inhabited their vast continent for at least 60,000 years with no significant cultural change and little concern for the future. The two factors that made Maori particularly vulnerable to the negative effects of European contact were lack of political unity and susceptibility to a host of new pathogens to which they lacked resistance. Yet, as we will see, Maori agency survived despite the overwhelming numerical and technological superiority of the European settlers. Although white settlement produced many adverse consequences, Maori resistance and adaptability ensured that contact could never be dismissed as a fatal impact.

3

An Australasian Colony and an Apprenticeship in Race Relations, 1792–1840

From the founding of Britain's penal colony in Australia in 1788 down to 1840, New Zealand developed as an extension of the Australian frontier. During that time the formerly isolated Maori learned ways of coping with the European intrusion. During the 1820s crippling disease and musket wars severely reduced their numbers from around 100,000 to something like 60,000. Yet, although considerable, the European impact never proved fatal, as some historians claimed in the 1950s and 1960s. Such population loss appears relatively modest when compared with the collapse experienced in postconquest Central America (where numbers fell from perhaps 30 million to 2 million within a century), or the drop from perhaps a million Aborigines to 60,000 within a century in Australia.

Rather than surrendering meekly, after shrugging off the devastating impact of such diseases as measles and influenza before 1840, Maori set themselves to make painful adjustments to their rapidly changing world. They, in turn, influenced the predominantly British and other European explorers, sealers, whalers, timber workers, missionaries, and settlers with whom the came into contact. Right from its beginnings, the colonization of New Zealand was a two-way process, with Maori agency continually subverting and challenging attempts to impose British authority. Maori also continued to act out of their own motivation. In the process of pursuing their own agendas, in the years before 1840 Maori and the newcomers they dubbed Pakeha served a long and troubled apprenticeship in race relations. This painful learning process helped shape a complex and distinctive pattern of relations between European colonizers and indigenous people.

EXPLORERS

The first European to discover New Zealand was a Dutchman named Abel Janzoon Tasman. He sailed there in 1642 on behalf of the Dutch East India Company, in pursuit of the so-called great south land. Many geographers still believed that the known world had to be balanced by a large southern continent, and Dutch entrepreneurs hoped that its discovery would open up new trading opportunities. But instead of a continent, Tasman found only parts of the New Zealand coast. After a bloody conflict with Maori at the top of the South Island, he retreated in haste. His reports condemned this part of Statenlandt (as he called it) as dangerous and of little interest to Europeans. Dutch cartographers later added the name Nieuw Zeeland to acknowledge the contribution made to the Dutch East India Company by investors based in Zeeland. A less appropriate name is hard to imagine. New Zealand is, in Tasman's own words, "a land uplifted high," whereas Zeeland in Holland is dead flat. Tasman's fleeting visit also produced little impact on Maori, as the tribe he encountered (supposedly Ngati Matakokiri) seemingly disappeared, and there is scant record of Tasman in Maori oral tradition.

The world largely ignored Tasman's apparently insignificant discovery until Lieutenant James Cook and the famous botanist Joseph Banks rediscovered New Zealand for Britain and for science in 1769. The British Admiralty sent Cook, Banks, and an astronomer, Charles Green, to Tahiti to observe the transit of Venus (the passage of the planet across the sun), as this celestial event would not be viewed for another 105 years. Cook was also instructed to check out Tasman's findings to ascertain whether a great south land indeed lay hidden behind Nieuw Zeeland.

After an apparently successful observation of Venus (the expedition lacked the sensitive instruments to do the job properly), Cook sailed southwest and sighted New Zealand on October 7, 1769. His and Banks's account of the potential of the new land aroused much interest in Britain, especially when popularized by author John Hawkesworth. Guided by prevailing scientific theories of soil fertility, the navigator and the botanist guessed that rich soils lay hidden beneath the dense rain forest that seemed to cover the country. Parts of northeastern North America had produced soils well suited for cropping once settlers had removed the trees. But Cook and Banks were not to know that New Zealand's forests leach the soil of nutrients rather than improving it. Banks was also influenced by his father's success in draining his estates in swampy Lincolnshire and believed that New Zealand too might easily be drained and converted to smiling farmland. Both explorers also favored New Zealand's temperate climate over the heat of tropical Tahiti. They deemed the big islands of the new land—similar in size to Britain—to be an ideal place for British settlement. Banks later admitted that he found the predominantly green vegetation a little dull compared with the tropical luxuriance he was to find in Australia, and missed the opportunities to discover unusual animals like marsupials. But New Zealand's mild climate and apparently limitless potential for farming held out enormous appeal.

Cook possessed a number of advantages over Tasman that helped him in mapping New Zealand's coastline with considerable accuracy. These included more navigable ships than his predecessor and the ability to calculate longitude (east-west) as well as latitude (north-south) instead of relying on dead reckoning. Even so, it would be churlish to deny Cook's great skill as both sailor and navigator, especially as he lacked accurate clocks (or chronometers) until his second voyage of 1772–1775.

While circumnavigating the country on his first voyage, Cook claimed the area of Mercury Bay southeast of Auckland and the tranquil waters of the Marlborough Sounds (at the top of the South Island) for the British Crown by right of discovery. He and Banks renamed many prominent topographical features after fellow officers and scientists on board (including Banks Island, which is actually a peninsula, Cook Strait, and Solander's Isle), patrons such as admirals of the Royal Navy (Hawke's Bay and Mount Egmont), and familiar places in Britain (the Firth of Thames and the River Thames). Sometimes the phlegmatic Yorkshireman indulged in flights of whimsy or little jokes as he named the landscape (Cape Foulwind, Dusky Sound, the Poor Knights Islands, Hen and Chickens, and Doubtless Bay).

Cook's first visit suggested that the existence of a great south land was extremely unlikely. His second voyage in 1772 proved the matter beyond reasonable doubt when he explored the edges of Antarctica. His remarkably measured observations on Maori, however, proved more influential in firing the European imagination by confirming notions of the noble savage influenced by the contemporary Romantic movement. Nonetheless, Cook sailed to New Zealand as a man of the Enlightenment who believed in the capacity of rational thought to overcome cultural difference and who viewed all forms of humanity as dignified, even if not all were equally civilized. He shared none of Tasman's fears of goblins, monsters, and giants and remained insatiably curious throughout his life. Although he made criticisms, especially of cannibalism, and killed perhaps 20 Maori in the course of his travels, he nevertheless regarded them as an intelligent, brave, modest, and healthy people who lived in harmony with their environment. This positive response contrasted dramatically with the negative image of ignoble savages promulgated by contemporary French explorers.

In contrast to Cook, the French generally had a miserable time in New Zealand. Scurvy ravaged the crew of Jean Francois Mare de Surville's ship in 1770 as the leaky *St. John Baptiste* sailed around New Zealand in Cook's wake. De Surville fell out with Maori on the northeastern tip of New Zealand following the theft of a yawl or small sailing boat, and he responded by burning villages. In 1772, in the northwest corner of the country, Captain Marion du Fresne offended Maori custom and overstretched tribal resources, with the result that Ngai Puhi murdered him and 26 of his men. The remaining crew responded by massacring 250 Maori villagers. Another French explorer, de la Perouse, disappeared at sea in 1788 soon after the first fleet reached Botany Bay in Australia. Artists on these voyages portrayed Maori as strange, exotic, and debased savages, while journals kept by crew members revealed only modest enthusiasm for New Zealand's potential for trade and settlement. No equivalent to Hawkesworth emerged in France to promote New Zealand as ideally suited to European settlement. In turn, Maori developed a deep suspicion of the French after the excesses of de Surville and du Fresne's crew. British interests later manipulated this mistrust in persuading Maori to opt for the British rather than the French variant of colonization.

Later British explorers, such as Vancouver in 1791, and Malaspina, the Italian leader of a Spanish expedition in the same year, generally confirmed Cook's judgments. These expeditions produced little impact on Maori beyond encouraging more extensive cultivation of the nutritious potato and greater use of iron tools. Partly as a result, there occurred what historians Gordon Parsonson and James Belich have labeled an agricultural revolution, enabling *iwi* to move to new locations nearer whaling stations, especially in the colder southern areas. The potato proved easy to grow compared with the *kumara* and permitted more sustained military campaigns. Carving also flourished as Maori craftsmen acquired metal tools. Thus sealers, and later whalers and timber workers, soon came to play much more prominent roles in contact than explorers.

SEALING, WHALING, TIMBER FELLING, AND FLAX

The sealing industry pulled New Zealand into the orbit of global capitalism from as early as 1792. American and Australian-based operations slaughtered every animal they could find to supply the new Chinese craze for felt hats. China also happened to supply the tea craved by the English, thereby encouraging the growth of a truly international trade. Once the seal population of Bass Strait (south of Melbourne) had been decimated (by about 1802), attention turned to the chilly waters of southern New Zealand, mainly around Stewart Island and the sub-Antarctic islands. The reckless slaughter that followed peaked around 1806, when John Grono gathered 60,000 skins. The same sealer sold another 35,000 skins to the Sydney market in 1810, when in a single week seals'-skins traded fetched a record £100,000 (about US$500,000). Not surprisingly, the rough sealers, frequently ex-convicts, had hunted the seals of this hostile southern environment almost to extinction by the end of that year.

Numbers recovered a little as operations declined, and another burst followed in the late 1820s. John Boultbee, one of few literate sealers, recorded details of this second wave of hunting in a journal in which he described a life of extraordinary brutality. Captains treated their men badly, often abandoning them to their fate by leaving them on lonely islands without adequate supplies for months. The men, chronically undernourished and frequently drunk, generally approached local Maori in similar fashion. Fighting broke out constantly between the two groups. In 1817 Kai Tahu (the southern branch of Ngai Tahu) from Otakou near Dunedin attacked and killed two American sealers who had tried to buy the shrunken and mummified heads of tribal enemies as curios for the amusement of English and American gentlemen. The Americans razed a village close to modern-day Dunedin in revenge for an earlier attack. Thereafter, an uneasy truce prevailed, with Maori remaining deeply suspicious of sealers and their grisly tastes. The name of Murdering Beach encapsulates the fragility of these early racial encounters. Even so, some sealers established long-term liaisons with local Maori women, and many Ngai Tahu families incorporate Europeans into their genealogies from the early 1800s. This otherwise unhappy apprenticeship in race relations came to an end by the early 1830s, when overhunting killed off the seals completely.

Whaling proved much more important in both economic and social terms. Compared with sealing, enormous fortunes could be earned through whaling—specifically, by gathering the fine-grained spermaceti oil used in precision machinery from the brain of the sperm whale and boiling blubber down for fuel. Whaling also involved ships visiting from as far away as Nantucket in New England, Britain, and Europe (especially France, Norway, and Russia).

Whaling in New Zealand took two forms. The first was on the Bay of Islands in the far north, where crews stopped for rest and recreation after hunting the fast and dangerous sperm whale. Visits by whalers to the Bay of Islands averaged 118 per year in the 1830s. Historian Harry Morton estimated that about 26,000 men visited between 1820 and 1840, about 20,00 of them in the 1820s. Visits by American ships declined in the later period in contrast to the so-called British decade of the 1820s. Northern tribe Nga Puhi responded to the obvious trading opportunities by becoming expert wheat growers and supplied the visitors with food and provisions. Many of the British and Australian crews drank heavily and treated local slave women as prostitutes, a category of humanity unknown in the pre-European Maori world. Chiefs manipulated these women to exchange sex for iron tools, cloth, money, and sometimes muskets. Venereal disease—hitherto unknown to Maori—spread rapidly, especially gonorrhea, and lowered the level of Maori fertility. In contrast to the British whalers, the Quaker captains on the American ships enforced strict discipline on their men.

As with sealing, careless exploitation involving the indiscriminate taking of cows and pups meant that the northern fishery was largely destroyed by about 1840. Historian and anthropologist Anne Salmond notes that many Nga Puhi men worked on these ships and visited Hobart Town in Van Diemen's Land (Tasmania) as well as Sydney on a regular basis. Indeed, Maori first met Christian missionaries on such a journey to Sydney. Some Nga Puhi traveled even further afield to America and Britain. Such journeys convinced northern Maori that Western culture had much to offer, especially in terms of useful technology. This Maori experience of the wider world must not be overlooked in understanding why Maori chiefs willingly signed a treaty with the British in 1840.

The second major form taken by the whaling industry—shore-based or bay whaling—was carried out from about 80 stations down the east coast of both islands from Mahia Peninsula in northern Hawke's Bay to Riverton near modern-day Invercargill. This produced a much greater impact than activities in the Bay of Islands because whalers stayed semipermanently in these bases. Onshore whalers chased the slow southern right whale, so named because it floated once harpooned and was the right kind of whale to hunt. They then towed the animal back to shore and boiled down the blubber for heating and lighting purposes. Clothing manufacturers used whalebone for the corsets and undergarments that so restricted the movement of nineteenth-century women.

Hunting could occur only during winter, when the hapless southern right whales migrated down the coast, so that whalers had to commit to farming during the summer months. Some, such as Johnny Jones, based at Matanaka north of Dunedin, became expert farmers. Jones flourished by combining the operation of seven whaling stations and substantial farming interests; he employed 280 men and later became a big landowner in North Otago. Such endeavor also encouraged Maori farming, and many *hapu* moved around the coast to supply these whaling-based settlements with food. The potato spurred on a quiet but vital agricultural revolution within the Maori world.

Long-term relationships inevitably developed between Europeans and local women, especially among the southern Ngai Tahu. Some Ngai Tahu, such as the prominent chief Tuhawaiki (called Bloody Jack by the whalers because of his constant use of an expletive they taught him), actually ran their own whale ships. The sharp-ended whale boats, in which crews of five to eight men set out to harpoon their prey, also proved popular with Maori. These strong and highly maneuverable boats proved more suited to the rough seas of southern New Zealand than open *waka* (canoes).

Both Australian and Maori whalers made plenty of money before whale numbers collapsed in the 1840s in both the northern and southern fisheries as a result of overhunting. Until then, the chief beneficiaries of the industry had been its financial backers in Sydney (especially Thomas Campbell and his family), Nantucket, and London, as whaling pulled New Zealand even more firmly into the orbit of international capitalism. Although the total returns from onshore whaling have never been calculated, in one good year a middle-sized station like that at Cloudy Bay at the top of the South Island could earn £20,000. Exports of whale products to the main receiving port of Sydney grew from around £58,000 in 1830 to around £224,000 in 1840, before collapsing dramatically. High overheads and wages offset profits, and bankruptcies were as common as runaway successes. Estimates of the capital required to run a station vary from £1,200 to £5,000 per year. Johnny Jones spent some £15,000 on his seven stations in 1839 alone. Skilled harpoonists and helmsmen could make up to £35 for three months' work—about double the average wage.

Economic historians categorize whaling as a depletable industry because it self-destructed once the resource was exhausted. Consequently, like all the other exploitative industries pursued in nineteenth-century New Zealand, it acted as a tributary rather than a mainstream of development. Even so, the major historian of the industry, Harry Morton, argues that whaling played an important role in shaping race relations, in stimulating economic activity, and in raising Maori expectations of greater trade prospects and the advantages of contact with Europeans. Whaling also left its imprint on the landscape—boiling pots and buildings survive in many isolated and windswept parts of the country. It produced a major environmental impact by virtually removing whales from New Zealand waters until relatively recently, and a more subtle impact through the introduction of rats, dogs, and cats that set about feasting on the slow flightless native birds. And whalers, along with explorers, sealers, timber workers, and traders, unintentionally introduced a host of exotic plants, many of which would soon be viewed as weeds in this newly rediscovered land.

TIMBER, TRADE, AND RESOURCES

The tall trees reported with such enthusiasm by Cook and Banks seemed ideally suited to meeting the demands of the British Navy, especially once the supply of good timber from the Baltic area began to dwindle. New Zealand appealed to naval authorities in much the same way that timber-rich New England appealed to Britons in the seventeenth century. On closer inspection, however, it became apparent that New Zealand's tall native trees produced soft timber, while the hardwoods generally grew too short for the tall masts required by vessels of the Royal Navy. (Masts needed to be 74 to 84 feet long, 21 to 23 inches in diameter, and perfectly straight.) Nevertheless, intensive milling of the giant *kauri* tree, whose timber was ideally suited to building houses and boats, began as early as 1793 in the Thames area southeast of Auckland and took off in the Hokianga (in New Zealand's northwest) in the 1820s. By the late 1830s millers had also returned to the Thames area in strength.

Timber remained a major staple of the New Zealand economy throughout the nineteenth century and won considerable prosperity for millers in the Auckland area in particular. Production increased from 300,000 super-feet (length, width, and depth) in 1843 to 1 million super-feet by 1847. Life proved tougher for the saw men and mill workers, who had to endure harsh working conditions. Pit sawing was exhausting and dangerous work, especially in the wet environments where trees grew in profusion. There were other dangers to be faced. Australian and British millers learned from American whalers the skill of building trip dams that could be released in a flood so that the logs could be floated downstream to the coast. As in New England, this proved a treacherous business. Accidents happened frequently, and blood poisoning became a major killer in nineteenth-century New Zealand. Loneliness, a very monotonous diet, and lack of female company also encouraged drunkenness. Although workers' wages stayed low, some entrepreneurs won handsome profits down to the early 1900s, by which time they had cut out over 2 million acres of *kauri.*

Flax milling also grew into a major industry in early New Zealand. The abundant native flax *(Phormium tenax)* initially appeared to provide an ideal resource for making rope, but it soon proved even less useful than the tall but soft-wooded *kahikatea* trees. Traditional European methods of converting flax to linen simply did not work, and the job of processing the fiber was handed over to Maori. Flax became the subject of some farcical incidents. As early as 1793 Lieutenant-Governor Gidley King of Norfolk Island tried to promote this industry by kidnapping two Maori men, Tuki Tahua and Ngahuruhuru, only to discover that they knew nothing of cultivating or weaving flax, which was regarded as women's work. Thereafter, flax continued as New Zealand's Cinderella industry, promising much and delivering little. Maori processed about 10,000 tons in 1830–1831, an arduous process as buyers required that about 40 tons of raw material had to be processed to produce 1 ton of dressed flax. Traders shipped this hard-won bounty to Sydney, but supplies spluttered along intermittently thereafter. Tough Pakeha workingmen later eked a living out of cutting the course, fibrous plant but, although 300 mills were operating in the peak years of the 1870s, flax never accounted for more than about 2 percent of exports. More importantly for our story, Maori exchanged hard-won dressed flax for muskets, so escalating the intertribal musket wars that dominated the 1820s.

Interaction between Maori and Europeans in this period yielded mixed results. A mixed-race group known as Pakeha-Maori was involved in the whaling and timber industries and played an important intermediary role in the trading of goods. Although the Pakeha-Maori passed on a limited knowledge of Maori beliefs to later settlers, they contributed little to a more sophisticated understanding of Maori culture. A trader like Philip Tapsell married into the Arawa tribe after setting Tauranga and founded a important local dynasty. However, these half-caste families tended to operate outside the mainstream of settler society until much later in the nineteenth century.

Intermarriage also helps explain Maori demographic recovery from the 1880s, although initially the influx of new genes occurred on too small a scale to help build immunity to European diseases. Common infections such as the cold, influenza, and measles wreaked havoc on some communities at first. However, New Zealand's relatively large size and extreme isolation (the sea journey from Europe was too long for the deadly smallpox virus to survive) meant that imported diseases did not cause a demographic catastrophe as in other parts of Polynesia or in Central America. Maori population fell from around 100,000 to about 60,000 by 1840 as a consequence of both disease and the musket wars. Yet even at its low point of 46,000 in 1896 (almost certainly a serious underestimate), the decline of the Maori population never approximated that of Central America or Australia, where population numbers fell by a factor of 12 or more.

Although Maori health problems certainly escalated rapidly after contact, these comparative statistics emphasize that the Maori adjusted better than many other indigenous peoples to the onslaught of European colonization. The milder impact of colonization also underscores the power of Maori agency and their ongoing dominance down to around 1850 as they continued to use potatoes, maize, and wheat as economic tools and turn European technology to effective use, developing new skills in traditional areas such as carving and canoe-building. Many *iwi* also took strategic advantage of their resident Europeans, "parking Pakeha in the tribal garage," in the arresting phrase of historian James Belich.

DUAL COLONIZATION AND RESETTLEMENT

The major exception to the generally positive effects of contact stemmed from a simple piece of European military technology—the musket. As a result of its introduction, the 1820s were marred by large-scale intertribal fighting, and Aotearoa/New Zealand was effectively resettled in a number of major tribal movements before full-scale European settlement began. By the early 1830s Maori capacity for military engineering had largely nullified the initial advantage given by the musket. After that, the older balance of power seems to have been restored, but not before the musket had brought about the deaths of some 10,000 Maori. For the first time in Maori history, slaves were taken on a large scale during these wars, and their eventual release would play a key role in the spread of the new faith of Christianity. Wandering bands of warriors (or *toa*) also strengthened the genealogical links between many tribes that had formerly lived very separately. As a result, alliances changed dramatically. All this fighting, loving, and childbearing would prove critical to the eventual signing of the Treaty of Waitangi and the Maori choice of British rather than French imperial rule.

The first major musket wars spread from the north as the powerful Nga Puhi tribe ventured south to avenge old grievances. Raids in 1818 under

Murupaenga pushed as far south as Hawke's Bay and stimulated the emergence of another powerful tribe known as Ngati Kahungunu. Fighting intensified after the northern warlord Hongi Hika traveled with the missionary Thomas Kendall to England in 1820 and returned with over 300 muskets. Hongi then led devastating raids against his southern neighbor, Ngati Whatua, driving the tribe out of the Auckland isthmus before crushing two more tribes, Ngati Maru and Ngati Paoa, in the Thames/Coromandel area. Arawa of Rotorua and the Tainui confederation of the Waikato also felt Hongi's wrath before he lost support of powerful factions within his own *iwi* around 1826. Hongi was wounded in inter-*hapu* skirmishing in 1827 and died in 1828. Although he failed to win any new territory, he took many slaves and transformed the political landscape.

Some tribes were not beyond using Pakeha to gain their ends. Historian Russell Stone has recently shown how Ngati Whatua were driven into the protective and all-too-often manipulative hands of Tainui, who used Ngati Whatua to win monies from the sale of Auckland to the settler government. Once armed with the all-powerful musket, Tainui turned their attention to harassing the small Ngati Toa *iwi* based at Kawhia as well as making numerous raids southwest into Taranaki. Ngati Toa responded to constant military harassment by moving south under the skilful leadership of the formerly minor chief Te Rauparaha. Some of the northern Taranaki tribe of Ati Awa and Te Rauparaha's inland allies and relations, Ngati Raukawa, joined him. These migrations of the mid-1820s pushed smaller *iwi* such as Muaupoko and Rangitane out of their traditional homelands. Te Rauparaha eventually settled in the island fortress of Kapiti, north of Wellington, while Ati Awa put down roots at Waikanae, and Raukawa settled in Otaki.

After 1830 Te Rauparaha, who had grown rich from whaling and trading flax, turned his attention to the South Island and inflicted several severe defeats on Ngai Tahu from 1830 to 1832. Thereafter, Ngai Tahu fought back and confined Ngati Toa to the top of the South Island. Some Ati Awa meantime traveled all the way to the remote Chatham Islands and virtually wiped out the peaceful Moriori. Fighting also flared across the central North Island—involving Tuwharetoa of Taupo, Arawa of Rotorua, and Ngati Kahungunu in particular—until exhaustion and the construction of what Belich calls fireproof "fighting pa" restored some kind of balance.

By the late 1830s skirmishing had taken on a ritual character; opposing warriors stood so far apart that they were able to use boys to retrieve spent ammunition for further volleys. It is understandable why some historians have attributed the signing of the Treaty of Waitangi to the desire for peace. Without doubt, these catastrophic wars had caused immense damage to the fabric of Maori society. The number of deaths resulting from the use of the inaccurate and unreliable musket was put at 40,000 by historian Keith Sinclair. Even if we accept the more conservative figure of 10,000, it still represents around a tenth of the precontact population—comparable to the devastation of modern-day Bosnia, or Serbia in the First World War, where over a quarter of men of military age were killed.

As an effective mechanism for keeping feuding in check and maintaining the balance of power between tribes, the sanction of *utu* had clearly failed. It is likely that that Maori realized that traditional social mechanisms were failing and sought alternative solutions, as the work of linguists Lindsay Head and Lachy Paterson on Maori-language sources suggests. Christianity provided one possibility, while British annexation offered another. In the climate of exhaustion and uncertainty that followed the musket wars, Maori reached out for more extensive and formal contact with the British authorities. European alternatives seemed more attractive following the tumultuous decades of the 1820s and 1830s, when Maori society and its institutional framework had been so thoroughly dislocated.

THE MISSION AND THE HUMANITARIAN IMPULSE

European alternatives also gained in popularity because of the considerable (but much misunderstood) efforts made on behalf of Maori by Anglican, Methodist, and Catholic missionaries between 1814 and 1840. The contribution of these dedicated, brave, but also stern and paternalistic individuals can easily be underestimated by students who have grown up in a more secular age. Certainly, missionaries tended to treat Maori as children and struggled to come to terms with their different systems of belief, but the stereotype of black-frocked, incompetent killjoys says more about the efforts of later-day intellectuals to cast off the country's puritan heritage than it does about the missionaries themselves.

The Anglicans were the first to begin their mission as the Church Missionary Society (CMS) in 1814. They soon became the most important mission but struggled until Henry Williams arrived in 1823. Williams broke the mission's dependence on Hongi Hika by building a ship—the *Herald*—and trading with other *iwi* and even with Australia. Williams, a former midshipman who had promised his life to God in return for being saved in a storm at sea, also overhauled the organization of the mission.

Before his arrival, Australian-based missionary and magistrate Samuel Marsden tried to run the Anglican enterprise from Sydney through tradesmen-missionaries based at Rangihoua on the outer edge of the Bay of Islands. However, their efforts often proved ineffective. Once the station moved to Kerikeri on the mainland, things improved, but firmer leadership was required. Williams won the respect of northern Maori and used the services of printer William Colenso to take advantage of the considerable Maori desire for literacy. The popular view that he reversed earlier practice by civilizing Maori before Christianizing them is a gross oversimplification. Slaves returning from Ngai Puhi in the north, however, spread the Gospel more rapidly than did individual missionaries. Maori soon warmed to the Old Testament emphasis on genealogy and amazed visiting missionaries by reciting long passages of scripture before they would allow themselves to be subjected to sermons or services.

Generally, the ritualized Anglican and Catholic services appealed to Maori more than the simpler pietistic services of the Methodists. The Anglicans also benefited from being first. The Wesleyan Methodist mission did not begin work until 1823, and the Catholics did not arrive until 1838. Because the Anglican missionaries, unlike their Catholic and Methodist counterparts, were not hampered by vows of poverty, they offered greater material advantages to Maori. The fact that the Catholics belonged to the French Marist order, when the great majority of missionaries, whalers, and traders were British, also reduced their authority. The Catholic practice of celibacy, although respected by Maori, struck such a family-oriented society as a little odd. Tony Ballantyne has shown that, despite recent stereotyping, Protestant missionaries held surprisingly relaxed views on sexuality within marriage. Certainly, their large families attested to healthy and vigorous sex lives and were close to Maori social ideals.

Maori soon adapted Christianity to a distinctive indigenous form. In 1833 a prophet known as Papahurihia emerged in the Bay of Islands as the first of many leaders of religious sects combining elements drawn from both cultures. His Te Atua Wera cult was the first of many such movements to appear throughout the nineteenth and early twentieth centuries as Maori adjusted to the challenge raised by British colonization. Te Atua Wera also represented an antimissionary sentiment that gained strength once major military conflict broke out in the 1860s. Mormon missionaries arrived much later, in the 1880s, but had little impact until after the Second World War.

The Anglicans ran by far the most mission stations, dominating the entire east coast of the North Island and confining the Methodists and Catholics to the west coast, especially the Hokianga harbor far in the north. Later, the Catholics added stations in places such as Meanee in Hawke's Bay as well as villages in southern Taranaki and the upper reaches of the remote Wanganui River. The Methodists struggled to expand after the mid-1830s.

By the late 1830s Maori began to show real interest in Christianity. The missionaries responded positively by accepting that this warlike native people had the potential to become sufficiently civilized to adhere to an often difficult faith requiring lifelong commitment. In 1840 the Church Missionary Society calculated that 30,000 Maori attended church on a regular basis at their 19 mission stations; the Methodists estimated that their church had 1,500 Maori members; and the Catholics claimed 1,000 converts. Some historians have questioned the sincerity of this so-called Maori conversion, but there is little doubt that Maori had shown considerable interest in the new faith before the Treaty of Waitangi was signed. Certainly, when George Augustus Selwyn, the first Anglican bishop, arrived in 1842, he found himself ministering to both a Maori and a settler church.

Today, new explanations are being sought for the Maori embrace of Christianity. Historians writing in the rapidly decolonizing world of the 1950s and 1960s, such as Harrison Wright and the young Judith Binney, argued that this growing interest in Christianity resulted from the collapse of traditional Maori beliefs and practices. This fatal impact type of explanation is now considered too simplistic by most historians, including the mature Judith Binney. Like Manuka Henare and others, Binney now stresses that Maori looked for some cultural advantage in Christianity, realized that literacy held the key to unlocking the secrets of Pakeha power, and genuinely enjoyed much of the ritual performance of church services. Many astute Maori leaders also saw that missionary influence could temper the worst excesses of European contact. The missionaries, for all their apparently strange ways and propensity to live on cultural islands separate from Maori communities, nevertheless followed clear moral codes of behavior, generally stuck to their marriage vows, and did not bring the problems caused by drunken whalers and timber workers. The few missionaries such as Thomas Kendall who fell into affairs with Maori women were condemned and ostracized by both sides. Maori also shunned *waipiro*, the fiery liquor consumed by the whalers, and appreciated the missionaries' sober lifestyles.

In wider terms, some of the more astute *rangatira* at higher levels within the enlarging tribes saw that the missionaries might be able to temper the effects of greater involvement with the British—as recent work by Anne Salmond, Angela Ballara, and Manuka Henare has shown. On visits to Sydney several chiefs had observed the plight of the Australian Aborigines and resolved that the excesses of Australia's white settlers should not be duplicated in their own country. Some missionaries, including Henry

Williams, concurred with this nightmarish reading of the future and did their best to maintain a kind of theocracy in New Zealand in an attempt to ward off large-scale British settlement.

These shared fears seemed to be borne out after the appointment of British Resident James Busby in 1833. The first official appointed from New South Wales to try to bring law and order to an increasingly unruly frontier, he had disappointingly little impact. Despite his grand title, Busby lacked soldiers, sailors, and ships to back up his attempts at keeping the peace. He soon earned himself the title of a "'man o' war without guns." Even so, he did secure one important agreement with the northern chiefs in 1835, as the work of Claudia Orange and Manuka Henare has revealed. In 1834 Busby presented local Maori with a flag to protect local shipping (basically a red ensign, with the red cross of Saint George on a white background and the blue, black-bordered top left corner featuring four eight-pointed stars), and the following year signed the so-called Declaration of Independence with 46 northern chiefs. This acknowledgement of tribal ambitions made the British authorities realize that negotiation would be the only option if they ever hoped to settle these far-flung islands. The Declaration of Independence, although nowhere near as significant as its American equivalent, also raised Maori hopes that some kind of agreement could be reached with the British that would bring the benefits of colonization without the kinds of problems witnessed by the chiefs who traveled to Australia. This long-neglected document has recently sprung into prominence as historians have realized its importance in establishing the idea of New Zealand as a Maori country.

The idealistic hopes raised in the Declaration of Independence were also shared by humanitarians in London, especially those who formed the Aborigines' Protection Society in 1837. They were determined that New Zealand should not witness the virtual genocide of its native peoples, as had happened in Tasmania. Continuing complaints of lawlessness in New Zealand made by missionaries, concerned settlers, and Busby himself persuaded them to lobby the British government. They pressured the Colonial Office to intervene by annexing New Zealand as a British colony on the basis of a full and fair agreement with Maori.

Things began to heat up in 1837 when the colonial reformer Edward Gibbon Wakefield, discussed in the next chapter, established his New Zealand Association. This was established to settle the islands as a private venture, along the lines of Pennsylvania in the United States. In the eyes of Victorian society, Wakefield's personal record—he abducted not one but two heiresses—made him a questionable figure, and his colonization theories had already failed in South Australia in 1836. Both the Church

Missionary Society and James Stephen, permanent undersecretary for the colonies, made sure that Wakefield did not win his royal charter. Wakefield changed tactics and in 1838 set up the New Zealand Company to settle New Zealand. Wakefield's dubious personal behavior, and the disclosure that his backers included several Roman Catholics, proved too much for the devoutly Anglican Stephen, who by late 1838 had made the decision to annex New Zealand. Wakefield, meantime, sent his Uncle William and son Jermingham to buy up as much land as possible before New Zealand became a formal colony. Hopeful settlers joined the Wakefield relations on the *Tory*, which sailed for Wellington (at the bottom of the North Island) in May 1839.

Although traditional accounts suggest that this action precipitated formal annexation, Sonia Cheyne, Peter Adams, and others have shown that the decision had been taken well before the *Tory* sailed. Recent research by Peter Tremewan suggests that fear of French colonization also persuaded Stephen and the new secretary for the colonies, Lord Normanby, to act. Certainly, French settlers arrived as early as May 1840 to settle at Akaroa on Banks Peninsula near Christchurch in the South Island.

Meanwhile Normanby and Stephen dispatched Captain William Hobson to treat with natives and win their assent. Although Hobson had no legal or diplomatic training—he had served in the Navy since age 10—he seemed undaunted by the size of the task allotted him. He sailed from England on August 14, 1839, and stopped over at Sydney for Christmas. While there, he talked at length with the humanitarian governor of New South Wales, George Gipps. Gipps persuaded Hobson of the necessity of a full agreement with Maori and confirmed Hobson's own view that he would need to annex the whole colony to ensure justice to Maori and to keep the French at bay. They agreed that New Zealand should become fully British for better or worse. The idea of a more limited protectorate, first proposed by Hobson in 1837, seems to have been rejected by the men closest to the action. Controversial historian Paul Moon has recently suggested that the Colonial Office never intended to govern Maori, but even if he is right the treaty itself, the input of the CMS missionaries, and the actions of Hobson as first governor all ensured that both races would be placed under a single British jurisdiction.

Hobson arrived on the *Herald* on January 30, 1840, immediately promoted himself to lieutenant governor (despite the protest of Captain Nias of the *Herald*), and called for a meeting of chiefs on February 5. He then set to work with Busby, a clerk named Freeman, and Henry Williams to devise a treaty. The language barrier was the first problem in drafting the document. Although Henry's brother William was expert in the Maori language, he was away on mission business at the time, and Henry had to rely on assistance from his son Edward, who had grown up bilingual.

The document produced by this unlikely group appealed to hopelessly high idealism on both sides. Given the amateur status of its architects, it is no surprise that it would later be condemned by historians as "hastily and inexpertly drawn up, ambiguous and contradictory in content, chaotic in its execution." Yet despite the later-day suggestion of some radicals and historians that it deliberately set out to defraud Maori, it was sincere in its aims—even if in its idealism it was no more practical than the fanciful notions of social engineering advocated by E. G. Wakefield. As W. H. Oliver has recently suggested, the new colony of New Zealand was founded on two kinds of idealism, both unrealizable: on the one hand, the treaty promised a harmonious pattern of race relations unparalleled in the annals of the brutal and messy business of colonization; on the other hand, Wakefield dreamed of building a better England in the antipodes, freed from the problems of overly rapid industrialization and urbanization.

New Zealand students are always surprised that such an important document could be so brief. It is no complex and sophisticated tome like the American Constitution, but rather a assortment of good intentions, expressed in just three clauses—not unlike a number of nineteenth-century treaties signed with tribes in Africa. First, it declares that the chiefs have signed over their full sovereignty or absolute power to the Queen of England. Second, the treaty guarantees existing powers of chieftainship and protection for all natural resources in Maori hands, while Maori for their part are required to offer land for sale to the Crown before involving any private buyers. Third, and finally, it guarantees to Maori the rights and privileges of British subjects. The Catholic bishop Pompallier also added the so-called fourth clause, which guarantees religious freedom. This proviso denied the possibility of any established or state church, a very important difference from Britain as we shall see later in the story.

Problems appeared even before the hastily translated document had been signed, however, with the great majority of chiefs signing a Maori version that differs from the English version in several important respects. Although there was no precise Maori equivalent for *sovereignty*, the 1835 Declaration of Independence had used *mana*, *tino rangatiratanga* (big or superior chieftainship cum overlordship), and *kingitanga* (king's power). Instead, the treaty uses the much less potent—and threatening—*kawanatanga* or governorship. Maori knew about governors as rather distant figures in New South Wales, or as the weak and vacillating Pontius Pilate in the Bible. *Governorship* suggested some limited form of cession rather handing over full and final authority to another nation.

The second clause is also fraught with difficulty. For a start, the English version guarantees Maori the "full, exclusive and undisturbed possession of their Lands and Estates, Forests, Fisheries and other properties," whereas the Maori version mentions only the "full chieftainship of lands, villages and taonga (treasures)." In addition to the problem of describing as property land that had not been valued, mapped, surveyed, or sold, the valuable resources of forests and fisheries were placed in a somewhat ambiguous category. Even worse, the term *preemption* (used in relation to land sales) is problematic enough in English, let alone in Maori. This arcane notion means the right of first refusal and had not been used in legal documents by the British Crown since the time of Charles II in the 1670s. Maori, not surprisingly, interpreted it in this traditional sense, but Busby and Hobson meant it to refer to the Crown's monopoly over land sales, which they saw as essential to ensure that Maori land could be bought cheaply before being sold to settlers to cover the costs of developing the colony. When Governor Gipps of New South Wales explained this to the southern chief Tuhawaiki in Sydney, the chief refused to sign because he realized that Maori would need to get market prices for their land if they ever hoped to generate enough capital to share in the benefits of development. The notion of a Crown monopoly over land sales also contradicted the third clause of the treaty—one of the rights of an Englishman is freedom of contract, that is, the right to buy from and sell to whomsoever he chooses. The simple Maori term *hokonga* (selling) could not hope to reflect this level of complexity.

Despite these problems, after some initial opposition 52 chiefs agreed to sign the treaty. They saw that its difficulties were outweighed by the advantages to be gained. Hobson, now seriously ill, instructed a group of naval officers and missionaries to take the treaty around the country to secure a more representative group of signatories. About 532 chiefs, or roughly half those eligible, signed, thereby providing a clear mandate. Taranaki Maori on the west coast of the North Island did not sign, for the simple reason that no one took the treaty to that part of the country. Some very high-ranking chiefs—such as Te Wherowhero of the Tainui confederation and Te Heuheu of Tuwharetoa—would not submit their *mana* to that of "a mere girl" (as they called Queen Victoria); however, some minor chiefs of those tribes signed just in case, as scholars have recently discovered. Fierce tribal and even intratribal rivalry ensured that various factions signed to ensure that their rivals did not steal an advantage over them.

The notion that Maori were somehow duped by the architects of the treaty simply will not stand up to historical scrutiny. International law at the time obligated a colonial power to secure a written treaty with a people who subsisted through gardening and tillage of the land. The British thus met a minimum set of obligations in presenting the treaty, and the early governors at least took the arrangement seriously. However, on May 21, 1840, Governor Hobson claimed the South Island by right of discovery to head off any French claims because he believed Ngai Tahu (who occupied the land) to be mere hunters and gatherers. He then established New Zealand as a colony separate from New South Wales in December 1840.

Troubled as its future history would be, the treaty soon proved useful to Maori, who ever since have resorted to it to address grievances and breaches. Yet, despite its genuinely noble intentions, it could do no more than temper the full force of the processes of colonization that were soon to impact them.

4

Building a Better Britain at Someone Else's Expense, 1840–1870

Pakeha or white-settler New Zealand began as a heady experiment in social relations thanks to the input of Edward Gibbon Wakefield and the New Zealand Company. Wakefield and his company's promoters based their deliberate efforts at building a better Britain on a hopelessly unrealistic reading of the productive capacity of the new colony, as well as on unrealistic expectations that Maori would be content to become claret-sipping, cigar-smoking squires confined to small reservations. Little wonder that this hard land, lacking both fertile soils for cropping and grasses suited to stock-raising, undermined Wakefield's grand designs. Maori resistance and hopelessly inadequate planning made the realization of Wakefield's fanciful schemes even less likely. Far from being a better Britain by the time the New Zealand Company folded in 1850, the new colony remained a chronically underdeveloped outpost of little importance to the greater British Empire.

WAKEFIELD AND THE NEW ZEALAND COMPANY

After abducting Ellen Turner in 1826, the widowed Edward Gibbon Wakefield spent three years in Newgate Prison. Here this rather turbulent man, whose father's friends included the radical intellectuals John Stuart

Mill and Jeremy Bentham, dreamed of making colonization more beneficial to the mother country. In his *Letter from Sydney* published in 1829, Wakefield outlined a new and supposedly scientific and systematic theory of colonization. He believed that the dangerous pressure resulting from overly rapid urbanization and industrialization could be removed if organizers based in Britain planned emigration to the colonies more carefully. He also devised a theory to avoid the disaster of penal colonies such as Australia and what he perceived to be the raw, crude democracy of the United States. The imaginary immigrant who supposedly wrote from Sydney suggested that an improved version of preindustrial Britain could be transplanted if the New Zealand Company sold land at the so-called sufficient price. By this Wakefield meant that land should be sold at a relatively high price so that only capitalists could afford to buy it. Laborers would have to work for those capitalists for 10 years or more before they could buy land and become farmers in turn. This way the chronic shortages of both capital and labor, which had so afflicted Australia and North America, would be avoided by the simple act of setting the price of the most important commodity in any colony.

Wakefield also regarded colonial roughness with horror and insisted that instant civilization could be achieved by basing these colonies around market towns and ensuring that women and children at least equal the number of male immigrants. He blamed the high crime levels of frontier societies on the imbalance of the sexes and the propensity of settlement to sprawl across vast areas of land. Wakefield also believed that cheap or free land encouraged land monopoly, whereas he wanted a society based on middle-sized family farms rather than vast estates. The principles of concentration and contiguity (settlements should grow out from central points and be interconnected) would make it much easier for colonial leaders to maintain social control and order. Consequently, churches and schools would play a central role in building these new communities and aid the search for order.

Raising crops, especially growing wheat, would supposedly provide the economic engine that drove these new colonies. Unlike sheep farming, cropping required long-term commitment to one place and relatively intensive use of land. In combination, then, the sufficient price, concentration and contiguity, family-dominated migration, and wheat-growing would create an improved version of an idealized preindustrial southeastern English society—harmonious, orderly, hierarchical, and conservative. Such a world had, of course, never existed in reality. This improved Old World social model would remake the forest-clad landscape into a replica of southeastern England with its manicured fields and tidy, carefully planned market towns.

We should note, however, before dismissing the theory as hopelessly impractical and fatally flawed, that other political economists of the day, including Karl Marx, took it seriously because it built on many of the concerns of both the Scottish Enlightenment and the Romantic reaction against the tyranny of reason. Indeed, Erik Olssen has labeled Wakefield's vision a "post-Enlightenment experiment." Like the radical intellectuals who regularly visited his father and his Quaker grandmother Priscilla, Edward Gibbon (he was named after the famous historian) believed that rational thought could reform the whole colonial project. At the same time, he took on board the criticisms of the new industrial order made by the Romantic poets and idealized the rural way of life over the urban. Having lost a father at a young age, he also tended to sentimentalize the nuclear family. Above all, he believed and learned from his spell in prison that the best colonies would be born free and peopled by respectable persons of some education and means.

Consequently, he pitched his whole enterprise to the group he called the "uneasy class," that is, middle-class persons who felt that their opportunities in Britain had been blocked by the difficulty of owning land, or blighted by the competition for jobs in the burgeoning professions and government bureaucracy. South Australia and New Zealand provided such persons with a real chance to start again, marry, have large families, and improve their lot. Such promotion, of course, held out sinister consequences for Maori, as it implied that there was plenty of room for everyone. Worse, Wakefield's misplaced belief in the abundance of New Zealand suggested that modest reserves would suffice for Maori, meaning that most land was in fact waste and ready to be used more productively by persons with farming skills.

Wakefield and his company established three settlements in the North Island (Wellington in 1840, Wanganui in 1840, and New Plymouth in 1841) and three in the South Island (Nelson in 1842, Otago in 1848, and Canterbury in 1850). The three North Island settlements and Nelson all struggled desperately, but the two more southerly colonies fared better.

THE EARLY SETTLEMENTS, ASSERTIVE MAORI, AND INTERFERING GOVERNORS

The 146 settlers on the *Aurora* had their hopes dashed when they arrived on January 23, 1840, to find that the settlement had been planned but not prepared in any tangible way. Instead of cultivated, smiling park land, they found steep and scarred hills, thick forest, and an apparently untamed country. The original town of Britannia, laid out in classical grid pattern, soon had to be shifted because it had been sited on the floodplain of the Hutt River. Taranaki Maori who conquered the area in the 1830s kept the 800 or so settlers who had arrived by March supplied with basic foodstuffs. Unfortunately, these Ati Awa gardeners occupied the only land suitable for settlement. The English and Scottish settlers responded to Maori hospitality by driving them out of the Lambton Harbor area in May. Thereafter, the settlers concentrated their efforts on what is now central Wellington. Ati Awa meantime joined forces with their Ngati Toa allies and hemmed the settlers into the Hutt Valley.

To make matters worse, the wild weather and steep country made the growing of wheat difficult, at least until forest had been cleared. Absentee ownership and the system of distributing land by lottery in England did not help either. Some setters found their promised farms to be in fact a sheer cliff face. Even if they had received proper farms, London-based speculators owned the majority of the surrounding farms and left them to appreciate in value under an accumulation of weeds. Fences could not stop the spread of weeds from these neglected properties, and agriculture soon began to contract. Things deteriorated further when the first two governors—Hobson and Robert FitzRoy—called in Commissioner William Spain to investigate the New Zealand Company's claim to 20 million acres of land. By the time Spain completed his investigation in 1844, the company's land had been reduced to a paltry 220,000 acres.

Most settlers responded to this hopeless situation by running subsistence farms or small businesses in town, or by migrating to Auckland in the north. As a result, by 1846 Wellington had attracted only 3,977 settlers, whereas Auckland, free of the strictures of Wakefield's sufficient price, had grown to 4,655. Things only began to improve from the late 1840s once Governor Grey overcame the resistance of Te Rangihaeata to the northwest and sheep farming began to flourish in the dry country of the Wairarapa to the northeast. Sheep farming on an extensive scale represented the opposite of Wakefield's theories, and his dream collapsed along with the New Zealand Company in 1850.

The other northern settlements fared little better. Maori hemmed settlers in around New Plymouth and Wanganui, and like Nelson, each struggling beachhead of settlers suffered from undercapitalization, absentee ownership, and a lack of farmers and employers. In each case preparations also turned out to be hopelessly inadequate. Things became so bad in Nelson that settlers revolted in 1842 and had to be allowed to exist as peasants in the interest of survival. When Nelson's settlers tried to expand across to the Wairau Valley to the east, disaster ensued. A series of misunderstandings resulted in the so-called Wairau affray of 1843 in which Ngati Toa killed 22 settlers. This incident scared away immigrants for several years.

Nelson began to achieve modest progress only when sheep farming developed in Marlborough from the late 1840s. Both Wanganui and New Plymouth struggled until after the major wars of the 1860s. Significantly, none of these settlements progressed until they abandoned two of the core elements of Wakefield's scheme: the sufficient price for land and wheat-growing. None of them could match the growth of Auckland either, which, ironically, also developed along more obvious class lines, whereas widespread hardship forced Wakefield's northern settlements to develop as relatively egalitarian communities lacking a wealthy ruling class.

The other reason for Auckland's greater success involved Governor Hobson's decision to remove the capital from Okiato in the Bay of Islands to Auckland in September 1840. Capitals tend to benefit from the operation of rudimentary administrations, and Auckland was no exception. When Nga Puhi led by Hone Heke and Kawiti protested the loss of trade and *mana* between 1844 and 1845, Auckland also gained impetus from the arrival of sailors and soldiers brought in to quell the so-called rebellion.

Hone Heke made his dissatisfaction clear by chopping down the British flagpole at Kororareka (modern-day Russell) several times in 1844 before sacking the town on March 10, 1845. Heke demanded that the flag associated with the 1834 agreement with Nga Puhi be flown alongside the Union Jack, but Governor Robert FitzRoy refused to contemplate any such suggestion of shared sovereignty.

Initially, the strategic skills of Kawiti secured the Nga Puhi several victories, until the arrival in November of the tougher new governor, Captain George Grey. Grey had many more soldiers and much heavier artillery in support and wore Nga Puhi down after heavy fighting at Ruapekapeka (the Bat's Nest) over Christmas. Nga Puhi discovered that although they could counter heavy bombardment with clever engineering works and trench systems, they could not sustain a long war against a professional army and navy. Once Grey secured a truce in January, he succeeded in persuading Nga Puhi, still one of the most powerful tribes in New Zealand, to remain neutral thereafter. This achievement should not be underestimated because it made British domination easier. Nevertheless, this northern war made clear Maori disappointment at the failure of the Treaty of Waitangi to deliver on its promise of some kind of smooth, trouble-free colonization experience based on partnership with rather than subjugation by the British. Significantly Nga Puhi also never attacked civilians or mission stations, to underscore the point that their dispute was with the British Crown, that is, the governor, and not settlers as such. On the contrary, they made it clear that they wanted settlers to stay and provide access to the advantages of trade and improved technology.

Russell Stone's recent work on the sale of Auckland has also suggested that the town moved ahead more rapidly than the Wakefield settlements because control of the Auckland isthmus by the Tainui Confederation, based farther south in the Waikato, made land available at cheap prices. Had Ngati Whatua not been so decimated by Ngai Puhi raids in the 1820s, things could have been very different. Instead, few Maori occupied Auckland when settlers arrived. Both colonizers and patron tribe Tainui thereby forced Ngati Whatua to sell land cheaply.

British settlers took considerable time to take advantage of this cheap land because they had to learn how to farm Auckland's volcanic soils. Once they did from the late 1840s, Tainui to the south of the city soon began to grow wheat successfully. During the early 1850s, Waikato Maori even exported wheat as far away as California and cornered the Sydney market. Governor Grey encouraged their endeavors in a very miserly way, but this relatively smooth coexistence began to disintegrate from the mid-1850s as settlers came to outnumber Maori (about 56,000 Britons as against 54,000 Maori). Most tribes began to realize that their remaining lands were now under threat of seizure. Cattle owned by settlers sometimes chewed down wheat crops, while Maori pigs rooted up settlers' gardens, further adding to the tension between the races.

Meantime settlement had spread significantly in the South Island, where Wakefield attempted to help establish two more settlements. Governor Grey helped move matters along from 1846, when he realized that Maori resistance would inevitably slow the progress of the North Island. His solution was to promote the development of the South Island by instructing officials to buy up as much of the South Island as quickly as possible, for as little as possible. He also instructed the likes of Captain Kemp and Walter Mantell to extinguish Maori title so that the vast and apparently unused acres could be made available for farming. Ngai Tahu lacked the numbers to resist and so sold the vast 20 million acre Kemp block (comprising most of modern-day Canterbury and much of Otago) for a mere £2,000 (about US$10,000 at this time). By the time of Grey's departure in 1853, most of the mainland areas had been bought up for less than £10,000. Government completed the purchase of the both the South and Stewart Islands by 1863 for under £15,000, leaving less than 2 percent of this land in Ngai Tahu hands, far less than the 10 percent originally proposed by the New Zealand Company. This buying spree made possible the rapid expansion of settlement in the South Island.

THE LATER WAKEFIELD SETTLEMENTS

The first settlers to benefit from this buy-up were the Scots led by the Liberal politician George Rennie, by Captain William Cargill, the grizzled veteran of Indian campaigns and the Peninsula War in Portugal, and by the Reverend Thomas Burns, nephew of the poet Robbie. Rennie and Cargill set out to build a New Edinburgh at the bottom of the world from 1842. Wakefield supported their notion of Presbyterian settlement because he hoped that religion would provide the glue and cohesion missing in his earlier settlements.

The chances of this settlement being rather like that of New England seemed to increase in 1843 when Cargill and Burns forced out the more liberal Rennie and decided on a narrowly focused Free Church settlement. The Free Church emerged out of the so-called disruption that tore apart the Church of Scotland in 1843. This dispute involved the issue of who should appoint the minister—the local landowner or the ordinary people of the parish. Burns sided with the more democratic alternative, broke from the mainstream Presbyterians, gave up a comfortable living in a wealthy parish, and set his sights on the South Island. Cargill supported him, and together the two tenacious characters held together the scheme.

The Wairau affray frightened away many would-be migrants in Scotland, but by 1847 the doughty pair prepared to establish their New Geneva on a 400,000 acre block of land on the lower east coast of the South Island, bought by the New Zealand Company from Ngai Tahu for £2,400. They assembled some 294 emigrants in November and sailed late in the month on two small ships, the *John Wickliffe* and the *Phillip Laing*. The *John Wickliffe* arrived first on March 23, 1848, followed by the *Phillip Laing* on April 15.

Some lessons had been learned from earlier mistakes, so that the land had been surveyed and relatively few properties had been set aside for absentee owners. Even so, preparations remained inadequate, and the settlement lacked wealthy capitalists to employ labor or cover the high cost of breaking in the land covered in dense forest. Yet again, local Maori kept the desperate settlers alive for the first year or so. Luckily, the Reverend Burns was an expert farmer, and thereafter a small, law-abiding community began to develop around subsistence farming, combining cropping and stock-raising.

Cargill stuck rigidly to the Wakefieldian ideals of the sufficient price, concentration, and contiguity and promoted agriculture ahead of pastoralism. Once he lowered the price of land in 1856, however, the settlement began to prosper as sheep farmers moved in from the north. Extensive sheep farming began to undermine the New England–like experiment, and the discovery of gold in 1861 dismantled it. Yet something of the stern, puritanical determination of those first Scots Presbyterian settlers still persists in the small city of Dunedin (the old Gaelic name for Edinburgh), described as "Scotch" by Mark Twain when he visited in 1895.

The slightly later settlement (1850) of Canterbury farther north prospered much more rapidly than Otago because its leaders dropped the sufficient price within a year of arrival. This action attracted expert sheep farmers from Australia as well as Britain because Canterbury contains the country best suited to extensive pastoralism in New Zealand. Canterbury also happened to be the best planned and most surveyed of all the Wakefield settlements and lured many more wealthy capitalists. Its leaders—Anglo-Irish Robert John Godley (educated at Oxford) and James Edward FitzGerald (educated at Cambridge)—exemplified the settlement's success in persuading well-educated younger sons of the gentry to try their hand at colonizing. Those who stayed went on to dominate politics in the province for over a generation and used their capital to develop the hinterland into both cropping and sheep farms. As a result, Canterbury's population had risen to 16,000 by 1860, while Otago languished at a more modest 12,691.

Canterbury today is held up as the most successful of the Wakefield settlements, and Christchurch is outwardly the most English and Anglican of New Zealand's cities with its elegant parks, immaculate gardens, manicured river Avon that winds languorously through the middle of the city, and centrally situated cathedral. This judgment is nevertheless misleading because Canterbury prospered by rejecting Wakefield's ideals, whereas Cargill and Burns adhered to those ideals for eight difficult years rather than rejecting them immediately after arrival.

PASTORALISM

The woolen industry, which so benefited Canterbury, also saved the entire New Zealand economy from collapse. Pastoralism—that is, sheep farming carried out on a gigantic scale on runs of up to hundreds of thousands of acres leased from the colonial government at minimal rentals—was introduced by Governor Grey from as early as 1851. It earned New Zealand by far the greatest part of its export earnings throughout the nineteenth century. Gold would challenge its dominance for a few short years in the 1860s, but wheat-growing, so favored by Wakefield, won a significant export income during the 1870s in only two provinces—Canterbury and Otago. Over the century as a whole, oats, which constituted the oil of the horse-powered world of nineteenth-century agriculture, won a greater share of exports in cooler Otago.

Pastoralism grew as an offshoot of the older Australian industry, which supplied the burgeoning textile mills of Britain with the bulk of their wool once the Spanish industry went into decline from the early nineteenth century. Consequently, fine-wooled merino sheep and Australian farming techniques dominated sheep farming down to the 1870s. Sheep spread north from Wellington into the Wairarapa and Hawke's Bay from about 1846, then moved across to Marlborough soon after, and more slowly into Canterbury and Otago. Sheep numbers surpassed 2 million as early as 1860, and wool became the golden fleece that attracted both capital and labor. Banks and special firms known as stock and station agencies—which supplied materials, seeds, and equipment; transported wool; made credit available; and were run both by local entrepreneurs and established Australian companies—multiplied rapidly as sheep farming expanded through the 1850s.

New Zealand's more regular rainfall made it an easier country than Australia in which to raise sheep, and early arrivals, especially those with adequate capital, made rapid fortunes. The famous English novelist and philosopher Samuel Butler, for example, arrived with £2,000 in his pocket and quadrupled his money within four years. This success enabled him to return to England and live the life of a literary gentleman. The apparently abundant fertility available on land that had never carried four-legged herbivores also produced high returns in the early years. All a farmer had to do was burn the native tussock, oversow some English grasses, and leave his sheep to flourish free of attack from natural predators other than a few wild dogs.

Unbeknown to the early pastoralists, however, their pursuit of fast profit had set in motion an ecological revolution. Sheep, which eat lower than any other herbivore, and fire soon upset the very delicate ecological balance of the high country. Carrying capacity fell suddenly from as early as the 1870s, and early farmers remained baffled by this unexpected reverse. Unexplained droughts and floods, in addition to anticipated snowstorms and constant wind, added to their problems. Erosion soon compounded these difficulties as the tough tussocks succumbed to the onslaught. The rabbit, introduced as early as the 1860s, enjoyed grasses eaten low by sheep and, free of predators, expanded to plague proportions. Disbelieving witnesses reported that whole hillsides appeared to move with rabbits by the 1870s. Shooting, poisoning, building long rabbit-proof fences, and the later introduction of mustelids such as stoats and ferrets in the 1880s seemed impotent in repelling the plague. A small mite known as sheep scab also soon made its appearance, and the colony failed to remove this scourge until 1893.

Consequently, what biogeographer Peter Holland has described as "people, plants and animals behaving badly" sent several runholders crashing into bankruptcy as early as the 1870s. This environmental uncertainty limited profitability. Although the majority of runholders still made comfortable livings and exercised considerable political power, they never exerted anything like the influence of their Australian equivalents, who began life as squatters, free of any form of state control or regulation. These Australian sheep lords ended up running much larger properties, sometimes millions of acres.

Consequently, pressure developed as early as the 1870s to find other ways of utilizing the land, as extensive sheep farming reached its environmental limits within a generation of large-scale white settlement. Combining sheep raising with large-scale grain farming offered one alternative in Canterbury and Otago, but the wetter North Island also proved difficult for merino sheep as well as cropping. Experiments began, therefore, with many different sheep breeds from the 1860s. Despite much trail and error, these coarse-wooled animals produced little tangible gain until refrigerated shipping, to which we shall return, made fat lamb farming possible from 1882.

VIRTUAL SELF-GOVERNMENT AND THE WARS OF RANGATIRATANGA

Before the South Island made rapid advances over the North Island thanks to the development of pastoralism and the discovery of gold, major war erupted in the North Island between the colonial government and tribes determined to defend their lands and chiefly authority. Governor Grey did not help matters when he virtually denied Maori participation in the political process by basing the suffrage on property ownership under his constitution of 1852. Maori still owned land communally, so most did not qualify for the vote. This meant that as colonists busied themselves with setting up a federal system of government, initially with six provinces, Maori found themselves excluded from influencing government policy.

The first assembly of the new bicameral legislature (consisting of a Legislative Council of 11 to be appointed by the governor and a House of

Representatives of 24 to 42 to be elected every five years), which meet at Auckland in 1854, compounded this problem by seizing control of land sales from the governor. Some Maori responded quickly from as early as 1854 by setting up the so-called king movement, or *Kingitanga,* as a kind of alternative government. Grey's offer of minimal support for Maori education, justice, and agriculture failed to buy much time as resistance grew steadily.

Tamihana, the missionary-educated son of Te Rauparaha, and his friend Matene Te Whiwhi had traveled to England and had taken great interest in the British system of constitutional monarchy. Encouraged by Archdeacon Octavius Hadfield, they toured the North Island advocating *kotahitanga* or unity and urged Maori to select their own king and establish their own parliament. Tribal suspicion limited the appeal of this idea. Large meetings at Manawapou in south Taranaki in 1854 and Taupo in 1856 split into more moderate and radical camps. One group wanted to stop land sales by driving Pakeha into the sea, while their opponents believed in coexistence on more equal terms. Eventually the moderate and Christian Wiremu Tamihana of the Tainui confederation persuaded the Ngati Haua and Ngati Mahuta *iwi* to join forces with Ngati Maniapoto and the Hauraki tribes and elect the aged *ariki* of Ngati Mahuta, Te Wherowhero, as king in 1858.

Te Wherowhero accepted very reluctantly and took the name of Potatou the First, devised his own flag, and clad some of his warriors in a special uniform. He never saw himself as a rival to the governor or Queen and had lived in Auckland for many years, trading happily with Pakeha settlers. The British authorities, however, viewed his election quite differently, believing that two sovereign powers could not exist in one land. Te Wherowhero died soon after in 1860, but his son Tawhiao—a priest rather than a warrior—continued the work of overseeing a ruling council or *runanga* (a parliament or *kahanganui* did not emerge until the 1890s) and running a newspaper. As both Tawhiao and Tamihana pointed out, clause 71 in the constitution allowed Maori autonomy at the local level. Indeed, the king movement expressed a desire for partnership as promised under the Treaty of Waitangi. Proponents argued that they represented one side of a meeting house and the Queen's government the other, while God acted as the ridgepole holding this union together.

It is most important to note that the great majority of tribes, most noticeably the powerful Ngai Puhi of the north, Ngati Porou of the east coast, and Tuwharetoa of the central North Island, did not join the *Kingitanga.* Some dissension also persisted among even its own immediate supporters. Nevertheless, it represented some kind of pan-tribal and proto-nationalist grouping in advocating that formerly divided tribes and clans unite against further land loss and British domination. Historians used to argue that the major war against the British led by this movement in the early 1860s was essentially about land, but today James Belich, Judith Binney, Ann Parsonson, Keith Sorrenson, and others stress that it also involved issues of sovereignty, or power. Students will find these wars variously described as the Maori Wars, the Land Wars, the Anglo-Maori Wars, and the New Zealand Wars. All four labels have some worth, but we must not forget that the majority of tribes did not participate in the wars, that the bulk of British soldiers were in fact Irish, and that no fighting associated with this resistance occurred in the South Island. For these reasons, the terms Wars of Resistance and Wars of *Rangatiratanga* (chieftainship) are probably most accurate.

Hostilities did not break out in the Waikato, however, but farther south in Taranaki. As the Taranaki tribes returned from their southern excursions, tensions rose when settlers attempted to expand out from the confines of New Plymouth. Would-be farmers especially envied Maori ownership and control of the rich soils of Waitara district about 10 miles north of the town. A chance to access the rich soils of the district came in 1859 when an internal tribal dispute apparently made the land available for sale. Teira, a minor chief of the area, felt aggrieved because the predominant chief of Te Ati Awa, Wiremu Kingi, had given sanctuary to a girl who had been betrothed to Teira's nephew. Kingi had acted correctly according to Maori custom by providing Teira with generous *utu* in the form of a horse and 20 sovereigns. But Teira remained unsatisfied. He then decided to secure *utu* through a peculiar distortion of seeking satisfaction known as *whakahe,* described earlier in the book. This involved selling the Waitara block to the new governor—Thomas Gore-Browne—who has little idea of land sale protocol. Senior officials such as Robert Parris and Donald McLean knew better, but the sale went ahead anyway. Kingi and his people protested vigorously, with the support of the Anglican bishop George Augustus Selwyn. Such protest produced little result, so Kingi began to remove surveyor pegs and occupied the block. Local setters and Governor Browne judged this a hostile act, and Colonel C. E. Gold led troops against Kingi from March 17, 1860. When Governor Grey returned to replace the disgraced Browne in 1861, he expressed support for the justice of Kingi's case by returning the block to Ati Awa, but his generosity came too late as a bitter war had ensued before his return.

The Taranaki War lasted only a little over a year, with Wiremu Tamihana negotiating a peace on April 8, 1861. It involved fierce fighting between about 3,500 imperial troops and 3,000 Maori warriors, with some 1,500

Kingites supporting Ati Awa and their other Taranaki allies. Initially, the Maori forces held the upper hand, winning a stunning victory at Puketakauere in June 1860. Maori surprised the British with their sophisticated fighting pa, which could be abandoned at a moment's notice. Eventually, however, under a new leader, Major-General T. S. Pratt, the British forces wore down Maori resistance through the use of spas or deep trenches, which soldiers dug in a zigzag pattern up to the fighting pa.

The part-time warriors had to return home to tend their crops and became weary fighting a full-time professional army. Much to the embarrassment of the colonial press, 238 British were killed or wounded, as against Maori losses of about 200 warriors, many of whom were killed. Neither side really won this small war, which can best be summed up as an inconclusive draw. Maori, though, learned again, as they had in the Northern War, that they could never best the British in straight-out frontal attack because their shotguns and *taiaha* (spears) were no match for the British bayonet. Serious losses of Ngati Haua warriors at Mahoetahi taught them never to repeat that mistake.

Governor Grey returned from South Africa soon after in September 1861 and talked of peace while preparing for war. Grey arrived under instruction of the Colonial Office to hand over control of native affairs to the Colonial Assembly in the hope that this would reduce the cost of any further military engagements. The colonial politicians, in contrast, hoped that the British government would continue to fund any future wars. This clash of imperial and local interest placed Grey in a difficult position. He responded by behaving autocratically and acted as if he knew what was best for settler and Maori alike.

On the one hand, Grey advocated the return of the Waitara block, introduced *runanga* or councils to increase Maori participation in government, and increased expenditure on schooling and hospitals. On the other, he built a military road south of Auckland leading to the Waikato and kept all 3,500 imperial troops in New Zealand under the pretext that Auckland faced imminent invasion. Meantime, Grey reoccupied the disputed Tataraimaka block south of New Plymouth on April 4.

Rewi Maniapoto, the Kingite leader of the powerful Ngati Maniapoto *iwi*, assumed that this meant a resumption of hostilities and ordered an ambush on the British blockade on May 4. His men killed nine soldiers in the raid. This action seemed to support Grey's portrayal of the Kingites as extremists, even though both King Tawhiao and Wiremu Tamihana pleaded for peace. The unpunished rape of a white woman in Kingite territory soon after seemed to support Grey's argument that Maori were incapable of ruling themselves. The incident inflamed settler racial prejudice against Maori, and even humanitarian opinion fell behind the governor, with the formerly critical Bishop Selwyn agreeing to serve as chaplain to the troops. In Selwyn's view, Maori had become the equivalent of naughty children who need to be taught a painful lesson. Most colonists agreed, while the Methodist missionaries remained silent. Only Archdeacon Hadfield remained firm in his opposition to any kind of war.

Grey prepared enthusiastically for war, knowing that the relatively flat Waikato offered an easier fighting ground than hilly Taranaki, while the Waikato River could be used to considerable effect by powerfully armed gunboats. Auckland businessmen and land agents supported him in the hope of winning access to excellent farming country. Their representatives in the Colonial Parliament made sure that politicians backed the governor against the protests of some South Island representatives who feared the cost of further war. Grey and Premier Alfred Domett (New Zealand had no prime ministers until it became a self-governing Dominion in 1907) easily won the debate. Grey retook Tataraimaka on June 24 before invading the Waikato on July 12. The Kingite leaders did not receive the governor's advice that all Maori had to swear the oath of allegiance or be expelled to Kingite territory, or that Grey intended to build military posts on their side of the Mangatiwhiri stream until July 17, the same day that the tough and experienced Scottish general, Sir Duncan Alexander Cameron, crossed that very stream. In other words, the governor ruled out any chance of diplomatic negotiations by his precipitate actions.

Historian Alan Ward refers to the invasion of the Waikato as the "climatic moment in New Zealand race relations" because it unleashed large-scale fighting followed by land confiscations still resented by Maori with great bitterness. Grey had built up troop numbers to over 4,000, out of a total imperial force of about 40,000. By 1865 that figure would rise to about 12,000, one of the largest imperial armies assembled outside India. Consequently, overwhelming numerical advantage and superior firepower enabled the British to win some easy early victories, as at Meremere. Fiercer fighting occurred at Rangirerere, but Cameron managed to take the Kingite capital of Ngaruwahia without a fight on December 8. Thereafter, the king's men stiffened their opposition to the Queen' forces.

Elaborately built fighting pa caused the British many problems, especially as they moved inland up the Waipa River, and proved effective in withstanding fierce artillery bombardment. American military historian John Gates has questioned James Belich's claim that these structures anticipated the trench system of the First World War by pointing out that such engineering can be found in many places since the invention of the cannon. But Belich is correct in stressing that the British never expected a supposedly savage and primitive people to be able to engage in such a sophisticated level of military engineering. Consequently, Maori often caught them out and slowed their advance.

Even so, Cameron inflicted heavy losses on Rewi Maniapoto at the remarkably chivalric battle of Orakau between March 30 and April 2, 1864. Rewi refused to surrender against overwhelming odds and fought on with wooden bullets. He lost 80 warriors but escaped capture with a remnant of his force. The British soldiers expressed their respect for his bravery by erecting a memorial at nearby Te Awamutu, only one of two instances in the annals of the British Empire that imperial troops made such an acknowledgement. (The other such memorial was erected at Rorke's Drift in South Africa in honor of Zulu heroism.) The severe loss at Orakau did not constitute a final battle such as Wounded Knee or Culloden, however, because resistance continued for a long time yet.

Indeed, the next major clash resulted in a stunning Maori victory at Gate Pa near Tauranga on the east coast on April 24, 1864. Ngai Te Rangi allies of the Kingites lured overconfident soldiers and sailors into a trap by building false fortifications behind deeply dug trenches. After a very heavy bombardment carried out from the sea, overconfident troops rushed the shattered ramparts, imagining that most of their enemy had been decimated. Instead they were caught in deadly crossfire. The 111 casualties and 31 killed represented the British low point in the war. Revenge followed soon after on June 21 at Te Ranga, when British troops caught the now-overconfident Ngai Te Ranga warriors and killed 120 of them.

This battle represented the end of the formal Waikato war as British troops slowly withdrew, to be replaced by colonial militia and progovernment Maori known as *kupapa*. Both the colonial soldiers and the Maori loyalists proved far less disciplined than the professional troops, and the conduct of the war degenerated as it entered a looser guerilla phase. The prophet Te Kooti Arikirangi, who had been falsely arrested as a rebel and shipped to the Chatham Islands, returned in 1868 to lead the colonial militia a merry dance around the central North Island. On November 10, 1868, he committed the notorious Matawhero massacre of 37 Maori and 33 Europeans. The *kupapa* leader Ropata Wahahwaha exacted revenge a few days later by summarily executing 120 of Te Kooti's followers at Ngatapa Hill near Gisborne. Te Kooti eventually sought refuge with King Tawhiao in 1872 and received a pardon in 1883, although the colonial authorities never allowed him to return to his home at Rongopai near Gisborne. After the fighting ended, Te Kooti also founded the pacifist Ringatu religion, which survives to this day.

The Ngati Ruanui warrior Titokowaru matched Te Kooti's resistance in the west. Titokowaru controlled southern Taranaki throughout 1868 and 1869, raiding as far south as the river port of Wanganui. He put up resistance from his diamond-shaped pa at Tauranga-ika and succeeded in killing the infamous Prussian mercenary, Major Gustavus von Tempsky. Then suddenly Titokowaru lost support, perhaps because he indulged in a sexual liaison with the wife of one of his warriors. Thereafter, warlike Titokowaru gave up the ways of the warrior and saw out his days living in Te Whiti o Rongomai's pacifist community at Parihaka.

General Trevor Chute and Colonel George Whitmore, who tracked Te Kooti and Titokowaru, engaged in a scorched-earth policy with as much enthusiasm as General Sherman. They burned villages, destroyed crops, and killed woman and children. Recently, a Waitangi Tribunal report has described these actions as a holocaust. This is undoubtedly an exaggeration, although these tough and ruthless professionals bequeathed a legacy of bitterness to southern Taranaki in particular. On the other side, the so-called Hauhau movement also raised the temperature of war by reverting to ancient practices such as ripping the hearts out of enemies and eating them. The prophet Te Ua Haumene established a religion known as Pai marire (literally good and peaceful religion), but some of his followers carried his teachings to fanatical extremes and put real fear into the minds of many settlers.

This degeneration into bloody chaos helps explain the considerable impact of what was a large war by the standards of a small and new colony. The king's forces had some 2,000 men killed as against 560 British troops and 250 *kupapa.* Maori losses were therefore very severe, with about 4 percent of their population wiped out as against the less than 2 percent of the total New Zealand population killed in the First World War. It took Maori a generation or more to overcome the trauma of these losses, yet it should be noted that they were modest compared with the devastation caused by the musket wars of the 1820s. In combination, though, the killing of about a quarter of the pre-European population as a result of exposure to the deadly military technology of Europe seems to support Jared Diamond's claim that "guns, germs and steel" hold the key to understanding the success of European colonization around the globe.

Even though the British never won a clear-cut victory as they did, say, over the highlanders of Scotland, it had become clear by 1872 that Maori could never win against such overwhelming odds. So they changed tactics from military to passive resistance, and like the First Nation peoples of the United States began to utilize legal and constitutional avenues to redress their grievances.

The wars of Rangatiratanga also produced three other major impacts upon Maori. First, they accelerated the loss of Maori land. The main engine for appropriation of Maori land was the Native Land Court established in 1865. Soon dubbed the land-taking court by Maori, it processed some 5 million acres in the North Island for sale by 1891. When this vast area is added to the 7 million acres already sold before the wars, Maori found their estate reduced to a mere 11.5 million acres by 1891. Most of the good farmland had also been wrestled from their control by this time, as some *hapu* were forced to sell to pay for their military campaigns, even if they supported the government. Land sharks won the 10 signatures required to buy land through getting owners drunk, or by buying their right to sell (formerly the consent of all the collective owners of land had been required for legitimate sale). The costs of surveying if a *hapu* decided to lease to Pakeha farmers, or of attending the sittings of the Native Land Court in Wellington, forced yet more sales.

The introduction of enforced confiscation known as Raupatu of 3.5 million acres by Governor Grey and a majority of colonial politicians in 1863 deepened the intense sense of grievance associated with the loss of their most valuable asset, in both the economic and spiritual sense. This action was supposedly to punish the rebels and fund the cost of the wars, but it failed to achieve either of these objectives. New Zealand continued to pay for the wars throughout the remainder of the nineteenth century, and *kupapa* also had land confiscated, while so-called rebels like Ngati Maniapoto held onto their land. Eventually, about half of the less valuable confiscated land would be returned, but this gesture did not satisfy Maori. The emotion tied up with a deep sense of betrayal still rankles with Maori in the twenty-first century because the confiscations continue to be equated with the abolition of habeas corpus, or the right to fair trial, under the Suppression of Rebellion Act of 1863. Despite a formal government apology in 1995 and the fact that the Native Land Court removed far more land from Maori control, many *iwi*, Tainui in particular, continue to feel deeply aggrieved about the Raupatu.

Second, land alienation on such scale confined Maori to more remote parts of the colony in the central North Island, the east coast, and the far north. Interaction and intermarriage continued but slowed as the two races tended to live in separate worlds until Maori moved en mass to the cities after the Second World War. Some *iwi* kept contact to a minimum, while others decided to increase contact, but economic survival soon forced most *hapu* to engage in seasonal farming tasks such as shearing sheep, digging drains, and erecting fences. Once they completed these tasks, most Maori laborers retreated to their remote pa until compelled to return by the need for more cash. So they survived on the margins of British settlement as a kind of rural proletariat who owned just enough land to subsist. Housing remained very poor; health problems escalated; and astute visitors confirmed a growing Maori complaint that they lived at much lower levels of affluence and comfort their Pakeha neighbors.

Third, physical separation of the two peoples encouraged the development of a powerful myth that good race relations characterized the New Zealand experience. Indeed, the notion of the noble Maori, the best of all native peoples, took hold of the national psyche. What had once been viewed as arrogance and insolence became reinterpreted as courage. After the wars, New Zealanders placed Maori on a pedestal with other famous martial races of the British Empire, such as the Zulu, Sikhs, and Pathans. The new attitude toward race—summed up as social Darwinism—built on an older idea that Maori sat at the top of the second division of the so-called tree of man. Some settlers even questioned the suggestion that Maori were in any way inferior to such lesser Caucasians as Slavs and Latins. At the other end of the scale, settlers gave unanimous support to ranking Maori far above the Chinese, effete Hindus, and black people such as the Australian Aborigines. Maori had, therefore, the capacity to elevate themselves to become brown-skinned Englishmen. Amateur ethnographers such as Edward Tregear even elaborated ornate theories to prove that Maori were at least proto-Aryans who came from India, or possibly Egypt. Such beliefs appear odd and eccentric today, but they constituted the greatest compliment that an ethnocentric nineteenth-century Englishman could pay a colored race.

This high estimate of a brave and noble adversary translated into a few meaningful concessions. The most important involved granting four seats in the House of Representatives and two in the Legislative Council to *kupapa* or loyal Maori. This action has subsequently been dubbed tokenism, but no other British colony granted indigenous people such advanced constitutional rights so early. Australian Aborigines, for example, did not win the right to vote until 1962. At the same time, a rather condescending attitude toward Maori emerged in the 1870s that suggested that, according to the teachings of Charles Darwin and Herbert Spencer, they were a dying or doomed race that would be displaced by a stronger race. Consequently, settlers should make the passing of the Maori as comfortable as possible by "smoothing their dying pillow." Fortunately for the future history of Aotearoa/New Zealand, Maori had other ideas and set about pursuing a range of strategies to cope with the loss of the wars and so much land.

THE MAJOR GOLD RUSHES OF THE 1860S

Settlers migrating to New Zealand had long hoped to find gold, the most precious mineral in the nineteenth-century world. Numerous guidebooks and immigration pamphlets had promised that gold lay below ground in abundance, but it proved remarkably illusory for two decades. After numerous false rushes, the experienced Tasmanian geologist Gabriel Reid found gold in early June 1861 in Central Otago's Tuapeka River, shining "like the stars in Orion on a cold frosty night." This discovery started the first of New Zealand's three major rushes, all of which occurred in the 1860s.

The timing ensured that, by the end of 1861, 17,000 Victorian miners poured in from Australia because the gold there had been largely worked out. Otago's population rose dramatically from 12,000 to 30,000 by the end of 1862, and Dunedin boomed. The sleepy village of 2,000 grew rapidly to 6,000 by the end of 1862 and to 14,000 by the end of the so-called golden decade. Its prim 3 hotels increased to 30 by 1862, as speculators threw up ramshackle buildings across its plunging gullies. Open drains and sewers saw rates of infection for diphtheria and dysentery climb above those of contemporary London. As shanties, grog shops, and brothels mushroomed, it became clear that the orderly village of Wakefield's dream had become a wild frontier town. Business benefited, particularly brewing to quench the miners' big thirst, brick-making for construction, and soap to cleanse miners at end of a hot and dirty day's work.

Gold exports obviously stimulated financing, with the Auckland-based Bank of New Zealand and the Sydney-based Bank of New South Wales securing most business out of this rush. Local businessman responded more slowly, only founding the ill-fated Bank of Otago in 1864, but local farming soon flourished in response to the stimulation of a much larger population, with sheep numbers climbing from 600,000 in 1860 to 2.4 million by 1867. Stock and station agencies, referred to in the section on pastoralism, emerged to service the needs of this sector for finance, marketing, and supplies. Wright Stephenson and Donald Reid were the most important of these firms in Otago.

In combination, these new activities converted Dunedin into New Zealand's leading city, and it proved its right to premier status by founding the colony's first university in 1869 and first public school for girls in 1871. Such dramatic growth and development spelt an end to the old hierarchical and rather static Wakefieldian order, as did the influx of democratically minded miners.

These men held egalitarian views and had won the universal franchise in Victoria. They soon secured this right within their own special Goldfields electorate. The Otago rushes were very orderly compared with those in California and Victoria. Dunedin's Scottish establishment ensured that they were strictly regulated, bringing in Vincent Pyke from Victoria as Goldfields' warden to oversee their administration. Pyke and the Provincial Council insisted on a 24-square-foot rather than an 8-square-foot claim as in Victoria, reduced the unpopular miner's right or annual fee, and avoided any kind of uprising such as the Eureka Stockade in Victoria. No gangs ever attempted to attack the mounted gold escort manned by tough Crimean War veterans. Indeed, the Otago rushes were probably the most orderly in history. Even the solitary bush ranger Henry Garrett treated his victims well before being imprisoned by the provincial authorities.

Much of the credit for this orderliness must go to the miners themselves, who were a little older than in California and Victoria, where they had learned many painful lessons. They were also surprisingly well educated because many of them had trained in skilled trades. Consequently, they set up libraries (or athenaeums, as they called them) and mechanics' institutes in many settlements to encourage self-improvement within their predominantly male communities (men outnumbered women three to one on average). Lectures by visiting speakers were very well attended, and the most popular book among miner readers was none other than Samuel Smiles's best-seller *Self Help*. Most miners also seemed determined to work within the system by drawing up petitions, lobbying politicians, and avoiding direct violence. This is not surprising, given that some had experience of the earlier chartist movement in Britain, which attempted to bring about social reform through constitutional channels rather than by direct action.

Historical geographer Terry Hearn has shown that these men also soon turned to the central state to solve their problems through the passing of special laws rather than relying on the Provincial Council, which remained dominated by farmers and businessmen with different objectives. This strategy proved so effective that miners received many more concessions in their use of precious water resources than did miners in either California or Victoria. As a result, New Zealand rivers were fouled on a much grander scale than elsewhere, even though this was a relatively small rush by world standards. The miners also dumped debris at will, and the landscape remains scarred by the sluicing and dredging that soon followed the initial diggings.

The Otago rushes pushed inland as the American Horatio Hartley and the Irishman Christopher Reilly made a huge find worth £2,000 near Cromwell in August 1862. Discoveries at nearby Cadrona (note the direct naming reference to the Californian rushes), Queenstown, and Arrowtown soon followed, and the rush became a little rougher. The hordes of miners soon worked out the easily accessed alluvial gold and turned to hydraulic sluicing instead. The building of hundreds of miles of pipes to power the hoses required more cooperative effort, and individual miners tended to group together in small companies, often run along ethnic or family lines. Cornish miners, who had experience of this technique in England, became more prominent, and the Otago Provincial Council brought in Chinese miners from 1866 to rework mined areas, especially with high-pressure hoses. The Chinese received rough, discriminatory treatment as in California and Victoria, but suffered less violence. Even so, legislation discriminated against them down to the 1920s, persuading the prime minister of New Zealand to make an official apology for their wretched treatment in 2001.

Some of these sluicing operations persisted into the twentieth century in places like Blue Spur, where the rush first started, but sluicing generally gave way to quartz mining by large crushing machines from the late 1860s. Miners worked for wages for companies at these stamping batteries and adopted a lifestyle more like that of the coal miners of Europe. Large dredges worked rivers such as the Clutha in the 1890s and revived the industry. Dredge construction also stimulated heavy engineering in Dunedin, but this boom had largely ended before the First World War.

The same patterns repeated themselves on the west coast of the South Island from 1863 and in the Thames/Coromandel area southeast of Auckland from 1867. Gold mining created a province from virtually nothing on the west coast as Victorian miners who had given up on the cold and tough conditions of central Otago returned to try their luck once more. Because the Southern Alps blocked entry from the land, most miners came by ship. This transport pattern meant that this rush benefited Melbourne in Australia more than Canterbury in New Zealand. Consequently, the gold rushes produced only a very minimal impact upon Canterbury history as compared with Otago's. The concentration of Victorian miners also made the west coast of the South Island into the most Australian and Irish Catholic place in New Zealand. Much of this distinctive character survives to this day.

The alluvial gold around a string of rivers did not last long, so sluicing, and to lesser extent quartz mining, predominated from the late 1860s. Hokitika, which had grown from virtually nothing to 5,000 by 1867, boasting an extraordinary 102 hotels, lost its boom town character as gold mining gave way to coal mining as the major employer by the 1880s. This transition proved more difficult than the overconfident gold miners imagined, and they had to import some English experts to help them construct the safe underground cities that we also know as coal mines. As in Otago, dredging flourished in the 1890s and lingered down to the 1940s, after which gold became of greater interest to tourists than mining companies.

The Thames/Coromandel rush was somewhat different in that it concentrated much more on quartz mining from the outset. Consequently, it was a much more capital-intensive rush based around expensive machinery and the employment of miners on wages. This rush lasted longer than elsewhere because the cyanide method of extraction gave it a new lease on life in the 1890s. It lingered into the 1920s, but the cyanide process proved less happy for both workers and the environment. Labor historian Erik Olssen has estimated that miners in this area had a life expectancy of 44 years, against a national average of 61 years. Devastation and scarring of the heavily forested landscape is still easily seen today, and the mess involved has persuaded locals to continue to fight against any revival of mining activity in the area. The town of Waihi features a big water-filled hole like that of Butte in Montana, and many houses are now collapsing into abandoned underground mines. Little wonder that this area has been home to New Zealand's Green Party.

The three rushes produced similar amounts of gold (the west coast 6.55 million ounces, Otago 6.52 million ounces, and Thames/Coromandel 3.7 million ounces), but although significant regionally this only constituted 9 percent of the world's gold during the peak years of the 1860s and 3 percent for the nineteenth century as a whole. This is modest compared with Victoria's 13 percent, South Africa's 15 percent, and 47 percent from the Americas. Both Victoria and California also produced about a quarter of the world's gold at their peaks. The net result is that today Dunedin is a respectable little city of about 120,000 people, whereas Melbourne and San Francisco are important international metropolises of about 4 million, approximately the total population of New Zealand.

Gold certainly revitalized a flagging colonial economy, winning up to 70 percent of New Zealand's export earnings in 1864. It increased the population from 99,000 to 248,000 by 1870, pushed the South Island well ahead of the North, helped Auckland recover from the traumas of war, and unleashed a more egalitarian impulse into colonial political life, but it never represented more than an important tributary in New Zealand's economic and social development. Farming had been the mainstream of New Zealand's development since the late 1840s and became so again from the late 1860s as gold production waned. The quelling of Maori military resistance and the resulting acquisition of so much Maori land opened the way for stock farming to flourish on land formerly controlled and gardened by the tribes. Better Britain could now be erected at great speed.

5

Boom and Bust, 1870–1890

EXPANSION, CENTRALIZATION, AND EXPERIMENTATION IN THE 1870S

Waning gold production and low wool prices made New Zealand into the ugly duckling of the Australasian colonies by the late 1860s. It seemed that, unless someone took drastic remedial action, the colony was destined to be little more than a giant sheep walk. It lacked all three key ingredients for development—capital, labor, and infrastructure. The only organization with sufficient managerial expertise and financial clout to attract capital and labor was the state because tiny New Zealand lacked large corporate organizations like those of Britain or the United States. Colonial politicians had increasingly realized this need by 1870, but it took the leadership, vision, and nerve of Julius Vogel to set New Zealand on a more dynamic course.

Vogel came from a family of Jewish merchants in London and made his modest fortune as a newspaper journalist and editor in the Victorian gold rushes. He moved on to the Otago rushes and established the colony's first daily newspaper, the *Otago Daily Times,* in 1861. Vogel's entrepreneurial flair soon found him involved in numerous business ventures, several of which would benefit from his holding a seat in parliament and the Otago Provincial Council. He succeeded in both objectives in 1863, serving as the member for Dunedin North and representing Waikouaiti on the Provincial Council. Vogel used his position to advance his own interests, as did many other so-called businessmen-politicians. At the same time, he was a very able administrator and soon rose to become provincial treasurer in 1866 and, after changing from Dunedin North to the Goldfields electorate, colonial treasurer in 1869. Vogel seized the chance to reinvigorate the stagnant economy in his public works budget presented on June 28, 1870. He proposed to borrow £10 million over the next decade to fund a massive program of public works and immigration and to buy up large areas of Maori land for development.

Most politicians supported the general public enthusiasm for this grand design. A few more-cautious parliamentarians expressed concern about the size of the loan and the difficulty of servicing such a huge debt, but hardly anyone questioned the concept. Most developing colonies had to borrow if they hoped to grow, but none borrowed quite as heavily as New Zealand, especially once the loan expanded to £20 million by 1880. By then New Zealand's per capita debt outstripped that of every Australian colony and was four times higher than Canada's.

Some contemporaries, like several later-day historians, cited Vogel's bold plan as the major cause of the sharp depression of the 1880s that followed the boom years of the 1870s. Such an interpretation is unfair because this depression resulted from the collapse of an increasingly inefficient British farming industry overwhelmed by the overproduction of wheat by New World producers such as Canada, the United States, Australia, and Argentina. New Zealand would have been seriously affected by the subsequent downturn in international economic activity even without the loan. The loan rather exacerbated short-term economic problems while bringing mid- and long-term advantages. Later development, especially that related to the frozen meat industry, would have been considerably hampered without the 1,100 miles of railways, 2,500 miles of road, and numerous bridges built in the 1870s over New Zealand's turbulent and dangerous rivers. Over 4,000 miles of telegraph poles erected in the 1870s and connection to the international telegraph cable in 1876 plugged New Zealand back into the global village and broke down much of what Australian historian Geoffrey Blainey calls "the tyranny of distance."

Equally important, nearly 200,000 immigrants helped double the colony's population. Financial institutions flourished in response to the influx of capital and people. Two new banks, the London-based National and the Dunedin-based Colonial emerged in 1872 in response to increased business activity. The Auckland-based South British Insurance Company and the Dunedin-based and London-backed National Insurance Company also became established in 1872 and 1873 respectively to cater to the needs of the rapidly growing colony. Similarly, the National Mortgage Agency joined other stock and station agencies in supplying the burgeoning farming sector with credit and supplies.

Large land companies, most notably the Glasgow-backed New Zealand and Australian Land Company, stepped up their activity and pumped money into developing both grain and stock farming. Their input helped produce the first dual-purpose sheep for the production of good quality meat as well as wool. Known as the Corriedale, this big, tough sheep could be run on wetter country than the Spanish merino, which flourished only in dry areas. Not surprisingly, the New Zealand and Australian Land Company also played the leading role in the development of refrigerated shipping to create a market for its meat-producing sheep.

The 1870s also witnessed the emergence of New Zealand's two largest shipping companies, the Dunedin-based Union Company and the New Zealand Shipping Company based in Christchurch. The Union Company benefited particularly from its monopoly hold over the San Francisco mail run and grew to become one of the 10 largest shipping companies in the world. Not to be outdone, the government added a Government Life Insurance Company in 1869 and a public trust to sort out wills for persons of modest means in 1872, and it greatly improved the postal service.

Grain-growing boomed in Canterbury and Otago in response to these inputs of capital and their associated superior technology and expertise. Grain exports rose from £130,000 in value in 1871 to £1.2 million pounds in value in 1881. Land in cultivation over the same period also increased nearly five times, from 1.2 million to 5.2 million acres. Almost 7 million acres had been fenced by 1880, 4 million with wire. Imports of agricultural machinery, especially from the United States, as well as local manufacture of horse-drawn reapers and binders flourished. But the boom induced by borrowing and the associated grain bonanza burst when the initial soil fertility ran out, and prices for both wheat and oats crashed in the late 1870s.

This busy burst of development by both the private and public sectors won New Zealand a reputation as a workingman's paradise. Even unskilled laborers could earn two pounds a week, almost twice the going rate in England, and they generally worked an 8-hour day rather than 10 hours or more as they would in Britain. Some economic historians suggest that during the mid-1870s New Zealand achieved the highest per capita standard of living in the world.

Vogel and other politicians also abolished New Zealand's cumbersome provincial system in 1876, primarily to secure more favorable terms on the London money market. A unitary entity called New Zealand had far more chance of producing the equity to secure large loans than a place called Auckland or Otago. In short, as Vogel's biographer Raewyn Dalziel has shown, his imagination and faith in the future potential of the colony helped hasten economic recovery once the international economy began to recover in the mid-1890s.

Things would have been better if parliament had agreed to accept Vogel's proposal that 6 million acres of native forest be set aside as a national estate. Vogel had read the American G. P. Marsh's important book *Man and Nature* and became concerned about impending timber shortages after a tour of the country. Unfortunately, most politicians did not share his farsighted and pragmatic vision and rejected conserving resources for future use. Development became wanton. The interest bill soon grew into a serious burden; no one undertook any kind of cost-benefit analysis; and self-seeking politicians had roads, bridges, and railways built in the wrong places. Branch lines, for example, tended to run onto the properties of wealthy landowning parliamentarians rather than linking port to hinterland in any systematic fashion. Already developed Canterbury and Otago raced ahead of the North Island, although Hawke's Bay on the east coast benefited enormously from the virtual removal of its giant forest. Easy credit encouraged speculation, and land values soared to unsustainable levels. Levels of indebtedness of both large-scale and small-scale farmers increased alarmingly along with the national debt.

The immigrants who arrived in such large numbers from Britain and Australia ameliorated some of these problems. Lured by descriptions of New Zealand as a land of milk and honey, about 115,000 came from Britain, Scandinavia, and Germany as assisted immigrants. A further 60,000, mainly from Australia, made their own way to win high wages and the chance to own land.

Initially, immigrants assisted by the government received very bad press. Older settlers labeled them "certificated scum" and blamed everything from an increase in drunkenness to the economic depression on their arrival. The research of Rollo Arnold, Charlotte Macdonald, and others has shown this judgment to be completely unfair and wildly inaccurate. The great majority were, in fact, hard working, law abiding, and highly literate, despite the fact that most were from low-status occupations deliberately targeted by the government, such as agricultural and general laborers, domestic servants, and navvies (specialist railway builders who had already worked in Canada and the United States). The absence of any representatives of the lesser gentry or the professional classes constituted the major difference from earlier waves of immigrants. The 1870s also saw the first major influx of single women, especially from Ireland. Traditionally, historians suggested that these women came in search of husbands in a more favorable marriage market, but Charlotte Macdonald's work shows that they came primarily to improve their individual lot, even though most eventually married. Otherwise, the 1870s group was very similar in demographic terms to earlier groups, with about 60 percent being male and young.

The ethnic composition was also more diverse than formerly, although these settlers remained more than 90 percent British in origin. About 4,500 Scandinavians (predominantly Danes) and 2,000 Germans came to convert the forest of Hawke's Bay to farms. Generally, this Protestant group integrated easily into a very Protestant colony, and most succeeded in improving their lot. A handful of Italians who tried their luck in the very wet southwest corner of the South Island has less success, and many returned to Italy. A small group of Poles who settled near Dunedin fared better, but New Zealand remained determinedly Anglo-Celtic and did not encourage European migrants like the United States did. For the first time in the colony's history, about 34,000 Irish outnumbered 22,000 Scots. This influx strengthened the Catholic community sufficiently to enable it to run its own separate school system after the government established a secular state system in 1877. Some of the Irish and Scots from cities such as Dublin and Glasgow struggled with the harsh frontier conditions, but the majority thrived on their newly found independence.

The biggest single group of around 25,000, though, was made up of English agricultural laborers from the southwest counties of Devon and Cornwall, Kent and Essex near London, and Oxfordshire to the west, who had been locked out in a bitter dispute with their landlords. Rollo Arnold has shown that members of this group generally succeeded as small farmers and helped push New Zealand in a more egalitarian direction because their Methodist faith taught that all men were equal. Consequently, they strove to overcome privilege and ostentatious wealth. These families, along with the Scots and Irish, also bolstered family life, especially as the women proved remarkably fecund and produced more than six children on average. These rapidly growing families shared with single women migrants a dislike of high levels of drunkenness and violence associated with male-dominated communities. They soon set about challenging this rough and visibly unequal frontier order.

These new groupings found much to protest. The grain bonanza in particular had encouraged sheep farmers to freehold their rental properties into giant estates on which they also grew grain. Subdivision also occurred alongside these aggregations of farmland, but the trend moved inexorably toward monopoly as these big properties earned handsome profits. Some estates made up to £30,000 in good years, the equivalent of about US$5 million in modern money. Such earnings enabled the building of grand houses in the east coast downland areas from South Otago all the way through Canterbury, Marlborough, Wairarapa, and Hawke's Bay to Gisborne in the North Island. Exclusive schools also began to appear, especially in Christchurch.

Some big landowners, particularly in Canterbury and Hawke's Bay, aped the lifestyle of the English gentry and carefully controlled the marriages as well as the education of their children. Many historians refer to this group of around 500 families as a gentry, but the term is questionable for a number of reasons. First of all, only a relatively small number came from the ranks of the British gentry. Furthermore, most other colonists refused to behave deferentially toward these families, thereby removing much of their power. Big landowners also controlled far fewer levers of power than in Britain because New Zealand had no established church, and the state rather than beneficent squires looked after social welfare, even if in a most preemptory way. Outside of Canterbury, the big landowners never even dominated local politics; farmers running more modest properties, small businessman, and skilled workingmen contested their power. Farmers won seats alongside the estate owners on the provincial councils and in the county councils that replaced them, and made sure that they too became justices of the peace. Trevor Burnard's and Jim McAloon's work on inheritance has also shown that the would-be gentry tended to self-destruct by practicing partible division rather than primogeniture as in Britain; that is, they divided their properties among all their children. Before the breaking up from inside occurred, however, this conspicuous elite became very unpopular, especially after an inquiry in 1890 found that a mere 584 individuals and companies owned 56 percent of New Zealand's freehold land.

Although this concentration of ownership was not nearly as bad as in Latin American countries, it was worse than in England, where the great estate owners controlled only about a third of freehold land. Migrants who had traveled halfway around the world in uncomfortable small ships to escape the evils of a class-dominated society had little tolerance of such replication of Old World evils. Literacy rose from an already high 70 percent in 1870 to nearly 90 percent by 1890 as a result of the introduction of compulsory schooling in 1877. This made New Zealand into one of the most literate societies on Earth, and newspaper circulation rose at twice the rate of population growth between 1870 and 1890. Reading widely in the often-radical press, many people determined that this state of affairs should not be allowed to continue indefinitely. Even small-town newspapers along with the specialist rural press introduced them to the ideas of English radicals such as J. S. Mill and of the California radical Henry George, and to the soft socialism of the dreamy American Edward Bellamy. Protests by the American populist movement were also reported at length as ordinary New Zealanders on farms and in small towns and cities learned about possible solutions to the problems of gross maldistribution of land and wealth. It took the pressure of a decade of depression and hardship, however, before the lower-placed groups in society could organize themselves to bring about some big changes in their "Britain of the South."

Maori, meantime, regrouped as the Native Land Court systematically bought up their land. Vogel's roads, bridges, and railways made the movement of troops much easier, and this development ruled out the possibility of future military resistance. So Maori turned to other forms of protest. In Hawke's Bay, Ngati Kahungunu shamed the government into appointing a commission to inquire into the dubious purchase of land in the area. The two Maori chiefs on the commission reported that they had found ample evidence of such conduct, but the Pakeha majority won out and little changed.

Farther west Te Whiti o Rogomai and Tohu Kakahi founded a thriving pacifist community at Parihaka in South Taranaki. Supported by the former warrior Titokowaru, this community began to dispute local farm ownership by tearing down fences and plowing up land. This all proved too much for the colonial government, which waited for the pro-Maori governor Arthur Gordon to leave the colony before invading the peaceful community on November 5 (Guy Fawke's day on the English calendar) and making mass arrests. This shameful action constitutes one of the real low points in the history of New Zealand race relations, but it did not break the spirit of Te Whiti and Tohu, who continued to resist, despite intermittent imprisonment, until their deaths in 1907.

From 1882 tribes outside the Kingitanga, especially Nga Puhi of North Auckland, Ngati Kahungunu of Hawke's Bay, and the Wanganui River tribes, began to organize themselves into the Kotahitanga or unity movement to lobby government. They sent a delegation to London in 1883 and prepared the way for more effective action in the 1890s. King Tawhiao meantime, refused a seat on the Legislative Council, called for the establishment of a Maori parliament and attempted to visit Queen Victoria in

1884. He had no more success than the Kotahitanga in actually meeting with the monarch, but caused considerable embarrassment to the colonial government nevertheless.

Te Kooti continued to develop his Ringatu community in the remote Urewera ranges. Maori farming, especially amongst the wealthier Ngati Porou *iwi* of the east coast, began to slowly recover. Despite the alarmingly high rates of infant mortality (about one in three Maori children failed to make it through the first year of life, about the same as the shocking statistics for back-country Mexico at this time), the birthrate lifted and population numbers began to increase. Maori may have achieved few tangible gains, but they weathered their worst years with dignity and patience, which helped produce more tangible advances from the 1890s.

THE LONG DEPRESSION OF 1879–1896

The boom years of the 1870s ended rather abruptly in 1879 when the City of Glasgow Bank collapsed. This institution backed the New Zealand and Australian Land Company, so investment in the colony dried up fast. Indeed, British investors tended to withdraw their money out of New Zealand in the 1880s and redirected it to the more fashionable Palatinate region (Argentina and Uruguay). Initially, this removal of capital hit the South Island worst, with Auckland surviving thanks to the ongoing Melbourne building boom sustained by Melbourne's elevation into one of the great cities of the late nineteenth century. The region's *kauri* forest continued to supply the builders of "marvelous Melbourne" with excellent timber, and unemployment did not become obvious until this bubble burst in 1885.

From this time, the whole of the New Zealand economy remained depressed until around 1896. The massive migration inflows of the 1870s turned into a steady outflow to Australia; bankruptcies increased; many small farmers clung to mere subsistence levels; and unemployment rose to at least 10 percent of the workforce. The new frozen meat industry, promoted by the New Zealand and Australian Land Company, failed to produce much beneficial impact until the 1890s, except for the great estate owners who built the first freezing works. Yet this industry, along with dairying, which really only took off from the late 1890s as New Zealand farmers learned how to run dairy cattle rather than sheep, would completely change New Zealand's economic direction in the late nineteenth and early twentieth centuries. Several generations of historians, starting with Guy Scholefield in 1909, have emphasized the huge importance of the technological innovation of refrigeration in confirming New Zealand's role as Britain's far-flung grassland farm. Recently, James Belich has caught the public imagination by referring to this development as "recolonization," but his racy phrase merely supports the conclusions of many other scholars.

In contrast to the consensus over how refrigeration made New Zealand much more dependent upon the London market and three basic export staples (frozen, fatty lamb; yellow butter; and wool of often indifferent quality), historians have wasted much ink arguing about whether 1879 to 1896 constituted a long depression. Suffice to say that although we do not know exactly how the downturn in prices impacted upon such modern measures as gross domestic product, contemporaries felt that the New Zealand dream, promised in such rosy fashion by the borrowing of the 1870s, seemed to be disappearing fast. We cannot calculate the exact level of unemployment either, but it clearly was the worst in the colony's short history. Several of Auckland's merchant princes went bankrupt in spectacular fashion, along with some heavily indebted sheep farmers who had purchased land at highly inflated prices during the 1870s. Confidence dropped to an all-time low. Government policies of retrenching on spending did little to help ease the sense that the colony had apparently lost all sense of direction. Talk of some kind of pension system by Premier Harry Atkinson in 1882, experiments with leasehold tenures by the supposedly conservative government of John Hall and William Rolleston, and easier terms for buying and leasing land introduced by John Ballance in 1885 and 1886 did little to restore confidence. New Zealand still constituted the third biggest economy in Australasia after New South Wales and Victoria, but its appeal to both investors and immigrants waned. Even a change of government in 1891, which saw the reforming Liberals come to power, did not lift the gloom completely because prices for frozen lamb, butter, and wool did not recover until 1896.

British consumers had to learn that frozen lamb could be more palatable than canned beef from Argentina and that cheap New Zealand butter represented better value than its Danish or Victorian counterpart. The rising standard of living of the English working class also had to come to New Zealand's rescue because workers, and not the well-heeled gentry and middle classes, provided the market for these rather unappetizing-looking food products. New Zealand entrepreneurs and financiers had originally imagined that they would sell at the top, luxury end of the market. Instead the bottom end saved the day. Coincidentally, falling shipping costs helped overcome the problem of exporting over such vast distances.

Before these developments rescued the struggling economy, however, some entrepreneurs attempted to pursue a different path by trying to develop textile manufacturing. New Zealand could still produce cheap wool, so visionaries such as the Jewish Bendix Hallenstein and the Scots John Ross, Robert Glendining, and John Roberts set up large mills in the 1880s, especially in or near Dunedin. Unfortunately, this effort to diversify New Zealand's dangerously narrow export base did nor succeed because both Australian and American politicians pursued a policy of industrialization behind hefty tariff walls at this time. A modest tariff instituted in 1888 could not offset this disadvantage, and the textile industry floundered thereafter. By the early 1900s New Zealand was once more exporting most of its wool raw, only to buy it back from Britain as finished garments.

A major protest against so-called sweating between 1888 and 1890 also undermined this rather desperate attempt at breaking colonial dependence upon Britain (whereas only about 50 percent of New Zealand's exports went to Britain in 1870, as against 46 percent to Australia; by 1900 New Zealand exported over 80 percent of its produce to Britain as against 14 percent to Australia). The Reverend Rutherford Waddell, an evangelical Presbyterian minister from Northern Ireland, delivered a very influential sermon on the "sin of cheapness" in late 1888. The local newspaper, the *Otago Daily Times,* investigated his complaints. The newspaper found that women and boys were working very long hours (around 72-hour weeks) for a pittance. A royal commission reported in 1890 that it could find few definite cases of outright sweating as in Britain, but the New Zealand public remained outraged and applauded the support given by manufacturers such as Bendix Hallenstein to the establishment of a Tailoresses' Union under the leadership of Harriet Morison, to prevent any further sweating. The reforming Liberal government then systematically withdrew women and children from factories immediately after its election in 1891, just as the United States began to build its economic power by employing hundreds of thousands of recently arrived female immigrants in its factories. Skilled male laborers also worked with the new Liberal government to keep women out of their traditionally male workplace. New Zealand thereby gained little advantage from the so called second industrial revolution, which the United States utilized to become the greatest economic power on Earth. So New Zealand followed a different path to modernity and higher living standards than most other places by industrializing its agriculture rather than by pursuing the development of manufacturing.

6

Britain's Experimental Farm, 1891–1914

THE 1890 ELECTION AND CREATION OF THE SOCIAL LABORATORY

The economic depression of the 1880s raised awareness among the electorate that supposedly Old World evils such as poverty, juvenile delinquency, and exploitation of labor had found their way to New Zealand. A large majority of voters also seemed alarmed that many of the evils of industrialization and urbanization were now appearing in a colony established expressly to escape the problems of dirty factories and sprawling, dangerous, and unsanitary cities. W. H. Oliver has described this process as the "loss of colonial innocence." Any party that appeared to offer solutions to such problems and seemed to have a semblance of a plan as to how New Zealand might be put back on the tracks had a strong chance of winning the election held in December 1890. The introduction of universal manhood suffrage in 1889 also helped create a mood conducive to reform.

The Liberals, under the leadership of the northern Irishman and Wanganui-based journalist John Ballance, constituted New Zealand's first modern political party. It emerged slowly from 1889 as a coalition of skilled workingmen, newly organized unions of such unskilled workers as coal miners and wharf laborers, and middle-class radicals. The unskilled organized themselves into Seamen's Wharf Laborers' and Coal Miners' unions in 1889 and then joined forces in an umbrella organization known as the Maritime Council in October 1889. This organization soon became embroiled in large strike from August 1890, essentially to support its Australian equivalent. The strike drew the unskilled unions closer to both the skilled unions and the middle-class radicals, but alienated potential small-farmer supporters. Consequently, it seemed unclear whether Ballance had enough support to win the government. Policies advocated by the Liberals and Harry Atkinson's government also seemed pretty similar, except that the Liberals promised to replace the existing property tax, which penalized improvements such as farm buildings, with a pure land tax.

As a younger man Ballance had talked a lot about J. S. Mill's idea of slowly nationalizing the land and had shown interest in Henry George's idea that a single land tax would break land monopoly more effectively than any other measure. But Ballance did not express anything so radical during the campaign and made it clear that the land tax would be accompanied by a progressive income tax. His caution seemed to backfire when a separate Labor Party emerged in Dunedin, so that humble working-class men such as brass finishers and boot clickers (the persons who attach the top part of a shoe to the sole) could stand for parliament for the first time.

Much to the surprise of the conservative press, Ballance won narrowly and soon gathered the support of five Labor members of parliament (MPs). Atkinson panicked and stacked the Legislative Council with his own supporters to prevent the passage of any radical legislation. This action infuriated the seven independent small-farmer MPs, and they too threw in their lot with Ballance. So the Liberals emerged as an unlikely coalition of both skilled and unskilled workingmen on the left; small-town businessmen, journalists, and lawyers in the middle; and small farmers on the right. In short, the Liberals constituted New Zealand's first broad-based democratic party. The Liberals also soon absorbed the Labor Party, so that a separate Labor Party like those in the Australian states did not reappear until much later, only becoming a permanent fixture on the political landscape in 1916.

By March 1891 the Liberals held a large majority of 50 out of 74 seats in the lower house and clearly had the mandate to initiate reforms. They set about their task with enthusiasm, concentrating their efforts on attacking land monopoly and overhauling the industrial relations system.

LAND REFORM AND MODERNIZATION OF AGRICULTURE

Ballance introduced his promised Land and Income Tax Act and immediately won favor with small farmers by exempting anyone who owned land valued at less than £500 from paying the land tax. He also set about reducing the power of the Legislative Council by appealing to the highest court in the empire, the Privy Council in London. Before Ballance died of cancer in 1893, the Privy Council upheld his claim that Atkinson had acted unfairly in stacking the upper house and granted Ballance the right to appoint councilors supportive of his government. Men from such humble backgrounds as boiler-making and printing thereby served on this body for the first time. Once he had thawed the legislative body dubbed "the freezing chamber" by his colleagues, Ballance handed control of the land reform program over to the six foot four inch, 18 stone Scottish highlander, John McKenzie. This big, angry, but realistic man became both architect and builder of the land reform program.

McKenzie had witnessed the highland clearances as small boy. He arrived in New Zealand in 1860 determined that the unequal patterns of land ownership that forced hard-working crofters from their homes should not be allowed to develop in New Zealand. When it became clear that the problem of land monopoly had found its way to the new colony, he decided to enter politics to rid his new country of what he viewed as a curse. He entered the House of Representatives in 1881; and despite a rather undistinguished career as a backbencher, he nevertheless won a reputation as an expert on land settlement. During the 1880s McKenzie also became more pragmatic and learned the important lesson that closer settlement could work only if it provided a viable living for settlers. Immediately, this pragmatism set him at cross-purpose with many urban-based radicals, who held a more romantic view of New Zealand as nation of superpeasants running tiny farms. McKenzie, in contrast, wanted middle-sized farms of 340 to 640 acres that would earn comfortable livings for farmers and their families. He also hoped to place many families on smaller but properly managed dairy farms. First, though, he had to persuade big landowning families and companies to sell. This meant that he would have to pay the market rate, or better, making reform costly.

In 1891 McKenzie tried to introduce a lease to be revalued every 50 years, only to have it rejected by the upper house. After a tour of the North Island in late 1891, farmers who wanted the freehold persuaded him to change tactics. In 1892 he responded to this demand by introducing a lease in perpetuity, or eternal lease of 999 years, which would never be revalued. This compromise infuriated the land radicals, especially the supporters of Henry George, because it earned nothing back for the state. In contrast, it proved very popular with farmers as it was a kind of super-freehold providing security at low cost. The problem remained, however, of finding sufficient money to buy up good land. McKenzie's colleague and close friend Joe Ward, a merchant from the southern port of Bluff and colonial treasurer, came to the rescue in 1893 by securing a £3 million loan at a low rate of interest. Before he put this money to work, though, McKenzie secured the prized Cheviot estate of 84,000 acres of prime North Canterbury land in 1893. The vendors wanted to rid themselves of the debt-ridden property and so deliberately undervalued it. Under the Land and Income Tax Act, such a action entitled the government to buy up the property. Ballance raised an internal loan, and the Cheviot estate, burst open from the inside by the Robinson family rather than the government, became a showpiece of the Liberal land reform program.

The Cheviot purchase also proved hugely popular with the electorate, and the Liberals won a record 56 percent mandate at the 1893 election. This enabled McKenzie to accelerate the program, and in 1894 he introduced the much better funded Land for Settlements Act, which made available £250,000 for purchase rather than the measly £50,000 under the 1892 act. The Land for Settlements Act empowered the government to take land compulsorily from private owners for closer settlement. Such draconian powers were only used in full four times and in a more limited form nine times, but this constituted a far more radical reform than any ever instituted in Australia. Many of the properties purchased under this legislation proved very successful.

McKenzie also realized that new farmers needed capital to get on their feet. He worked with Ward to devise an advances to settlers' scheme, also introduced in 1894, to provide these new settlers with adequate capital on very reasonable terms. The loans could be repaid at low interest rates over a working lifetime of 36 years and proved very popular.

At the same time, McKenzie spent another half million pounds in 1894 and 1895 on buying up Maori land for dairy farming. By reintroducing Crown preemption in 1894, he succeeded in securing some 2.7 million acres of this land for very little. Whereas government paid the great estate owners more than 84 shillings per acre, Maori landowners received a paltry 6 shillings, well below the market value of their land. Maori also received far less generous compensation in the form of 50 acres of first-class land as against the generous 640 acres made available to the great estate owners. Whereas the estate owners took a small step down the landowning ladder but continued in considerable comfort, Maori farming became even more marginalized.

Matters would not have been as bad had Maori been included under the advances to settlers scheme, but they were excluded until the 1920s, far too late for any kind of successful revival of Maori farming. Consequently, the great estate owners were successfully integrated back into the political system and broader society, while Maori became even more excluded. Maori pressure groups, especially the Kingitanga and Kotahitanga, protested this treatment vigorously throughout the 1890s, as did the Maori parliamentarians, but the Liberals heeded little. Under pressure from the half-caste James Carroll, who served as representative of the Maori race in the cabinet throughout the 1890s, Richard John Seddon, who became premier on Ballance's death in 1893, made a few concessions. The Maori councils scheme introduced in 1900 gave Maori a little more say in controlling their local affairs, slowed land sales, and brought about some improvements in health, but the experiment largely expired as early as 1907 because of underfunding, public hostility, government indifference, and Maori suspicion.

McKenzie also realized that, if New Zealand hoped to compete with other agricultural producers, its agriculture had to be run on as modern and scientific lines as possible. He set up the Department of Agriculture in 1892 to provide both quality control and advice to achieve this result. New Zealanders knew little about dairying, so the government brought in Danish and Scottish experts as advisers and appointed inspectors to ensure that farmers produced milk in as clean a manner as possible. A rigorous system of branding also ensured that butter and meat reached the English market in reasonable condition. As a result, by 1900 New Zealand had won a reputation for producing frozen lamb and butter of good quality and value. Although the Department of Agriculture initially undertook little research and little diversification occurred outside of stock farming, McKenzie virtually restructured New Zealand farming by consulting constantly with farmer organizations and instituting strict quality control.

This very practical assistance probably made a greater contribution to the development of New Zealand as Britain's outlying farm than did the land reform program. Historians remain divided over the efficacy of these reforms. Many argue that the Liberals were a lucky government because commodity prices rose at the right time, technological innovations such as refrigeration and the cream separator worked to their advantage, and big business generally supported the move to more intensive farming. On the negative side, revisionists also point out that Maori did not share in the new prosperity, creating a major social cost for the future, and the environment suffered as settlers burned over 3 million acres of bush to make way for farms. Much of this land turned out to be of poor quality and would have been best left under timber. On the other hand, although the program took some time to gather momentum, the Liberals did redistribute 1.3 million acres of highly improved land along with 3.2 million acres of undeveloped Maori land, broke a deadlock in rural land sales, restored confidence in the colony's future, and ensured that New Zealand became a land of family farmers rather than great estates. They thereby revitalized the countryside for a time and brought considerable benefit to small towns, which remained loyal Liberal supporters until the 1920s. Ironically, as the perceptive French visitor Andre Siegfried predicted, the very success of small farming also guaranteed that these former allies would soon become very conservative as they concentrated on entrenching their personal gains. Subsequently, the Liberals lost small-farmer support from around the 1905 election.

Overall, the Liberals' capacity to establish a successful working partnership between government and business and ability to borrow and adapt models from overseas that worked in everyday practice constituted real contributions to New Zealand's development. Their land reforms must, therefore, take much credit for heading off any major form of agrarian protest such as the populist movement in the United States. John McKenzie also helped establish New Zealand's first national park, Tongariro, in 1894, along with several bird sanctuaries on offshore islands. He made provision for scenery preservation under the 1892 Land Act and ensured that New Zealanders had largely free access to the open country under clause 110 of the same act by hardwiring the so-called Queen's Chain, or 22-yard strip around the coast and all waterways. His namesake, Thomas Mackenzie, a storekeeper from South Otago, built on these early conservation initiatives in the early twentieth century. In sum, the Liberal land reform program can be judged relatively successful.

INDUSTRIAL RELATIONS AND LABOR REFORMS

Another powerful personality assumed the role of architect and builder of the reform of labor relations and conditions. William Pember Reeves, lawyer, journalist, historian, and poet, seemed an unlikely candidate for the job in that he had few connections to the trade union movement and came from a landed and privileged Canterbury family. His father William managed the *Lyttelton Times*, and William took over editorship of its weekly edition, the *Canterbury Times*, in 1885. Earlier, he had spent a brief time at Oxford before returning and being admitted to the bar in 1880. Although ill health cut short his formal education, he read widely and was far and away the most self-consciously intellectual of the leading Liberal politicians. Reeves won the St. Albans seat at the 1887 election and entered parliament as a radical critic of the new government. His biographer, Keith Sinclair, argues that Reeves thought of himself as a fabian socialist, that is, someone who believed that social engineering, brought about through gradual legislative reform, could improve the lot of the great majority of citizens. In 1889 Reeves threw his support behind John Ballance and emerged as the most knowledgeable speaker on labor matters by the time the Liberals won the government in 1891.

Reeves set to work immediately to end what he saw as destructive class conflict and to improve the working conditions of ordinary New Zealanders. Like many of his colleagues, Reeves aimed to make New Zealand into a classless, or one-class, society. Many overseas commentators who arrived in the late 1890s to examine his experiments, along with those of McKenzie, agreed that Reeves had succeeded in making New Zealand into a society without extremes of wealth and poverty. Later-day historians though have been less enthusiastic in their assessments.

Reeves's most important legislative contribution was passing, in the *annis mirabilis* of 1894, the Industrial Conciliation and Arbitration (IC and A) Act. This act established a system of compulsory arbitration and conciliation that lasted down to 1986. It involved the setting up of a special court to which all industrial disputes would be sent. Initially, employers balked at the prospect, while the shattered union movement greeted it with enthusiasm. Soon both sides accepted it as a reasonable way of sorting out their differences, especially once the union movement regained its strength. Initially, the system worked so well that the California progressive Henry Demarest Lloyd wrote a book about New Zealand entitled *A Country without Strikes* because no major strikes occurred until 1906. After that, the arrival of more militant philosophies and young migrants unaware of the contribution of the Liberals placed this system under considerable pressure. Yet, much to the amazement of critical English and American commentators, it survived for the long haul. Certainly, New Zealand avoided until 1912 the bloody and bitter strikes that disrupted social harmony in Britain and the Americas over this period. The success of the industrial and conciliation system also explains the late emergence of a separate Labor party along the lines of the Australian and British models.

Reeves set up a Department of Labor in 1891 to oversee the implementation of a host of small laws he passed to improve working conditions. These included truck acts to ensure that workers were paid in cash rather than in kind, some rudimentary provision of compensation for injury, and the introduction of a compulsory half holiday for retail workers. He ensured the stricter regulation of factory hours and conditions, removed children from factories, and considerably reduced job opportunities for women in manufacturing. In combination, these small reforms gave New Zealand workers rights that American workers failed to win despite the use of violent direct action. Only one New Zealand worker was killed before the First World War, as against hundreds in the United States. New Zealand has no songs about Joe Hills or other martyrs of the trade union movement. Labor historian Erik Olssen also points out that the skilled in particular gained a control of the industrial process that American workers had lost by 1910. In consequence, New Zealand factories became more like those of modern Japan, with power resting as much on the floor with the workers as with managers working in comfortable offices. On the other hand, Miles Fairburn and John Martin have shown that Reeves's reforms did not spread far beyond the cities, and rural workers still had to battle appallingly tough conditions, intermittent unemployment, and low wages.

Reeves soon became too radical for Premier Seddon when he tried to regulate conditions in small family businesses such as shops, so Seddon promoted him to the plum job of agent-general (the forerunner of high commissioner) in London. Reeves proved a most adept ambassador for his country. He promoted the idea that New Zealand had become the social laboratory or experiment station of the world so effectively that French, American, and English radicals all visited to check out the validity of this claim. Despite his departure, the reforms continued in more gradual fashion, thanks to the work of the extremely able undersecretary of labor, Edward Tregear, and the ongoing support of Premier Seddon, a self-styled champion of the workingman. Tregear's efforts, in combination with those of Reeves and McKenzie, led the Americans and French at least (the English found it harder to be gracious about one of their colonies) to conclude that New Zealand had indeed undertaken many successful experiments in social engineering, including their decision to grant women the vote in 1893.

WOMEN'S SUFFRAGE

Despite the praise of outside intellectuals, the Liberals granted women the vote very reluctantly. Ballance and Reeves were married to suffragists and liked the idea in theory, but feared that women would vote conservatively. Seddon and McKenzie shared that fear and also held more socially conservative views on the proper role of women. Seddon and the Liberal Party received much financial support from prominent brewers and feared that if women gained the vote they would force the introduction of prohibition, a prospect feared by his many male supporters as well as by the brewers.

In fact, the Liberals were outmaneuvered by a very well organized first-wave feminist movement and were undone by the vagaries of their political opponents. Women's suffrage was also a well-established cause in New Zealand, with bills to grant women the vote being introduced in 1878, 1879, 1882, and 1887, well before the Liberal Party came into being. J. S. Mill's influential book *The Subjection of Women*, published in 1869, seemed to have quite an impact, with women being admitted to university from the establishment of that system in 1869 and winning the right to vote for local bodies if they were property owners from 1877. Women could also serve on state school committees from their inception in 1877 and won the right to vote on licensing committees (which issued licenses to sell alcohol) from 1882. More important, the Married Women's Property Act of 1884 followed the British reform in granting women the right to own property after marriage. This change meant that a woman no longer lost her separate legal identity upon marriage. The success of girls' secondary schools since the establishment of Otago Girls' High School in 1871, and the advocacy of girls' education by feisty early graduates such as Kate Edger, also won the support of many male voters and politicians. In other words, women in colonial New Zealand had secured several important rights even before the so-called first-wave feminist movement became organized on a colonywide basis.

The women's suffrage movement as such grew out of the earlier Women's Christian Temperance Union (WCTU), established in the southern city of Invercargill in 1884 to end the gross abuse of alcohol by many colonial men. Under the influence of the American temperance campaigner Mary Clement Leavitt, who visited in 1885, the WCTU soon broadened its concerns to include dress reform, equality in marriage, and better nutrition for wives and mothers. More controversial and difficult matters were also raised when members challenged the prevailing double sexual standard. The WCTU demanded that the age of consent be raised from 12 to 16 to prevent abuse of children and called for an end to prostitution. They also wanted the blatantly discriminatory Contagious Diseases Act abolished. This measure had been introduced to stop venereal disease being spread by British troops in 1869 through the questionable empowerment of police to haul any woman suspected of being a carrier off the streets to undergo medical examination. As historian Barbara

Brookes has observed, the WCTU demonstrated a "weakness for strong subjects."

The effectiveness of the WCTU increased greatly in 1887 when it appointed the extraordinarily able Kate Sheppard as its franchise superintendent. The striking and charismatic 39-year-old Scotswoman had already won notoriety for her advocacy of absolute equality in marriage and through her role as a pioneer woman cyclist. More important, she was a superb organizer and propagandist who wrote articles for many newspapers, distributed pamphlets, and gave lectures all over the country. Her powers of persuasion won over reluctant newspaper editors and powerful politicians, including the leading conservative politician Sir John Hall. Hall feared the excesses of full democracy and hoped that the moral superiority of women would act as check upon the excesses of male politicians. Seddon and McKenzie feared that Hall was right, and the women's movement transformed itself from an eccentric and faddish group into a real power in the land.

Once the Liberals were elected, Sheppard converted the WCTU into a highly effective single-issue pressure group. She won the support of Harriet Morison and the newly formed Tailoresses' Union, and so broadened her support from its former almost exclusively middle-class, nonconformist Protestant base. With the help of Morison and the Dunedin suffrage superintendent, Helen Nicol, she gathered 10,000 signatures on a petition to parliament. A better organized effort in 1892 produced 20,000 signatures, easily the biggest petition in the colony's history. This success led to the creation of the Women's Franchise League (WFL) as a specialist suffrage organization separate from the WCTU.

The WFL set up branches in all the main centers and several smaller towns such as Gore in Southland and Feilding in the Manawatu. Larger and more frequent meetings helped raise consciousness of the issue, and several newspapers, including the *Auckland Evening Star, New Zealand Herald,* and *Dunedin Evening Star,* added their support. This crusade raised some noisy opposition from the likes of Henry Fish, former mayor of Dunedin and independent MP for South Dunedin, who argued that women's place was in the home. According to Fish, giving women the vote would be "analogous to taking the bloom off the peach—you destroy its beauty." He also organized two counterpetitions against those of the WFL, but obvious multiple signings undermined their credibility. Although such extreme sexism probably worked to the WFL's advantage, Seddon managed to head off their challenge in 1892 by adding allowing women the right to cast postal votes. Most of his Liberal colleagues were staunchly committed to the principle of the secret ballot, so they voted out the bill.

Undaunted, the WFL increased its efforts in 1893 and collected some 30,000 signatures, representing about a quarter of all the adult women of New Zealand, on a petition demanding the enfranchisement of women. Even the adroit Seddon felt threatened by such overwhelming support. He tried to appease his brewer backers and male supporters by legislating that an absolute majority of 60 percent of votes was required before an electorate could introduce prohibition and close its pubs. In addition, he once again added postal voting to delay the introduction of women's franchise to 1896. This time the Legislative Council called his bluff as an act of spite, and all New Zealand women, including Maori women, won the right to vote on September 19, 1893.

Historians have suggested several reasons why New Zealand women got the vote before any other centralized colonial entity. Wild-West Wyoming granted women the vote in 1869, Mormon-dominated Utah in 1870, and Colorado in 1893, but New Zealand beat the state of South Australia by a year and Australia, which federated in 1901–1902, by eight years. The United States and Great Britain lagged far behind, not admitting their adult females into the electoral process until 1919. Even then British women had to be over 30 to vote until 1928, when the age was lowered to 21, the same as for men.

Patricia Grimshaw argues that the newness of New Zealand and the resulting absence of strong conservative traditions proved critical, as did the favorable climate of opinion, the underdeveloped nature of party politics, the highly developed organization of the WCTU and WFL, and the drive, ability, and persuasive powers of Kate Sheppard. Raewyn Dalziel thinks that there were also deeper causes related to the role played by women in colonial New Zealand society. She points out that late-nineteenth-century New Zealand women led very different kinds of lives than their English contemporaries. Raw, frontier New Zealand had little time for ornamental females and rather wanted useful women who could act as partners in founding farms and businesses and raise large families to augment the labor force. Rural papers such as the *New Zealand Farmer* praised tireless homemakers who acted as a combination of laborer, domestic servant, and child-producing machine and bestowed high status upon women as result. Michele Knauf suggests that this elevation of women's status contrasts somewhat with Australia, where the family farm was not as central to colonial life. In addition, the work of Anne Summers and Miriam Dixon suggests that Australian men tended to stereotype their women as "damned whores or God's police." In contrast, the New Zealand stereotype was the fecund, hospitable, hardworking, and morally superior farmer's wife, a stereotype not unlike the prairie angel or Madonna of North America's Great Plains.

Australian historian Coral Lansbury further points out that women who did not earn wages did not threaten men in essentially rural areas such as New Zealand, the Australian wheat belt, or the North American Great Plains, in contrast to areas such as the U.S. Northeast and industrial Britain, where women's capacity to take over men's jobs presented a very real economic threat. In sum, the mature Grimshaw agrees with Dalziel and many others that the vote represented something of a reward for women's vital contribution to colonial development. In exchange, male politicians expected women to revert to the more traditional roles by retreating from factory to home.

Consequently, winning the vote did not produce any radical changes in New Zealand society, as numerous outside observers were quick to note. The relatively militant magazine of the WFL, *Daybreak,* had to revert to including recipes and knitting patterns as early as 1894. Similarly, the National Council of Women founded in 1896 went into abeyance in 1908 before sputtering back to life in 1918. Women's participation in the workforce remained much the same until the Second World War. Even so, the vote did secure women some tangible gains, especially once the populist Seddon changed his stance, gloried in the innovation of women's franchise, and supported the women's movement once he calculated that the bulk of women had voted for his party in the 1893 election.

As a result, the age of consent was raised from 12 to 14 and then to 16; divorce law became fairer to women in 1898; and deserting husbands had to provide maintenance for the first time under the Testators' Family Maintenance Act of 1900. The turn of the century also saw something quite radical in that New Zealand, under the influence of Lady Anna Stout and her chief justice husband Robert, became one of the first countries to move the crime of incest from the jurisdiction of canonical law to civil law. Nurses had to be registered from 1901 and midwives from 1904; free places in secondary schools became available to girls as well as boys from 1903; and Seddon founded special St. Helen's hospitals (named after his birthplace in England) in 1905 to make birth safer for working-class mothers and their babies. Abolition of the Contagious Diseases Act in 1910 and the introduction of a miserly widows' pension in 1911 completed the many concessions rung from the Liberals.

The majority of women felt reasonably satisfied with such gains because they only ever wanted to improve the lot of women and children with the family. More radical feminists such as Kate Sheppard expressed pleasure when women finally won the right to stand for parliament in 1919, but she still regretted that women had failed to win absolute equality in marriage, wages for mothers, equal pay for equal work, and a thousand and one other rights. These battles remained for second-wave feminists to fight from the 1970s onwards.

LIMITED WELFARE PROVISION

Generations of New Zealanders grew up believing that the Liberals laid the foundations of New Zealand's once-proud welfare state. The comment about widows' pensions above hints strongly that modern historians think differently. Essentially, the Liberals won this reputation because Seddon introduced old age pensions in 1898 to help shore up flagging electoral support. In fact, this pension was mean, limited, and very affordable. A residence requirement of 25 years and a clean criminal record knocked out many of the old, hard-drinking miners whom Seddon most wanted to help. He largely excluded Maori because most still owned some property and ruled out Chinese and other Asians on purely racial grounds. Consequently, less than 3 percent of the young colonial population meet the eligibility criteria. Even if people did, the princely sum of £18 a year, or about a fifth of the average wage, could hardly be described as generous, especially as evidence of property ownership or other savings sharply reduced the payment. On balance, historians judge this noncontributory scheme to be very inferior to the contributory national insurance scheme introduced in England by Lloyd George in 1909.

Taking this as a starting point, W. H. Oliver and his students Margaret Tennant and David Thomson have demonstrated that the Liberals established a minimalist form of welfare based on the notion that the poor could be divided into two categories: the deserving and undeserving. The 1885 Hospitals and Charitable Institutions Act supposedly provided for the deserving poor (that is, hard-working, thrifty, and sober citizens down on their luck) by outdoor relief in the form of food and fuel and indoor relief, or shelter in large institutions like the workhouses of England. David Thomson has described nineteenth-century New Zealand as an experiment in "a world without welfare." The new colony was supposedly so abundant that there should be no need for the workhouse made so notorious in the novels of Charles Dickens.

By 1885 the depression had forced a rethink, so the Stout-Vogel government introduced a limited welfare system. The Liberals barely added to it, except to provide some limited help to the unemployed by making work available in so-called cooperative gangs on railway and road building. A Labor Bureau also helped the able-bodied find work, but there was nothing like the dole. The unskilled had to live with the vagaries of New Zealand's inclement climate, which cost them many days' work. In the Liberals' eyes, the land reform program constituted their major form of welfare assistance in that it supposedly helped those who were prepared to help themselves.

If agricultural laborers failed to gain land under these schemes, however, they were condemned to lives of hardship and uncertainty. Education was intended to help citizens improve their lot, but some 80 percent of children did not attend secondary school by the First World War. The Liberals addressed the growing housing problem by building a mere 600 state houses, which tuned out to be too expensive for unskilled laborers to rent. The Liberals' harsh and judgmental treatment of the so-called undeserving poor—that is, drunks, spendthrifts, criminals, unmarried mothers, Maori who refused to live like Europeans, Asians, and non-British groups of migrants, especially the Lebanese (whom they called Assyrian hawkers) and Croatians (whom they called Austrians because of their membership in the Austro-Hungarian Empire) who came in the 1890s—compounded the shortcomings in the provision of welfare. Discriminatory legislation ensured the exclusion of all of these groups from whatever benefits accrued from the experiments carried out in the social laboratory. In short, the Liberals did not solve the age-old problem of poverty despite their propaganda to the contrary.

BENEVOLENT DICTATORSHIP AND A GROWING STATE

One feature of New Zealand life that caught the eye of many visitors was the growing power of the central state even though the Liberals only established a very rudimentary welfare system. The two examples that most impressed the California Progressive, Henry Demarest Lloyd, were the nationalization of the railway system in 1893–1894 and the rescue of the Bank of New Zealand between 1893 and 1895. American populists constantly complained of the exorbitant freight rates charged by the big rail companies, and here was a government buying the railway to force down freight costs while creating many jobs for both the skilled and unskilled. Similarly, when 28 banks collapsed in Australia in 1893 and more fell over in Argentina, the New Zealand government rescued the Bank of New Zealand. The Liberals stopped short of nationalizing the bank but guaranteed it all the government's business and thereby restored confidence in an extremely volatile financial situation. This move, yet again, was not far from what the populists wanted to happen in the United States. Praise for the government's decisiveness far outweighed complaints by conservatives like William Downie Stewart and the American professor of economics, James le Rossignol, that such action created distortions and inefficiencies.

Both the land reform program and the industrial conciliation system also considerably increased the power of the state in key areas of colonial life. Once Seddon ran a virtual benevolent dictatorship after the death of McKenzie in 1901, this trend accelerated. Seddon nationalized the coal mines in 1901, expanded the operation of the State Insurance Office, which he set up in 1903, and used the burgeoning bureaucracy to find jobs for the sons and daughters of his supporters. In a notorious case of favoritism, a clerk complained that a young cadet in his care could neither read nor write, and Seddon telegraphed back "larn him!." In such an atmosphere, opposition complaints of nepotism and corruption mounted; but in the small economy of colonial New Zealand, corruption never became anywhere as serious as it was in Australia, let alone the United States. Nevertheless, resistance grew amongst both Maori and Pakeha citizens against an interfering state and a government increasingly bankrupt of ideas.

The Kingitanga maintained ongoing criticism through its own assembly, the Kauhanganui (or great council) founded by Tawhiao in 1892 at Maungakawa in the Waikato. Tawhiao died in 1894 attempting to develop internal sovereignty for Maori. His successor, King Mahuta, decided to work more cooperatively with the government and served for a time on the Legislative Council before resigning in disgust in 1910 His successor, King Te Rata, made yet another visit to the meet the reigning monarch (George V) in 1912. For the first time, the Maori king meet his English equivalent, but the mission achieved nothing.

A prophet by the name of Rua Kenana emerged in the remote Ureweras and resisted Liberal attempts at buying up Tuhoe's land. At the same time, young professionals educated at the Anglican boarding school, Te Aute College, formed the Young Maori Party as a kind of lobbying group to keep the government honest while elevating the status of their own people. Even though the most famous pair of this group—the young Doctor Te Rangi Hiroa (or Peter Buck) and the lawyer Apirana Ngata—worked with the Liberal Party, they tried hard to support James Carroll's efforts to slow land sales.

Buck gave up politics after displaying considerable personal courage during his time with the Pioneer Battalion in the First World War. He went on to become a very distinguished academic, winning a professorship in anthropology at Yale and running the Bishop Museum in Hawaii. Ngata rather stayed loyal to the Liberals but worked strenuously to save the traditions as well as the land of his Ngati Porou people of the east coast. He succeeded in ending land sales by single Maori landowners in 1909, rescued vast numbers of Maori songs and stories, helped revitalize carving, and finally won some financial assistance for Maori farming in the 1920s. Many other lesser-known local leaders also led an ongoing struggle with government, and the slow recovery of the Maori population numbers suggests that despite appallingly bad housing and ongoing poverty they achieved moderate success.

CONSUMERISM, COMFORT, AND THE RISE OF THE REFORM PARTY

At the same time, the Liberals began to run into troubles with their increasingly prosperous European electorates. Small farmers, especially in the North Island, wanted to secure capital gains by freeholding their leasehold properties at their original valuations. Successful city-based businessmen moved out to the newly forming suburbs to live in much improved villa houses and determined to entrench their improved living standards. They wanted minimal state interference so that they could enjoy the very real gains in comforts brought about by the supply of electric power, hot and cold running water, and flush toilets located inside the house rather than in the corner of the backyard. The more successful also enjoyed riding bicycles and playing pianos in their good rooms. The very well off started driving motorcars around New Zealand's rather rudimentary roads, which remained impassable in winter. Expectations continued to rise as the 1912 Cost of Living Commission discovered. Above all, this new middle class wanted to gain respectability from being viewed as independent and successful by their neighborhoods. Too often, the increasingly impotent Liberals seemed unable to guarantee that this respectability and social distance from the rougher lower orders would be sustained.

A new party calling itself Reform emerged to champion the rising expectations of this burgeoning middle class of businessman, white-collar workers, and prosperous farmers. The Mangere-based farmer William Massey, who had long used his location near Auckland to build links between farmers and urban businessmen and property owners, built the party from the grassroots level from 1905. Although notorious as a bigoted Ulsterman who belonged to a rather strange Anglocentric organization known as the British Israelites, which argued that Christ was really British,

Massey was hardworking and a very good organizer. He began to challenge Seddon's dominance when he adopted the populist style of the Liberal leader and stumped the country meeting ordinary voters. He pragmatically accepted the popular policies of the Liberals such as old age pensions, but argued that the civil service needed streamlining and supported the new Farmers' Union in its call for the right to freehold farms rented from the government at their original valuation.

By 1905 the North Island had moved ahead of the South because dairying really took off in the early 1900s. Whereas there were only 5,000 specialist dairy farmers in 1901, that figure had risen to 15,000 by 1911. Sheep numbers in the North Island also surpassed those of the South Island as sheep farming reached its environmental limits in Canterbury and Otago. Auckland consequently became New Zealand's largest city and rocketed ahead as Dunedin stagnated. By 1911 Auckland boasted more than 100,000 people as against Wellington's 71,000, Christchurch's 80,000, and Dunedin's modest 64,000. This shift in the population dynamic caused problems for the Liberals, which had been a predominantly South Island party, with Seddon, McKenzie, Reeves, and Ward all representing South Island electorates. After Seddon's sudden death in 1906, the new premier, Joe Ward, tried to compensate for this problem by introducing more North Islanders into the cabinet. His response came a little late, however, as the Liberals lost support heavily at the 1908 election and only clung to power by a thread after the 1911 election.

The other major problem for the Liberals was that unskilled workers felt they were missing out on the huge gains made by the middle and professional classes and more established farmers. Instead of living in comfortable villas with all modern conveniences, most unskilled families still lived in small, cramped cottages without electricity, hot water, inside toilets, or telephones. When a large influx of single young men arrived from Australia to find such glaring inequality, it is not surprising that they soon became attracted to more militant philosophies spreading around the Western world at this time. Many of these ideas came from the United States, especially via the syndicalism movement based in industrial cities such as Chicago. New Zealand seamen such as Pat Hickey learned about these movements when they called in at San Francisco, and they returned with talk of the need for one great strike to bring capitalism to its knees. Movements such as the Chicago-based Industrial Workers of the World (popularly known as the Wobblies) advocated views closer to anarchism than socialism and spurned any attempt at working for reform through the parliamentary system. The De Leonites of Detroit rather believed that a revolutionary party should guide the unions, but they too agreed with various British variants of syndicalism that full-scale class warfare would bring down capitalism and secure big gains for workingmen.

These ideas found such fertile ground amongst the new migrants, who knew nothing of the Liberals' achievements, that they began to reject the IC and A system from as early as 1906 in the coal mines at Blackball on the west coast of the South Island. These miners seemed to gain more by striking than by working through the system. By 1909 they had formed the notorious Red Feds, or Federation of Labor, as wharf laborers, flax workers, and general laborers engaged in hard, dirty, and dangerous work joined forces with the coal miners. Gold miners in the Thames/Coromandel area joined the fray in 1912 and engaged in a very bitter strike that cost the life of a protestor.

Now the Reform Party had what it wanted—a clear-cut enemy that the Liberals seemed incapable of controlling. Massey and others convinced the electorate that the new Dominion (New Zealand became a self-governing Dominion in 1907) urgently needed a firm hand and stern measures to end industrial chaos. The Liberals were further undone by the breakaway of another left-wing grouping of nonconformist supporters of Henry George and the single tax who for some reason made their living as drapers, or sellers of cloth and materials. These land radicals did not seem to realize that a determined government breakup of high country runs in 1910 cleared out all but a handful of the original runholders and replaced them with men from much more humble backgrounds, many of whom have run those properties into the third and fourth generations. The complaints of the land radicals provided further evidence to support Reform's claims that unreliable and dangerous faddists were holding the country to ransom. Ward's efforts at appeasing this group by increasing the land tax and experimenting with different types of leases did not work as the old alliance of workingmen, small-town businessmen, and small farmers fell apart at the seams. A few Labor MPs who appeared for the first time in 1911 further frightened both farmers and urban property owners.

Ward resigned at the end of 1911, and Thomas Mackenzie, a former conservative, had little chance of clinging to power. He seemed almost relieved to hand over power to Massey in July 1912 when four Liberals crossed the floor to join Reform. The great Liberal era came to an end with a whimper. The apparently invincible monolith had been undone by deep and powerful changes within the broader society, as well as by the simple fact that the electorate became very tired of a government that had held power for an extraordinary 21 years—still a record tenure for any New Zealand government. The death of the charismatic and popular Seddon in 1906 did not help, but even he probably could not have held back the tide of change.

The new Reform cabinet was one of the best educated in the country's history. Interestingly, it contained the lawyer sons of several of the great landowning families, including the Bells and Rhodes, who had successfully readjusted to the inconvenience of McKenzie's bursting-up policies. Their abilities were soon put the test when a prolonged and extremely bitter waterfront strike broke out on October 22, 1913. The Red Feds, supported by Seamen's Union despite the relatively advanced age of most of its members, organized major strikes in Auckland and Wellington. Farther south the older workforce still remembered the gains they had made under the Liberals, and disruptions assumed much more moderate form.

Massey responded to the challenge with considerable force. Risking a potential civil war, he brought farmers in from country districts backed by the armed forces and police to break up the strike and load the ships. Farmers needed little persuading because they feared that their highly perishable products would rot on the wharves. Known as Massey's cossacks, they rode their horses into strikers with abandon and gave vent to the old, lingering urban-rural rivalry. The strike collapsed by November 24, although the coal miners held out until January 13, 1914. The combined power of the government and shipowners proved too great in what turned out to be something of a dress rehearsal for a different kind of warfare. Anger still smolders within the union movement over the treatment dished out by Massey's government, but it was forced to change tactics, and the parliamentary/reformist alternative became suddenly much more attractive.

7

The Most Loyal Dominion Loses Its Way, 1914–1935

THE WAR TO END ALL WARS

War brought temporary unity to a country that seemed intent on tearing itself apart. It was loyalty to empire rather than country, though, that provided the glue needed to restore social cohesion. New Zealand had been in a rather militarist and jingoistic mood from as early as 1899, when it declared war on the Boers of South Africa even before the British government did. Nearly 6,500 fighting men with their 8,000 horses won many accolades from the British for their service in this war. Along with Australians and Canadians, the New Zealanders earned themselves a reputation as fit and mobile troops well suited to the free-wheeling nature of the action. The fact that only 70 were killed in action, with another 158 dying from infection caused by wounds, made war seem rather glamorous, and these men received heroes' welcomes when they returned at the end of hostilities in late 1902. Memorials to this war are scattered around the country, and they tend to be confident, showing soldiers standing tall in white marble, in contrast to the gaunt and gray memorials erected in memory of the First World War. Little New Zealand proved its worth to empire, and soldiering became fashionable and popular.

School cadet numbers had escalated to around 15,000 by the time the government decided to introduce compulsory military training in 1909. The government brought out the imperial war hero Lord Kitchener in 1910 to advise on how to set up a citizen army and, in the process, raised enthusiasm to fever pitch. The austere, six foot, seven inch tall major-general Alexander Godley took up the job of commandant of the New Zealand forces in late 1910 and set about knocking this amateur army into shape. By the time war broke out in 1914, 18,807 men had been fully trained, along with 25,000 senior cadets. Godley estimated that a further 89,000 young men had been given some rudimentary training. New Zealand's willingness to support the empire was further reinforced when the government donated £2 million in 1909 to build a battle cruiser, the *HMS New Zealand*. Built in 1910 and commissioned in 1911, the ship served with the British Navy, leaving New Zealand to develop its own navy after the First World War.

In such a jingoistic climate shaped by the imperialist urgings of the new *School Journal* (founded in 1907) and promulgated by organizations such as the Navy League, there was no need to debate the matter of going to war. On August 5, 1914, New Zealand declared war on Germany. Recruitment proved successful as young men rushed to join, either out of sense of adventure or because of strong peer pressure. Women, in particular, shamed men who did not enlist. Young men wanted to be with their mates, and in some places whole rugby teams enlisted together. Things got off to a promising start when New Zealand took the German colony of Western Samoa without a shot being fired on August 29. New Zealand had already annexed the Cook Islands in 1901, and its dream of running its own small empire in the Pacific now seemed closer to realization.

Many young men brought up on unstinting imperial propaganda honestly believed that the war would be over in three weeks and that they would never see action. They need not have worried, but anxieties increased when no troops left until October 16 because the presence of a German cruiser in the Pacific threatened the safety of the convoy. The first 8,574 men who sailed with 3,818 horses on board imagined that, after they joined forces with the Australians in Perth, they would sail to France via Ceylon (modern-day Sri Lanka) and the Suez Canal. Instead they were dropped off in Egypt to train with the Australians in the sands of the Sahara. Their job was to help the British army fight the Turks who had joined the war on the German side.

The New Zealand troops enjoyed being tourists in an exotic place very different from their sleepy home country, but they soon became bored. Many succumbed to venereal diseases as the temptations of Cairo brothels proved too much. The refusal of the puritanical authorities to issue condoms did not help matters. Things got so bad by early April that the New Zealanders rioted along with the Australians out of boredom, racist dislike of their Arab hosts, and frustration at their treatment by local hotel and brothel owners. Finally, the waiting was over when on April 25 they joined their Australian peers in the ANZAC (Australian and New Zealand Auxiliary Corps) attack upon the Gallipoli Peninsula in Turkey.

Lord of the Admiralty Winston Churchill imagined that, if the Gallipoli Peninsula could be taken and Constantinople (modern-day Istanbul) seized, the Allies could easily join forces with the Russians on the other side of the Black Sea, attack the Germans from the rear, and bring the war to a rapid end. The British government agreed to this fanciful plan because the war had bogged to a stalemate on the western front. Before the troops invaded, the British Navy made an ineffectual series of raid on the area, which only alerted the Turks to the likelihood of full-scale attack.

The ANZACs had no idea of the incompetence of the British Navy, however, and lulled by arrogant British tales of Turkish weakness happily joined the invasion force of April 25. Their job was to assist the Australians in taking a low part of the peninsula before marching to the other side and moving on to capture Constantinople. Unfortunately, true to form, the British Navy did not allow for the strong currents in the area, and they ended up a mile or so north of their designated landing point. Instead of flat land, they found themselves hemmed in on a tiny beach beneath steep cliffs covered in dense scrub. By the time the New Zealanders arrived on the beach around nine o'clock in the morning, the Australians had been engaged in heavy fighting with the well-armed Turks since dawn. The Fern Leafs, as they were known, arrived to find hellish chaos. Somehow they managed to help the Australians cling to the narrow strip of sand. Most commanders would have abandoned such a debacle immediately, but not Sir Ian Hamilton. Instead he ordered the men to "dig, dig, dig, dig for your lives." The ANZACs dug in so successfully that they would cling to this unlikely base of operations until nearly Christmas.

The determination of the extremely able Turkish commander Mustapha Kemal, who later became Ataturk, founder of modern Turkey (see Douglas A. Howard in the Greenwood series), compounded their problems. The ANZACs only survived his constant harassment by becoming very well organized. The New Zealanders produced their own highly efficient commander in Colonel William Malone, who disciplined his men to the point where they managed to hold the Turks at a point-blank range of only 22 yards. An ill-judged attack in broad daylight farther south on the peninsula, carried out by men withdrawn from the cove, escalated casualties. The combination of incompetence and efficiency at killing one another caused such massive slaughter that both sides agreed to a truce on May 19 to bury the dead bodies rotting and bursting in the heat. As summer set in, temperatures soared over 100 degrees, and stalemate resulted. Casualties still mounted, although the deeply dug trenches offered reasonable protection from constant Turkish bombardment.

Then in August the generals decided on a bold plan to take the high ground known as Chunuk Bair. They entrusted the Australians with diverting the Turks on both the left and right flanks and ordered the New Zealanders to sneak up the steep slopes under cover of darkness. Everything soon went wrong. The Turkish forces on the right turned out to be much more heavily concentrated than intelligence had reported, and this attack bogged down in bloody hand-to-hand fighting in well-constructed trenches. Nearly 2,200 Australians were killed at Lone Pine. On the left the Turks slaughtered the elite cavalry unit known as the West Australian Light Horse when the Navy and Army failed to synchronize their watches.

Meanwhile, the New Zealanders had set off to climb the steep and treacherous cliffs leading to Chunuk Bair in the pitch black of night. Somehow they made it onto the heights on August 7, only to hesitate, allowing the Turks to regroup. The Auckland battalion tried attacking in broad daylight, but the better-organized Turks forced them back. Finally, on August 8 the Wellington Battalion under Malone's command took and held the top of Chunuk Bair for a few hours. The soldiers could actually see Constantinople in the distance. Visions of a glorious victory and a shortened war soon faded when wave after wave of Turkish defenders finally drove them off the crest. Malone died a martyr's death, according to tradition killed by a British shell, and only 70 of his 760 men survived unscathed. Meantime supporting but inexperienced British troops, who had landed at Suvla Bay to the north, hesitated. Their help arrived too late on August 9 to save the situation, and the one chance of breaking the stalemate was lost.

A few more adventures in other parts of the area, all involving foolish daylight attacks, added to the casualty list. Winter then set in, and, remarkably, the British command managed to evacuate all the troops by Christmas without losing a man. The New Zealand losses were terrible indeed. The casualty rate reached an astonishing 88 percent, whereas military manuals suggest that the rate should never rise above a third. An appalling 2,721 of the 8,556 New Zealanders who served on Gallipoli were killed. The entire rugby 15 of the small north Auckland town of Rawene lay in marked and unmarked graves of a far-off country most New Zealanders knew nothing about. Another 4,526 suffered serious wounds.

Such reckless wastage along with totally inadequate support and inferior weaponry made the New Zealand soldiers deeply suspicious of the British high command. Unsurprisingly, a more nationalist attitude began to flourish among the troops. They also had gained an enormous respect for their Australian allies. In contrast, politicians and the public back home expressed great pride in the fact that their boys had proven their worth in a most difficult situation. Such military achievement only made defense of the empire seem an even more glorious enterprise. As a result, New Zealand still commemorates this horrible failure because it represented the young Dominion's first real engagement in war and established a proud military tradition. Revisionist historians are now questioning the part played by the incompetence of New Zealand commanders and the hopelessly antiquated rifles supplied by the New Zealand Army, but their critique seems unlikely to remove the romance of such a glorious failure.

Bad as Gallipoli was, worse soon followed on the nightmarish western front. This term summed up the 25,000 miles of trenches, enough to circle Earth, that ran from the English Channel to the French Alps. Most of the fighting, though, concentrated around the champagne-growing area of northeastern France and tiny Belgium on flat or undulating swampy ground. The British and French commanders believed that trenches should be used only for offensive purposes, so they deliberately kept them damp and uncomfortable. Often trenches ran with water and were infested with lice and rats. In contrast, the German soldiers had comfortable and well-constructed deep trenches that offered protection and enabled them to sleep more easily. This difference helps explain why the heavily outnumbered Germans resisted for so long.

This system of trench warfare, in which the opposing armies often faced each other a mere 20 or so yards apart, dragged to a stalemate very quickly. By the time New Zealanders joined the fray in April 1916, the war was already a weary 18 months old. They arrived first in the so-called quiet sector of Armentières, where the German and British soldiers had developed a system of live and let live. The enthusiastic New Zealanders would have none of this and soon upped the action, carrying out numerous night raids. Tensions escalated, and 375 men were killed, many of them in one disastrous bungle on the night of July 16, 1916.

This initiation was relatively mild, nevertheless, compared with New Zealanders' engagement in the second phase of the notorious battle of the Somme. The Allies lost 60,000 men killed or wounded when this badly organized and ill-conceived campaign began on July 1. The New Zealanders joined the moribund battle on September 15. They found a desolate no-man's land of smashed trees and wrecked buildings in which the only living thing was the adaptable rat. One old soldier described the by now muddy battlefield as worse than a Taranaki cow yard after weeks of rain. Futile charges into German machine guns cost the increasingly disillusioned New Zealanders 1,560 lives by the time they withdrew on October 4.

Other pointless engagements followed before the New Zealanders finally secured some success at the better planned battle of Messines between March 14 and June 10, 1917. New Zealand tunnelers, many with experience of working in the underground gold mines of the Thames/Coromandel area, played a critical role in digging under the well-constructed German trenches and blowing them up. This attack from below undermined German morale for a time, and in one of the few occasions in the war the New Zealanders took several hundred German prisoners. This battle represented a minor victory, but it cost the New Zealand Army, now supported by a Pioneer Battalion of Maori troops, 3,700 casualties with 780 killed.

Thereafter 1917 degenerated into disaster for the whole Allied Army as well as the New Zealanders. High command launched the third Battle of Ypres after the rains had returned on September 28, and it soon degenerated into a muddy bloodbath. Worse followed at Passchendaele when, between October 9 and 14, unopposed German machine gunners killed 1,000 New Zealanders, many drowning in the mud. Bombardment of the strongly constructed German pillboxes had failed, as had attempts at cutting the wire. In an horrific two hours, German machine gunners mowed down 640 New Zealanders. Even the Germans took pity and allowed the hapless Kiwis (as they were increasingly known) to try to extract their dead from the cloying mud.

This unmitigated horror, commemorated on many memorials around New Zealand, constituted the low point of the First World War for the small Dominion. The whole Allied Army threatened to mutiny as the Germans regrouped after the Bolshevik revolution of October 1917 in Russia produced a peace that enabled the Germans to draw their men back from the eastern front. Anticipating some kind of last-ditch German offensive in 1918, the Allied command pulled the New Zealanders and Australians back to the coast to prepare for repelling the onslaught. Rest and recuperation followed.

Both the Australian and New Zealand armies were fit and ready for battle when the exhausted British Fifth Army buckled and ran in March 1918. The German push almost worked as the elite, fresh, and strengthened German troops from the eastern front surged toward the British Channel. All that was standing in their way before the arrival of the Americans were these ANZAC troops, now fighting under their own commands. The New Zealanders slowly plugged up the gapping hole that had opened around Hedauville near Albert from March 25, while the Australians farther south held the Germans on the flat ground in the front of Amiens. The delay caused by this stiff resistance stopped the Germans long enough for British and French troops to finish off the job from early April. Most New Zealanders and Australians are unaware of this very important contribution in changing the course of the war and European history, but the effort is well documented even though little celebrated.

After this time, the arrival of the Americans from mid-1918 turned the course of the war. The New Zealanders joined them and the other Allies on August 8 in slowly forcing the Germans back toward their old borders. Another 1,000 lives would be lost in this final push. Before it ended, in an ironical twist, the New Zealanders were finally presented with an opportunity to engage in chivalric action in their last action of the war. Le Quesnoy was a famous medieval walled town, and instead of bombing it the New Zealanders took it on November 6 by scaling a ladder one by one and rushing along its ramparts to seize it from German control. This gallant action so impressed the local people that they erected a special monument to the New Zealanders, which is still visited every November 6 by the New Zealand ambassador.

The war ended five days later on November 11, with New Zealand having lost nearly 17,000 dead (another 507 died in the deserts of Palestine where 18,000 New Zealanders fought on horseback and camel with Lawrence of Arabia against the Turks). A further 41,000 were seriously wounded, bequeathing New Zealand a casualty rate of 59 percent, second only in the British Army to Australia's horrific 65 percent, the price of British perception of them as the elite fighting force. New Zealanders would challenge this perception in the Second World War and win the title of best soldiers in the British Army from the Australians.

These losses for a country of little over a million people were very serious. The numerous lonely memorials that litter the country and the appallingly long lists of names beneath the columns on school gates and church walls reflect the sadness felt by everyone. In such a small community, virtually every citizen knew or was related to someone killed in the war. This shared grief helps explain why the 1920s in New Zealand could be characterized as sad and somber rather than swinging. Yet the impact of the losses was not as great as might be imagined because of a number of mitigating factors. First of all, most soldiers were single men, or, if married, they did not have children. Married conscripts with children only began to be sent at the very end of the war. As a result, the great influenza pandemic that arrived with the peace in November 1918 created more orphans (6,550 to 2,209) than did the slaughter at Gallipoli and the western front, and nearly as many widows (1,609 to 1,970). This lack of orphans was in dramatic contrast to a country such as Germany where many fathers were killed, thereby creating an opportunity for a charismatic leader to emerge promoting himself as a father figure.

Furthermore, awful as they were, New Zealand's losses appear relatively mild when compared with a place like Serbia, where a quarter of that troubled country's young men died fighting for their independence. Mechanization of New Zealand farming also meant that the many agricultural laborers who enlisted were not missed nearly as much as were skilled professionals such as veterinarians.

Then, there was the inability of the civilian population to identify with the sufferings of the soldiers. The public had been subjected to endless good news propaganda, and, despite the questioning of some newspapers, most citizens had little idea of what a war fought so far away was like. New Zealand lacked top journalists such as C. W. Bean, the English-born Australian who told his home audience in vivid prose about Australian valor and British bungling. Nor did New Zealand have a powerful newspaper magnate such as Keith Murdoch to challenge British management of the war in a very public manner.

The New Zealand soldiers themselves seemed unable to talk about their experiences outside the confines of their Returned Serviceman's Association (RSA). Most only let the emotion out if they survived into their eighties and talked to oral historians and television documentary makers. Consequently, little literature or art of merit appeared relating to the war. Several critical books appeared later, and it took the trauma of another depression to challenge the overwhelming sense of imperial loyalty.

Children too played their part because the war produced endless rounds of fundraising, picnics, and concerts. Most children of the era actually remembered the flu more vividly because it particularly hit adults in their prime and forced children to help run the country in the black fortnight of late November 1918. After all, the flu caused 8,500 deaths in New Zealand.

Similarly women did not gain real advances like their English counterparts because they did not put on uniforms as in the Second World War, and the First World War opened up few new job opportunities. Some 300 nurses served overseas, but the rest stayed at home, frustrated by being able to do no more than knit socks or pack food parcels. Numbers of women employees rose steadily in areas where they had made an advance, such as teaching, typing, and working in retail shops, but women were not required to make ammunition. English working-class women, in contrast, earned their first reliable wages in the munitions factories, ceased being endlessly pregnant with their men at the front, and thereby literally dragged up the vast urban-based British underclass. New Zealand possessed no equivalent group, and the war's impact consequently remained muted and often subtle compared with Europe, North America, and even Australia.

Life continued on much as before, but underlying tensions did come to the surface. The so called wowsers or temperance advocates had a field day in the absence of so many young men, with over 100,000 serving in the forces. While soldiers battled death, disease, and boredom, the temperance lobby managed to ban the buying rounds of drinks in 1916 and introduced six o'clock closing of hotels in 1917, a most peculiar practice that survived down to 1967 and promoted very unhealthy drinking patterns. Then, in 1919 New Zealand voted to go dry, but the soldiers' votes reversed the result. They figured that they at least deserved the right to drink beer and wanted New Zealand to return to the way it had been before the war. Their pre-1914 experiences seemed so superior and so much more comfortable than anything they experienced or witnessed overseas that they wanted to maintain the social laboratory exactly as it was in 1914. This further helps explain the surprisingly conservative impact of the war.

Like everywhere else in the Allied nations, xenophobic attitudes toward Germans produced several outrages. Enraged mobs burned German butchers' shops even though the sons of many German immigrants fought with the New Zealand Army. Street names of German origin were replaced with English alternatives; Brunswick Street in Dunedin, for example, was changed to Loyalty Street when a higher proportion of men living in the street volunteered for war service than in any other Dunedin street. German sausage suddenly became Belgium sausage. Bigots hounded the professor of German at Victoria University of Wellington out of his job and drove him to suicide. Similarly, Croatian gum diggers received discriminatory treatment even though the great majority wanted the overthrow of the Austro-Hungarian Empire even more desperately than the average New Zealander.

The old sectarian rivalry between Protestant and Catholic that had been imported from Ireland also flared under pressure of war. An organization known as the Protestant Political Association (PPA) formed in 1917 to expose the preference that the Catholic Joe Ward, coleader of the country under the coalition government established in 1915, had supposedly given members of his faith in the police force and civil service. These charges were largely baseless but caused much distress. When the leader of the

PPA, a Baptist minister called Howard Elliott, started to accuse both nuns and monks of dubious sexual practices, prejudice boiled over. After the abortive Irish rising of Easter 1916, the fiery rhetoric of southern Catholic papers such as the *Tablet* and *Green Ray* did not help matters. Things only cooled after the brother of one of the accused nuns horsewhipped Elliott and the ardently Protestant prime minister, William Massey, disassociated himself from the PPA. Thereafter, this issue simmered away, with the PPA claiming a very high membership of 220,000. The trial of Catholic archbishop James Liston for sedition in 1922 brought the division into prominence once more, but thereafter it healed slowly as New Zealand became an increasingly secular society.

Race relations also worsened under pressure of war, despite the good press won by Ngata's recruiting efforts and the performance of the Pioneer Battalion of 2,227 men. A special police unit arrested the pacifist prophet Rua in 1916 on very dubious grounds. Rua told of a vision that the kaiser would come with King George V to witness the New Zealand government hand the country back to Maori in exchange for a giant diamond he had been shown by the Archangel Gabriel near his settlement at Maungapohatu. This visionary statement alarmed the authorities, but they had to trump up a charge of sly grogging (illicit dealings in alcohol) to find a pretext to send in a force. Although Rua was later cleared by a Pakeha jury, the judge locked him away for two years for sedition. Similarly, when Princess Te Puea of the Kingitanga opposed the conscription of Tainui men, the press unleashed a torrent of invective against her. Unfortunately for Te Puea, her grandfather had been a German, which meant that her passionate protest against land loss could easily be overlooked.

Some of this damage could have been repaired if the returning Maori soldiers had been included in the rehabilitation program, but they were ignored completely and gained nothing for their service. Then the flu pandemic ravaged Maori even worse than Pakeha New Zealanders, killing over 2,000 Maori and setting back their demographic recovery by several years. This health disaster alerted a few more-thoughtful Pakeha to the fact that Maori needed considerable assistance to be elevated above their unhealthily low status, but the great majority continued to ignore their plight. Te Puea, though, refused to accept this marginalization, and another prophet, Wiremu Tahupotiki Ratana, emerged in the west near Wanganui. He began his mission as faith healer responding to the devastation caused by the flu. He began as a religious prophet who established another Maori variant of Christianity, which still remains popular with about 15 percent of the population belonging to the faith today. As early as 1922, however, Ratana turned his attention to the more earthly concerns of politics.

Ratana's cause was helped by perhaps the most important internal development of the First World War—the emergence of the Labor Party in July 1916. Unlike Australia, New Zealand introduced conscription on August 1, 1916. A clear majority of citizens, including women, favored conscription because it ensured equality of sacrifice. Mrs. Jones's sons would have to fight along with Mrs. Smith's, and that was that. The revelation of a national survey in 1915 that some 40 percent of eligible men were not prepared to serve seemed to support the pro-conscription argument. A significant minority disagreed, however, arguing that there should be no conscription of men without conscription of wealth. In other words, they wanted stiff supertaxes and higher death duties, like those introduced by Lloyd George in Britain in 1917, imposed upon speculators and black marketers. Farmers, too, had done very well out of the commandeer, or buy up of all New Zealand's farm produce (frozen meat in 1915, cheese and wool in 1916, and butter in 1917) at highly inflated prices. The rural land market boomed in consequence, as inflation emerged for the first time since the gold rushes. Over the four and half years of war, prices rose by 36 percent, a staggering figure compared with prewar average of less than 1 percent per annum.

The New Zealand government did very little to control these developments apart from setting up a series of ineffectual boards. Working people thereby felt that they had received no compensation for the sacrifices made by their sons. The growth of Auckland and Wellington in particular provided a constituency where the staunchly Marxist views of a party set on nationalizing the means of production (land and factories), distribution (transport), and exchange (banks and insurance) held considerable appeal. A raft of important new politicians from humble backgrounds, many of them Australians, began to win their way into parliament. Their success spelled trouble for the old Liberal Party. When Joe Ward ended the coalition after the war, he failed to win back much of his traditional support. New Zealand politics was thereby split three ways, with the Reform government hanging on against the rising Labor and declining Liberal challenge. New Zealand politics became much less stable and much more unpredictable as a result.

THE DYNAMIC TWENTIES

New Zealand developed rapidly in the 1920s, especially in the material and technological sense. As a result, by the time the Great Depression arrived in 1930 it had become very similar to many Western societies and boasted the fifth highest standard of living in the world, a remarkable achievement for a former colony dependent upon a narrow range of farm exports for its livelihood. The first year of peace did not augur so well, however, and returning soldiers experienced much disillusionment.

The soldiers returned in late 1919, expecting heroes' welcomes. Instead they found a society traumatized by the savage death rate of the flu and seemingly at war with itself over such trivialities as temperance and sectarianism. Rehabilitation had been hopelessly badly organized. No one quite knew what to do with men who had lost their limbs, and few medical practitioners had much idea about how to treat shell shock and other psychological problems. Those supposedly lucky and fit enough to win farms under the returned soldiers' settlement scheme often found that they had been landed with overvalued, little developed farms located far from knowledgeable neighbors. Some farms were still covered in bush, and men from city backgrounds were supposed to be able to become expert frontier farmers without advice or assistance from either government agencies or kin with experience of the difficulties of bush farming. Consequently, this scheme produced many failures as well as success stories.

The soldiers soon found a lack of sympathy for their plight. Much to their surprise when they undertook direct action against the low rate of their war pensions in September 1919 by marching on parliament and breaking a few windows in frustration, they literally wiped out most of the country's good will. Pensions stayed at the same miserable level of £27 for each year of service as against the £75 they demanded. Thereafter, the former soldiers retreated into resentful silence. Even their own RSA organization seemed to lack the influence of its Australian equivalent. In this rather charged atmosphere, Massey's Reform Party apparently won the 1919 election comfortably by 46 seats to the Liberals' 19 and Labor's 8. This result did not ease Reform's concerns about the Bolshevik-like inclinations of Labor because they secured 25 percent of the vote, the same as the Liberals. Reform's modest 36 percent did not represent much of a safety margin.

The new decade began more promisingly because prices for all farm exports stayed high. Once the imperial government removed the commandeer later in the year and the world economy adjusted to postwar reality, things worsened rapidly. A short but sharp recession set in during 1921 and lasted until 1923. Massey responded in orthodox fashion by slashing government spending and reducing all civil service salaries by 7 percent. Unemployment rose quite sharply from virtually nothing to around 7 percent of the workforce. Farmer bankruptcies soared as the extravagant speculation of the war years caught out new farmers with large debts. About 2,000 of the 9,000 returned soldier settlers had walked off their land in despair by 1925. As a result, this recession caused more readjustment and farming failure than the longer Great Depression of the 1930s. Small businesses and small towns suffered along with the farmers. Labor benefited from disappointment with the peace and won 17 seats from a consistent 25 percent of the vote at the 1922 election, to the Liberals' 19 and Reform's 41 seats. Reform, though, managed to increase its share of the vote to 40 percent, a result that spelled even more trouble for the beleaguered Liberals.

The American rescue of the chronically ill German economy in 1923, however, turned things around for the entire world, and New Zealand recovered as prices rose. Good times had returned by 1924, and the country made real gains down to the late 1920s. Minister of works Gordon Coates built some 48,000 miles of properly formed roads to take advantage of the greater mobility offered by the motorcar. By 1929 the modest 60,000 vehicles of 1919 had risen to 213,000, the majority of them Fords, Chevrolets, and other American models. Cars, buses, and trucks revolutionized New Zealand as well as American life. Suburbs accessed by bus or car, rather than the older trams, mushroomed in the main cities, especially Auckland. Trucks could transport wool, meat, and butter to the ports much more rapidly than horse-drawn carts, and large, centralized dairy factories came to replace the multitude of small creameries.

The internal combustion engine broke down isolation and greatly improved opportunities for leisure and social interaction. Organizations grew apace, helped by the arrival of party lines to extend telephone service across the whole country. Radio licenses jumped from a mere 2,000 in 1923 to 17,000 by 1927. Now farmers could hear weather reports and check market prices before ringing one another to discuss how best to react to an oncoming storm or a dramatic shift in prices for wool, meat, and butter. Their wives could now meet together easily for the first time. Consequently, the Country Women's Institute (CWI), already flourishing in Canada and Britain, began to operate in small towns from 1919. Farmers' wives established its more rural equivalent, the Women's Division of the Farmers' Union, while husbands met at a national conference in 1925.

The rapid spread of electricity noticeably improved the quality of life of many citizens, while helping farmers in direct ways. Power lines increased more than three times between 1919 and 1925 from 1,900 to 6,000 miles. By the late 1920s New Zealand prided itself on having one of the most highly developed electricity systems in the world. Electric lights changed leisure patterns significantly and eased the lot of urban women especially. Washing became less time-consuming once housewives no longer had to heat the washtub and light the stove. Servants became less essential, and the number of female domestic servants fell from 32,000 in 1916 to 26,000 by 1926. Rural women gained less because reticulating electricity over long distances remained a problem until after the Second World War.

Farmers usually ran their own generators to power milking and shearing machines. The milking machine, whose numbers increased from around 2,000 in 1920 to 10,000 by the end of the decade, had profound effects upon the lives of farmers' daughters because they were no longer required to help with the milking. Many responded to this newly found freedom by leaving to work in offices or shops in towns and cities. New Zealand's population living in locations of less than 1,000 people (our somewhat idiosyncratic definition of rural) fell to 42 percent by 1926. Something of a white blouse revolution also occurred, as in the rest of the Western world, with the number of clerks, typists, and shop assistants escalating quite spectacularly.

Back on the farm, milking machines increased production significantly when combined with the use of electric fences to graze pasture more efficiently and with the introduction of herd testing. Massey Agricultural College, established in 1927 along the lines of an American land-grant college, along with the revitalized Lincoln Agricultural College and the new Department of Scientific and Industrial Research, aimed to make New Zealand farming more scientific and efficient. Prime Minister Massey tried to help too, by overhauling the marketing of frozen meat by setting up the Meat Board in 1922. Even though he espoused an apparently conservative philosophy, Massey realized that New Zealand was so small that it would do best on the British market by exporting through one centralized body. The shipping shortage after the war forced the issue, and this board did manage to make bulk agreements that lowered the price of freight and insurance. Gordon Coates added a Dairy Board in 1926, which had less farmer support and more mixed results. Although the combined results of their marketing reform and ongoing research and development took some time to benefit sheep farming, their contribution, along with machine milking and herd testing, saw butter production per cow rise nearly three times between 1919 and 1935.

The downside of the active modernization of New Zealand agriculture for women was that their usefulness on the farm decreased. The extra income earned through making butter and raising poultry no longer proved necessary, and wives did not have to milk cows as often as before. Their status declined in consequence. Both the CWI and the Women's Division of the Farmers' Union would have to spend much time trying to reverse this decline. Women couldn't help comparing their cold and inconvenient houses, still reliant on wood or coal stoves for heat, cooking, and hot water, with the tidy new bungalows with all modern conveniences being built all through the new suburbs. These smaller and better-lit houses, based upon the California bungalow model, suited the New Zealand climate and required much less timber than the older villas with their space-wasting halls, corridors, and high ceilings. For the first time since the 1880s, urban living became noticeably more comfortable than life in farmhouses. The gap would never be completely closed again, despite big advances made in the prosperous 1950s.

Puritanical disapproval slowly broke down so that New Zealanders were the biggest movie goers per capita after the Americans by the late 1920s. Hollywood swept all before it with baleful results for the surprisingly vigorous local film industry. It virtually disappeared until the 1960s. Other forms of local entertainment such as music halls and visiting shows also lost popularity, and classical music struggled. Indeed, many historians view the 1920s as a cultural wasteland during which little writing or painting of merit appeared. The poet R.A.K. Mason ended up throwing his poems into the Auckland harbor in despair, and the novelist Jane Mander gave up writing by the mid-1920s, disgusted at the lack of local support.

James Cowan and J. B. Condliffe wrote some solid history, and Herbert Guthrie Smith wrote a pioneer environmental history text, *Tutira,* published in 1921. Leading American environmental historians Richard White and William Cronon both credit this intensive study of a Hawke's Bay sheep station with converting them to a different approach to understanding the past. More popular writers such as Essie Summers fared rather better, but this was a miserable decade for New Zealand writing and the high arts.

New Zealanders seemed much more interested in and much better at sports. Achievements in this field included an unbeaten tour of Britain by the national rugby team, the All Blacks, in 1924 and Arthur Porritt's securing of a bronze medal in the same year at the Paris Olympics. Even so, given the apparent renaissance of both writing and painting in the 1930s, more must have been going on than historians have so far discovered.

Despite tangible material progress, the recession of 1921–1923 and an economic downturn from around 1927 made the 1920s into an anxious decade. New Zealand's best-known historian, Keith Sinclair, described it as "an aspirin age" in which the older generation became increasingly concerned by the apparent moral decline of youth. The drift to the cities was bad enough, but when the rate of venereal disease rose alarmingly after the war, their worst suspicions seemed to be confirmed. The obvious explanation was returning soldiers, but the authorities refused to admit that such heroes could be responsible. Instead, they set up a special committee of investigation in 1922, which blamed imbecile girls. The large back seats of Model T Fords and the dark movie theaters where patrons watched scantily-clad persons of exotic appearance engage in explicit kissing continued to worry the moral guardians. So too did the rapidly rising hems of the flappers who danced the Charleston to the jungle beat of jazz and smoked in public. Revelations in the 1926 census that one bride in three was pregnant on her wedding day threw the puritans into a frenzy of denunciation. This percentage of pregnant brides had probably changed little across the generations, but there remained a huge gap between public morality and private practice. Such moral guardians as ministers, schoolteachers, and mayors also continued to criticize the young for ignoring the Sabbath, but New Zealand lacked any equivalent of the Scopes trial. Darwin's ideas had always received wide acceptance in New Zealand, and an increasingly secular society seemed little worried about creationism. The strict puritanical code governing every aspect of life eroded slowly thereafter, until the post–World War II baby boomers dismantled it in the 1970s.

New Zealanders also feared an imminent Asian invasion in the 1920s and made sure that Chinese and Indians were kept at bay by restrictive legislation like the Immigration Restriction Amendment Act of 1920. Immigration did revive in the prosperous middle 1920s, but it remained exclusively British in origin. Unsurprisingly, a people so concerned with moral degeneration and threatened by sexual liberation and racial contamination also feared for their military safety. The obvious answer to nullify this fear was to cling to Britain's skirts as long as possible. New Zealand consequently remained the most loyal of all the Dominions and reveled in its title as the dutiful daughter. Australia and Canada questioned many British policies and refused to support Britain when war threatened to erupt with Turkey in 1922. In contrast, 15,000 young New Zealanders volunteered overnight to serve. Massey gave only lukewarm support to the League of Nations, supported the great European powers in barring Japan from membership, and made a mess of running the trusteeship of Western Samoa. New Zealanders imagined that Britain's Navy would still protect its farthest Dominion, so little was done about establishing its own Navy or Air Force until a more proximate threat emerged in Japan from the late 1930s. It will come as little surprise to the reader that by the late 1920s this psychologically and economically insecure people had become the most heavily insured people per capita on earth.

In such an atmosphere it is also unsurprising that politics became increasingly confused as the decade progressed. Gordon Coates, a war hero and the first New Zealand–born prime minister, easily won the 1925 election after Massey's death earlier in the year. This election involved the first use of modern electioneering techniques, including the hugely uninspiring slogan "Coats off with Coates." Despite his good looks, considerable ability, and key role in rapidly developing the country, Coates soon lost popularity. Declining export income and spiraling debts saw unemployment return by 1927. New Zealand had borrowed heavily to achieve so much material advancement, and this made the Dominion very vulnerable to any downturn in the international economy.

Then in 1928 Sir Joseph Ward returned to throw the political process into turmoil. Ward led a coalition known as the United Party. It joined the remnants of the old Liberal Party (which changed its name to National in 1925) with disillusioned businessmen and farmers from Reform who considered Coates to be too much of a socialist. Coates had introduced a modest family allowance in 1926, overhauled the treatment of juvenile criminals, and established the state-run Dairy Board. This proved too much for the orthodox conservatives in his own party. Even so, Ward would not have won but for a bizarre mistake in an election speech. The rather senile Ward read that he would borrow £70 million immediately. He meant that he would borrow this sum over 10 years, but the electorate refused to accept his denials. Buoyed by hopes of another glorious era like that of the Liberals, the electorate returned Ward with a narrow majority. It took the support of three independent candidates, also disillusioned by Coates's increasing use of state power, to return him to office.

Ward was an old man out of his time. The arrival of the Great Depression in 1930 rendered irrelevant his policy of yet again trying to break up more great estates. It was probably fortunate for a politician with such a long and distinguished career that he resigned on May 28, 1930, before dying a few months later on July 8.

DEPRESSION AGAIN

Coates's and Ward's borrowing meant that, once prices for New Zealand's export staples collapsed, the Dominion had to spend almost a third of its export income on servicing its debts. Like the rest of the world, New Zealand suffered because of the collapse of American prosperity brought about by overproduction of consumer goods and the panicky withdrawal of funds from ailing Germany. The Wall Street crash as such had little to do with the small Dominion's plight. Yet severe as it was, the Great Depression did not hit New Zealand as hard as it hit manufacturing countries. The rate of unemployment rose to high of around 100,000 or about 15 percent of the workforce. Even the most liberal calculations cannot lift the figure above around 20 percent. This represents a very serious figure by New Zealand standards, but it is a relatively modest one compared with Sydney's 25 percent, let alone the 33 percent plus experienced in the industrial northeast of the United States, the manufacturing regions of Britain, or the Ruhr in Germany. In short, the New Zealand figure was similar to other primary producing countries such as Denmark and Argentina, or the farming and mining state of Western Australia among its nearest neighbors.

This relatively modest level of suffering is important because it meant that the Depression unfolded in New Zealand as a very uneven experience. Big sheep farmers, for example, fared well because they took advantage of low prices and labor costs to increase their flocks and improve their properties. Some also splashed out on luxury cars and took cruises to Asia. Manufacturers such as the Fisher and Paykel who produced domestic appliances also benefited from low wages and reduced costs. Well-established farmers with low debt levels got by. So too did city dwellers who held onto their jobs. Some, like my own family, made modest sacrifices such as putting the car up on blocks, cutting off the phone, and dismissing the servant. Yet sales of electric stoves and water heaters rose through the worst years of the Depression. Students must remember that this depression was all about deflation. Consequently, costs went down along with wages. The new prime minister George Forbes, who replaced Ward, and Coates formed a coalition government in September 1931. They reduced the salaries of public servants by 10 percent. This caused inconvenience, but falling prices compensated the affected groups.

Things were different, however, for professionals and white-collar workers who had a long way to fall. Lawyers and dentists, for example, found that their work was nonessential to many, and they too had to join the work schemes building roads, digging tunnels, planting forest, and making gardens. The unskilled as always had a hard time of it and resented being broken up from their families by the notorious Number Five Scheme, which sent them off to camps in remote areas. Women experienced the brunt of declining wage packets and were the first to lose their jobs. They had to improvise and make do much like their pioneer grandmothers. Abortions increased as families could not feed extra children, and the marriage rate dropped alarmingly. The birthrate consequently hit an all-time low of little over two children per family. Most humiliating of all, many white-collar employees of banks, insurance companies, and government departments lost their supposedly safe jobs and had to forfeit their mortgages, sell their suburban houses, and move back into rental accommodations in the central city. Similarly, small dairy farmers were hard hit, and many simply walked off their land, never making it into the official bankruptcy statistics. Maori continued at the bottom level of society and suffered from the decline in casual work.

All this proved very traumatic in a land that Richard Seddon had described as "God's own country." The New Zealand dream was in tatters, and the whole point of emigrating so far from Britain seemed lost. In such an atmosphere, the great majority of people began to believe that everyone was suffering. Many accepted the Labor Party's argument that the system and not individuals should be held responsible for the widespread misery and that the country, therefore, required immediate remedial action to restore its fortunes.

Protest took several forms. Brief riots flared in Dunedin, Auckland, and Wellington early in the winter of 1932, but direct action never held much appeal to phlegmatic New Zealanders. Most rejected extreme solutions such as communism or fascism. Writers and artists joined in the criticism of the old order, but in a compassionate, humanitarian way rather than by developing a Marxist critique of the capitalist system like their Australian equivalents. The Labor politician John A. Lee wrote stirring realist novels about his poor childhood and First World War experiences. The poet A. R. D. Fairburn criticized financial orthodoxy in a long poem entitled "Dominion," but his alternative was Douglas Credit, not socialism. (Douglas Credit originated in Alberta and advocated an increase in the money supply as a way of solving the problem of underconsumption.) Novelist and poet Robin Hyde (real name Iris Wilkinson) wrote both realist and ironical accounts of family life and told the story of an ordinary First World War soldier in *Passport to Hell* and *Nor the Years Condemn*. She lived an unconventional life by raising a child outside marriage but disappeared from the scene to visit China and Britain before committing suicide. The predominately male writers of the time tended to marginalize her, but recently she has won stronger critical endorsement than any of the other writers of the 1930s. Other poets, such as Dennis Glover and Eileen Duggan, the novelist John Mulgan, and short-story specialist Frank Sargeson continued to critique the inhumane aspects of orthodox finance and the inadequacy of the puritanical moral code throughout the decade.

New painting also seemed to come of age in this era. Once again, artists actually had the time to paint in the midst of so much unemployment. Under the influence of the English trained teachers Robert Field and Christopher Perkins, women painters such as Rita Angas and Evelyn Page began to portray a distinctive New Zealand landscape rather than a watered-down version of English and European landscapes. Toss Wollaston and Colin McCahon pushed these experiments in a more abstract direction, while Lois White made explicit critiques of both capitalism and militarism in her symbolist paintings.

The Labor Party seized its chance after the riots by adopting a similar humanitarian stance. Rather than revolution, Labor politicians promised pragmatic reform. First, though, they had to wrest control of the unemployed from the communists before advocating a radical program of reform. They took a very different line from the Marxism of 1916, however. The nationalization plank, especially of land, had been dropped as early as 1927, and Labor became much more of a centrist party thereafter. They were above all humanitarians who simply wanted to bring relief to despairing, ordinary New Zealanders. Once the Christian Socialist Michael Joseph Savage took over Labor Party leadership on the death of the more militant Harry Holland in 1933, the party softened its appeal further. Basically Labor advocated policies not unlike those of FDR and the New Deal. Labor politicians may not have read Lord Keynes, but intuitively they realized that the economy had to be reflated through a sustained policy of public works. New Zealand desperately needed an overhaul of its aging housing stock, and this rebuilding program would provide many jobs. They also wanted to establish a maximalist model of the welfare state to provide free health care and education and adequate pensions. Their financial spokesman, Walter Nash, costed everything to the last penny and countered coalition government complaints that Labor was financially irresponsible. By 1934 the churches also fell in behind Labor, and Ratana made an alliance with the party to improve the lowly position of Maori.

The coalition government, which had won the 1931 election comfortably enough by 51 seats to Labor's 25, became increasingly unpopular. It did not introduce a dole until as late as 1934 and employed an army of busybodies to report on any visits to the pub or racetrack made by men on relief work. Coates did take some initiatives. In 1933 he removed the New Zealand pound from parity with Sterling to make exports more competitive, and he provided mortgage relief for farmers, hoping that a revitalized farming industry would trickle benefit through to the rest of society. He also established a Reserve Bank in 1933 to control fiscal policy in a more efficient manner and actually assisted some economic recovery. The public, however, cared little for such technical achievements and turned increasingly to Labor, which at least seemed to have a plan. Savage's vague pronouncements on making interest-free loans available and ending unemployment through a concerted public works program gave hope to many, and his party won comfortably in 1935 as the political right argued among itself. A rather stern Democrat Party split the conservative vote, allowing Labor to win 55 seats and 47 percent of the vote against the coalition's 19 seats and 6 independents. The election of this new radical government did not signal either revolution, as its supporters hoped, or disaster, as its opponents feared, but rather an energetic burst of reform within the strict confines of mainstream capitalism.

8

The Struggle for Greater Independence, 1935–1973

BUILDING THE WELFARE STATE

Labor had a clear mandate to undertake a program of rapid reform, but even so the new government surprised its opponents with the energy and efficiency with which it implemented a raft of new policies. Critics laughed at the fact that the new cabinet was easily the most working class in New Zealand's history. Prime Minister Savage was a barrel washer from a brewery; deputy leader Peter Fraser had been a wharf laborer; finance minister Walter Nash had worked as a small storekeeper and traveling salesman; and the rest of the group was made up of four miners, a French polisher, a boot clicker, and a railway caterer. Only one lawyer and one farmer, the groups that traditionally dominated parliamentary politics, served in Savage's cabinet. The ridicule only seemed to inspire this unlikely but remarkably well-read group to get on with the big job of putting the country to rights.

Labor's main aim was to make the economy less vulnerable to the vagaries of international markets through the encouragement of import substitution industries, such as domestic appliance manufacturing, and via greater control and planning of production and marketing. This insulated economy, condemned by its critics as fortress New Zealand, would defend every citizen from misfortune by building a full-scale welfare state. Savage and Fraser promised cradle-to-grave security, and the ebullient John A. Lee went one further by promising protection against poverty from erection to resurrection. His exuberance offended the straitlaced Savage and Fraser but caught the mood of the electorate very accurately.

First, though, Labor had to get the economy moving again if the nation ever hoped to defy orthodox economics by achieving full employment. Coates's healthy surplus of £38 million of overseas reserves helped expand public works and enabled government to undertake a major program of building state houses. Men on relief work building roads, digging tunnels, and planting forests were immediately paid a full award wage in an endeavor to restore consumptive power. The old Red Fed Bob Semple guided all the public works with enthusiasm and flair, but the more energetic Lee soon outshone even the colorful Australian soapbox orator. Even though Lee worked as an undersecretary outside the cabinet, he oversaw the construction of 5,000 new houses by 1939. He worked closely with the building magnate James Fletcher and personally ensured that every house was well built out of permanent materials. In a deliberate endeavor to counter criticism that socialism encouraged colorless conformity, Lee insisted that every house should be a little different from the others in its architectural design. Lee built one block of high-rise flats in Wellington. It so horrified him that he ordered all other state house to be built as stand-alone structures on their own sections of land, complete with lawns and gardens. He also ensured that these houses were scattered around older suburbs, rather than being concentrated in ghettos of new housing. In this manner he adhered to the New Zealand dream of owning one's own piece of land but, in the process, pushed the rentals out of the reach of the really poor. New Zealand, thereby, failed to develop anything equivalent to the council housing estates of Britain.

Finance Minister Nash tried to complement all this industry by developing a so-called mixed economy in which the state and private enterprise worked closely together. In 1936 he nationalized the Reserve Bank to gain firmer control of fiscal policy and passed the Primary Products Marketing Act to tighten central control of the various marketing boards. As promised at the 1935 election, he also introduced a system of guaranteed prices for butter and cheese to cushion struggling dairy farmers against adverse terms of trade. His idea of maintaining a steady average price (set at the extraordinary figure of 12 and 9/16 of a penny per pound of butter fat and 6 and 9/16 of a penny per pound of cheese—approximately 15 cents in American dollars) enabled farmers to plan for the future and recommence programs of farm and herd improvement. This idea of putting away surplus monies for a rainy day came as much from the Old Testament story of Joseph and the seven fat and seven lean years as it did from any socialist text. Initially the scheme proved popular with dairy farmers, some of whom threw over traditional prejudice against the left and voted Labor in 1935. Once prices rose sharply in response to the demands of war, however, farmers rejected the idea.

Passing legislation with a hefty majority is relatively easy, but insulating and diversifying a colonial-style economy is a much more difficult task. Nash soon found that English investors did not like the idea that New Zealand might develop import substitution industries and so deprive English manufacturers of a captured market. They showed their displeasure by withdrawing funds. By 1938 overseas reserves collapsed to a little over £8 million. Nash had to visit London to disabuse investors of the idea that New Zealand had engaged in an extreme Soviet-type experiment. He had some success, and things improved a little, but not before the crisis forced him to introduce exchange and import controls in December 1938 as a kind of surrogate tariff. The emergency measure enabled the minister of finance to limit the outflow of funds from New Zealand and introduce some restriction on imports, especially if they threatened to exceed export returns. This makeshift solution worked surprisingly well and provided New Zealand industry with much shelter until the radical reforms of the 1980s.

Labor, meantime, had carefully costed the implementation of a full welfare state before the exchange crisis broke. In a masterly display of political acumen, Savage announced on April 2, 1938, that his government would introduce new and improved pensions, free education, and free medical services. The electorate responded enthusiastically. The famous New Zealand novelist Janet Frame recorded a very common reaction: on hearing the broadcast, her father threw the family's many medical bills onto the fire. This promise earned Labor a huge popular mandate of 56 percent at the 1938 election, and the party won seven new seats even though it lost nine seats it had held in 1935. The so-called dairy seats reverted to their traditional patterns, voting for the new, mass-based National Party formed in 1936. National's complaint that the welfare state constituted applied lunacy, rather than the applied Christianity claimed by Savage, failed to gain traction with the clear majority of New Zealanders, and the welfare state was erected rapidly in 1939. Income tax literally doubled overnight to around 15 cents in the dollar equivalent, but the majority accepted this tax quite happily in return for greater economic security.

Nash's financial orthodoxy, though, meant that the government did not introduce a full, non-means-tested retirement pension at age 60, as Savage wanted. Staunch opposition from the doctors via their pressure group, the British Medical Association, also forced a compromise over delivery of health services. Labor did introduce free hospital treatment, but the patient still had to pay half of the fee for a visit to the doctor. This system worked well and discouraged abuse while guaranteeing doctors a comfortable living. Dentists too fared well, in that Labor never introduced free dental services. Instead, government greatly expanded the School Dental Nurse Service introduced in 1920 and made free treatment available to adolescents. Many dentists got their start under this heavily subsidized scheme.

Labor did rather better with education, making virtually free secondary education compulsory for everyone under 15 in 1944. University education became much cheaper and more widely available, and the dynamic new director-general of education, Dr. Clarence Beeby, overhauled the curriculum. Peter Fraser always had a deep interest in education and called a conference of international experts to overhaul the system in 1937. He followed their recommendations in an effort to make the system less narrowly academic and both more relevant and more enjoyable for all citizens. New subjects such as social studies were introduced in 1945 to replace the old rote-learned history and geography, and math and science teaching received a major overhaul. As a result, most New Zealanders received a solid education thereafter for over a generation.

Labor's sympathy for education constituted just one area of reform in the attempt to create a youth state. A family allowance of 10 shillings ($1) per child was introduced in 1946 to encourage the building of larger families. This supplement equaled another half a wage coming into the household if parents raised four children. Young couples were also entitled to generous tax breaks and cheap housing loans at a modest 3 percent interest from 1946. This pro-natalist policy worked, and New Zealand, like most of the Western world, experienced a spectacular baby boom after the war. Welfare historian David Thomson argues that in combination these benefits seriously advantaged the young adults and children of the late 1940s over subsequent generations. Feminist historians also complain that the high family wages paid to men since 1936, in addition to the family allowance, discouraged married women from entering the paid workforce.

The first Labor government achieved a notable record in two other key areas: pursuit of a more independent foreign policy, and patronage of cultural life and the arts. Savage, who was an Australian of Irish Catholic descent, did not hold nearly as fierce an allegiance to the British Empire as did the likes of William Massey. Similarly, many of his colleagues shared a rather internationalist outlook. As a result, during the heady years of 1936 and 1937 New Zealand pursued a line on foreign policy that deviated sharply from the policy followed by Britain and other Dominions within the empire. Under Savage's and Fraser's leadership, New Zealand advocated the cause of collective security and strongly supported the League of Nations. In 1936 New Zealand fell out with Britain by condemning Mussolini's invasion of Abyssinia (Ethiopia) and supporting a League of Nations intervention in the Spanish Civil War.

The Labor government loathed fascism and condemned General Franco outright, much to the embarrassment of British diplomats. At the Imperial Conference in May 1937, meek, loyal New Zealand amazed the Australians by criticizing both the League and the British government for not doing more to end the Spanish Civil War. In September New Zealand's refusal to recognize Mussolini's government of Abyssinia and stern criticism of appeasing Hitler further irritated the British. This independent attitude would emerge again under Labor governments in the 1970s and 1980s in opposition to French nuclear testing in the Pacific and to nuclear ship visits.

After the Munich agreement of 1938, however, New Zealand fell back into line as war became ever more likely. The threat of Japanese attack made it clear that New Zealand had to turn once more to protection from the Royal Navy while building up its own Navy and Air Force. As World War II drew to an end in 1944, however, Fraser played a prominent role in setting up the United Nations. In particular, he ensured that small nations had some say in the operation of the new international peacekeeper, and he made a large contribution to the drafting of the Declaration of Human Rights. Try as they might, revisionist historians have failed to deny the first Labor government's pursuit of a more independent foreign policy.

Labor's leaders also believed that citizens in a democracy needed more than full employment and better housing if the former colony hoped to flourish as a nation. Consequently, they tried to promote the development of a more vigorous cultural life and provided modest support for the fine arts. The by now popular medium of radio provided a ready means of encouraging such developments, so in 1936 they set up the New Zealand Broadcasting Service. This network offered commercial programs on the ZB network, run by their long-time ally, the Methodist minister and popular broadcaster Colin Scrimgeour (known to the public as Uncle Scrim), and also offered a more serious public radio modeled on the British Broadcasting Commission (BBC). James Shelley, the dynamic professor of education at Canterbury University College, won the job of directing this more high-minded broadcasting service. He set high standards and laid the foundations of what is still a world-class public broadcasting service offering news, analysis, and chat on the YA stations and classical music on the YC network. Eventually, the public came to demand a freer and more diverse system, but private radio did not return until the late 1960s. Government also published the *Listener* from 1939 as both a radio program guide and a serious middle-brow paper that commented on the key issues of the day. It has survived to the present.

Fraser, the Reverend Arnold Nordmeyer, and others had always been interested in adult education and, once in government, took several steps to promote this cause. They established the National Council for Adult Education in 1938; and the Workers' Educational Association, which had struggled along for years, received a government subsidy from 1937. A National Library service followed in 1938 and, with the help of the Carnegie Foundation in the United States, government built or improved many country libraries. New Zealand still boasts an excellent set of small-town libraries thanks to this American generosity.

The celebration of the centennial of the signing of the Treaty of Waitangi in 1940 gave government a chance to encourage writing and painting. Exhibitions of paintings traveled the country, while government organized competitions for writers and musicians. Such leading figures as the short-story writer Frank Sargeson and the composer Douglas Lilburn featured among other, long-forgotten prize winners. Several histories were commissioned, and a major exhibition held in the capital of Wellington gave New Zealanders a chance to show how far they had grown toward nationhood. Unfortunately, the advent of war sapped energy and reduced the funding available, so the celebrations were somewhat muted.

World War II, though, enabled the government to set up a War History Branch to record the deeds of New Zealand soldiers for posterity much more systematically than happened after the First World War. The government also founded a National Film Unit in 1941 to record the war effort. It went from making pure propaganda films to providing surprisingly perceptive documentaries on the war in both the Pacific and European theaters. After the war things improved further for the small community of artists with the introduction of grants for writers such as Sargeson in 1946 and the setting up of the National Orchestra (now known as the New Zealand Symphony Orchestra) the same year. Fraser also hoped to establish a national ballet school and a national opera, but neither eventuated. His educational reforms, though, did encourage the teaching of both art and music in much more imaginative ways than before.

Revisionist historians have naturally questioned the benefit of such overt state patronage and wondered whether something like a distinctive national identity can ever be forced into existence. Such criticism is not unreasonable, but the setting up of this basic cultural infrastructure did help many artists make their start in life.

Overall, then, the Labor government brought about tangible improvements in many areas of New Zealand life. By the advent of war in 1939 it had restored business confidence and reinvigorated the economy so successfully that New Zealand could boast the third highest standard of living in the world. On the other hand, it still had not overcome hefty dependence upon Britain for both markets and defense. New Zealand continued with a small and vulnerable one-engine economy, even if the engine was a little more powerful than before the reforms. Labor also seemed to be running out of ideas and energy by 1939. When the party expelled John A. Lee in 1940 for writing a scurrilous and ill-judged pamphlet criticizing the dying Savage, any hope of postwar innovation and reinvigoration evaporated. First, though, Labor had to fight a total war in which New Zealand's borders were seriously threatened for the first time.

NEW ZEALAND AND THE EXPERIENCE OF TOTAL WAR, 1939–1945

New Zealand entered the Second World War with much less enthusiasm than the First because the Dominion had lost its innocence after the slaughter at Gallipoli and on the western front. This time, though, there was little disagreement because fascist dictatorships represented a clear enemy that could be repulsed only by force. The introduction of conscription as early as July 23, 1940, caused little debate, although some muttered at the irony of its introduction by Peter Fraser, who had been imprisoned for his opposition to conscription during the First World War.

War was no longer distant and remote, but far too close for comfort. In one of his last speeches the seriously ill Savage mumbled, "Where she [Britain] goes, we go," and ended, "we march forward with a union of hearts and minds behind the sure shield of Britain." He sounded reluctant because, as an Australian of Irish Catholic heritage, he did not share this high imperialist vision, and he almost had to be forced to make the speech. Like Fraser and others, he also doubted Britain's capacity to defend his small country. From 1937 his government began to build its own Air Force as a separate branch of the defense forces and to expand its rudimentary Navy in case of Japanese attack. The light cruisers *Achilles* and *Leander* were also commissioned in 1936 and 1937 to serve in the New Zealand division of the Royal Navy. Very quickly, though, the Air Force concentrated its efforts on supplying men and aircraft to help the Royal Air Force.

It did not establish any of its own squadrons until 1942, after Japan had entered the war. By 1944 the Air Force had grown from a modest 750 to 15,000 men.

As in the First World War, New Zealand's greatest contribution would be its fighting soldiers. About 194,000 men put on uniforms, and 105,000 of them served overseas. This represented the greatest effort per capita outside Soviet Russia and taxed both the government and the people severely. Remarkably, the great bulk of those men would serve in the European rather than the Pacific theaters. When Australia called its troops home to stave off the Japanese, New Zealand's remained in North Africa, forcing the inadequately defended small country to turn to the United States for its defense. This shift of defensive allegiance constituted a key change in both New Zealand's military and cultural history, to which we shall return.

Over 12,000 men signed up in the first week of recruiting. By the time conscription was introduced in July 1940, 59,664 had joined. They were the same mixture of youthful adventurers, people looking for a way out of difficult life situations, and ordinary citizens intent upon doing their duty as those who served during the First World War. On balance they were slightly older than their fathers and uncles because the government raised the upper recruitment age from 35 to 40 early in 1940.

This time the New Zealand soldiers adopted a more hard-nosed attitude, but they were very conscious that they had a high reputation to uphold. They had their own commander, the dental mechanic turned major general and First World War hero, Bernard Freyberg. Nicknamed Tiny with typically laconic Kiwi irony by his troops, this big, charismatic man soon earned a reputation for being somewhat reckless, but he always held the respect of his soldiers.

Maori also had their own separate command and served in the 28th or Maori Battalion. They were recruited along tribal lines to avoid some of the rivalries that disrupted the Pioneer Battalion in the First World War. Ngati Porou from the east coast and Ngai Puhi from the far north—that is, the traditionally loyal *iwi*—dominated. Princess Te Puea disapproved of Tainui men serving but did not stop them from going, as in the First World War. Apirana Ngata recruited enthusiastically once more. About 3,600 saw action overseas, and over 15,000 Maori volunteered to serve in some capacity.

Before the army arrived in Europe, 103 New Zealand fighter pilots played a vital role in the Battle of Britain during September 1940, which greatly reduced German aerial bombardment and ended the threat of Nazi invasion. One pilot in 12 during this famous air war was a New Zealander, representing a contribution out of all proportion to the Dominion's size. Several war aces won decorations, including Keith Park, Johnny Deere, and Cobber Kain. Over 10,000 New Zealanders went on to serve in the RAF's bomber command, with 3,000 losing their lives in raids over Europe.

Once the New Zealander soldiers arrived in 1941, they began their campaign with another humiliating loss in Greece between March and May. Ironically, Winston Churchill, architect of the Gallipoli debacle, moved the New Zealanders there to stop the Nazi drive down the Greek peninsula into the eastern Mediterranean. Churchill seriously overestimated the capacity of the poorly equipped New Zealanders to repulse the overwhelming number of well-supported Germans. Pistols proved little use against tanks supported by Stuker bombers. The New Zealanders fought on valiantly against the odds, but lost 291 men killed and 599 wounded. Any New Zealand tourist to Greece today soon learns of Greek appreciation of that brave, if hopeless, effort. The Germans took another 1,614 prisoner.

This loss of men to prisoner of war camps in Germany constituted a big difference with the First World War, in which only about 500 New Zealanders were taken prisoner. In contrast over 9,000 New Zealanders would see out the Second World War in prisoner of war camps in Germany, amusing themselves by making largely futile attempts at escape, with only 716 actually evading recapture. About 400 died in captivity, 160 drowning when British submarines torpedoed prison ships. Generally, even Maori prisoners received reasonable treatment from the Germans, in stark contrast to the Italians and Japanese, who treated their prisoners with great cruelty.

Worse followed for the exhausted and dysentery-ridden survivors on Crete. Between May 20 and 27, 1941, the Kiwis joined some Australians and Greeks in defending the island against what was then the greatest aerial invasion in history. The heavily outnumbered Kiwi soldiers put up a very stiff resistance. Indeed, they shot so many German paratroopers that the Nazis never again used this form of mass attack in the war. The Maori Battalion shone in particular in its numerous attempts to reclaim control of the Maleme aerodrome. Some revisionist historians argue that aging commanders such as James Hargest and Edward Puttick lost their nerve at critical points of the battle. Such armchair critics forget the chaos of battle and such mitigating factors as poor transport and communications and lack of air support. It seems unlikely, therefore, that any army could have beaten off such overwhelming odds. The Germans killed an appalling 634 New Zealanders in this single invasion and took another

2,217 prisoner. A further 967 of those evacuated by the Royal Navy carried serious wounds. The battered and demoralized New Zealand Army had some serious regrouping to do in North Africa.

The deserts of North Africa allowed much greater mobility than Greece and Crete, and rapid movement in trucks, tanks, and armored cars seemed to suit the New Zealand soldiers, especially the Maori Battalion. Things began badly, though, because the astute German general Erwin Rommel, known as the Desert Fox, held the upper hand throughout 1941 and the first half of 1942. Rommel seriously mauled the New Zealanders at Belhamed in Libya during late November and forced them to withdraw to Egypt. In June 1942 the New Zealanders had to execute another retreat when surrounded by Axis forces at Minqar Qaim. They also incurred heavy losses in July before surrendering the newly captured Ruweisat Ridge, but gained some consolation when Captain Charles Upham added a second Victoria Cross to one he had been awarded for daring action in Crete. This was a very rare honor in the annals of the British Army. Sergeant Keith Elliott also won a Victoria Cross in this gallant but unsuccessful action.

Things only really improved with changes in the British high command. Lieutenant-General Bernard Montgomery brought a new energy and enthusiasm to the men of the revamped Eighth Army. Equally important, he greatly strengthened the artillery resources, increased the number of tanks, and upgraded equipment. He acknowledged the New Zealanders' brave if formerly ineffective efforts by entrusting them with a key role in the huge battle of El Alamein in Egypt between October 23 and November 11. Montgomery's biographer credits this crucial victory to overwhelming superiority in artillery and the special contribution made by the Canadians, Scots, and New Zealanders. British military historians such as Liddell Hart and John Ellis support Montgomery's estimation that the New Zealanders became the best unit in the Eighth Army during this critical battle. Even the Australian historian Alan Moorhead accepts this high ranking.

Yet the victory that turned the war in Europe and won this glowing reputation came at the cost of 1,700 casualties. By the time the New Zealanders finished chasing Rommel over 1,800 miles from Egypt to Tunisia to help force a surrender in May 1943, 2,989 men had been killed, 7,000 wounded, and 4,041 taken prisoner of war. On March 27 at Tebaga Gap, Lieutenant Moan-nui-a kiwa of the Maori Battalion won a posthumous Victoria Cross for heroism. Recognition of the special contribution made by Maori soldiers also came when Colonel Arapeta Awatere replaced his Pakeha superiors as commander of the Maori Battalion at the end of the Italian campaign in late 1944.

Over 5,500 of these exhausted troops were sent home to New Zealand from North Africa on furlough for rest and recuperation. Once there, most refused to return, so that the army that joined the British and Indians in invading Italy on October 9, 1943, lacked battle-hardened veterans. This lack of experience would cost the New Zealanders dearly as a supposed sideshow soon degenerated into hard and bitter campaigning. The new recruits only arrived because Churchill begged Fraser to stay in the European war rather than withdraw his troops to the Pacific like the Australians. So for the first time the ANZAC comrades were separated, and the New Zealanders fought alone within the British Army. In many ways it seemed that this split weakened the ANZAC spirit, especially when Australian and New Zealand troops also fought in completely separate spheres within the Pacific theater.

Things went easily at first, especially against some ill-disciplined German units (Italy had already surrendered on September 8, 1943), but when winter struck it belied tourist brochure images of the sunny Mediterranean. At Orsogna in the Arbizzi Mountains, the New Zealanders' problems were compounded by their encounter with the crack 26th Panzer Division and 90th Panzer Grenadier Division. These highly disciplined troops defended the snow-covered mountain fortress with skill and held up the Kiwis until February 1944. Respiratory diseases wreaked havoc among the New Zealanders, and the efficient Germans killed 413 and wounded another 1,150. The retreating German army, though, did not take prisoners and mined every building it deserted with deadly efficiency. When the weary Kiwis arrived to relieve the Americans at the notorious battle of Cassino on February 13, 1944, they had come to realize that easy victory was nothing more than an illusion.

Worse followed as another stalemate ensued. Despite spectacularly heavy bombing of the ancient monastery, the town of Cassino had been converted into an virtually impregnable fortress by the ferocious Panzers and paratroopers. Tanks could not get anywhere near the town, and the rubble of houses provided ideal shelter for the defenders. Fighting often involved hand-to-hand combat as troops raced desperately from one *casa* to another. Even suicidal charges by the fearsome Maori Battalion could not dislodge the Germans. Eventually, the much greater mass of Allied troops forced a surrender in April. This largely pointless action had cost the New Zealanders 343 killed and 1,211 wounded.

Securing this hollow victory meant that the New Zealanders did not share in the joy of liberating Rome. Instead they slogged slowly up the peninsula, engaging in fierce fighting most of the way. As the months passed they became more efficient, coordinating air attacks with the efforts of their engineers to cross river after river. The terrible new weapon known as the flamethrower also helped them push back the tiring Germans. They helped recapture Florence in April and turned inland. By 1945 the New Zealanders had gained a certain momentum and began to race ahead of the following Allied army. They took Bologna on April 21, 1945, and moved on to Venice. From there they raced to take the important port of Trieste as a strategic objective. The New Zealanders secured the city on May 2, but nearly caused several international incidents in clashes with various groups of Yugoslav partisans. Luckily, the European war ended on May 8, and the communist leader General Tito withdrew in the face of the large Allied army.

Service in the Pacific theater was much less glamorous because New Zealanders did little more than support the east flank of the American drive against Japan, especially in the Solomon Islands and Rabaul, leaving the Australians to defend the west flank. In fact, the New Zealand government left defense of New Zealand to over 100,000 U.S. Marines after the supposedly impregnable fortress of Singapore fell in February 1942. Despite the lackluster nature of this contribution, over 20,000 New Zealand soldiers served with the Americans in the Pacific. Some 5,000 men from the Royal New Zealand Navy (formed in 1941) and 15,000 from the Royal New Zealand Air Force supported them at various times. New Zealand airmen also served with Fleet Air Arm on British aircraft carriers in the Pacific.

Casualties were serious, but not as horrific as in the American army. The Japanese killed 2,207 New Zealanders, wounded another 3,000, and tortured and ill treated about 100 unfortunate servicemen and 200 unlucky civilians taken prisoner of war. For those who avoided death or capture, this theater involved much waiting for action, and the troops became easily bored. Malaria and other tropical diseases also took a heavy toll. Numerous acts of gallantry occurred, but New Zealanders did not win accolades for their contribution to major battles as in North Africa and Italy.

The American Navy, not New Zealand troops, saved New Zealand from attack by winning the crucial naval battles of the Coral Sea in May 1942 and Midway in June 1942. By October 1944 the New Zealand government disbanded the generally unappreciated Pacific Division once the threat of immediate Japanese invasion had been removed. This action released troops to serve in Italy. Over 12,000 New Zealand men and a few hundred women known as Jayforce, though, did serve with the American occupation forces in Japan between 1946 and 1948.

This relatively unglamorous involvement in the Pacific and the threat of invasion were still very important to New Zealand, even though those who served there resented their lowly ranking relative to those who fought in the European theater as soldiers, sailors, and airmen. Apart from anything else, the arrival of over 100,000 American soldiers and sailors, with up to 48,000 in New Zealand at any one time, had a huge social impact on a small, isolated, and rather prudish country. Similarly, the threat of total warfare as well as the arrival of the Yanks impacted directly upon women's lives in a way that the remote First World War did not.

Initially, the Marines and New Zealand soldiers had to learn to live together. Racist taunts toward Maori by some Marines from southern states provoked a few brawls. New Zealand servicemen also resented the fact that the Americans were much better paid and fed. Disposable income spent on chocolates, flowers, and nylon stockings, though, made the Americans very popular with New Zealand women. Compared with many New Zealand men, the Marines possessed much more sophisticated social skills and seemed genuinely interested in women. Instead of retreating to one end of the hall to drink beer and talk to the boys, the Americans actually danced with local women. Many romances ensued, producing war brides and raising the rate of venereal disease alarmingly.

At a more prosaic level, many of the very young Marines enjoyed being billeted in ordinary homes, and such interaction made both groups realize that they had much more in common than they had formerly realized. On balance, this interaction liberated both New Zealand women and social life from some of the more rigid restraints imposed by the pervasive puritan code. New Zealand became more like middle America and less like a remote British province as a result. The relatively affluent Americans also raised expectations, both in terms of material comfort and quality of relationships. New Zealand women demanded more comfort in the home thereafter and asked more of their men. This encounter thereby explains much of the social conservatism and enthusiastic consumerism of the 1950s.

The Second World War offered many more opportunities for women to become directly involved or to join the workforce than the First World War. This time some did put on uniforms. The absence of over 100,000 men and the manpowering of another 90,000 into so-called essential industries provided access to occupations formerly debarred to women. Nearly 9,000 women served in the Women's Army Auxiliary Corps (4,589), Women's Auxiliary Air Force (3,764), and Women's Royal New Zealand Naval Services (640). They found the coarse woolen uniforms made to fit male bodies hideously uncomfortable, but reveled in the chance to be involved. Women carried out all kinds of useful support work, mainly clerical, but also flew planes around local airbases, drove heavy transport vehicles, trained airmen in bombing techniques, and prepared artillery for battle. Over 900 served overseas, mainly in the Mediterranean theater as nurses and orderlies.

The first women police were also employed during the war, but only a modest 30. More would have joined the forces, but nearly 3,000 were conscripted into the formerly male preserve of the metal and munitions industries, with another 2,000 being employed as land girls to make up for the labor shortage on farms. Consequently, the number of women employed in industry rose from 21,000 to 38,000. Women also served as train and bus drivers and conductors, drove bulldozers, and worked in bakeries for the first time (puritanical New Zealand did not like the idea of women working during hours of darkness). Maori women, too, shared in this participation in the paid workforce because the Maori War Effort Organization utilized their labor.

This experience gave New Zealand women a taste for paid employment, even if the land girls often were harshly treated by farmers and their wives. Revisionist historians such as Deborah Montgomery point out that the liberating effect of the war upon women should not be exaggerated because women soon retreated to the kitchen to contribute to the baby boom once the troops came home. Nevertheless, not all women returned home, and many hankered after the chance to earn their own money once again. This underlying desire helps explain the strong support that emerged for the quite radical second-wave feminist movement in the 1970s.

At first glance, the more modest 11,625 deaths and 17,000 wounded in this machine-oriented war seemed relatively mild compared with the hefty casualties produced by the more static battles of the First World War. The more practical memorials such as halls and swimming baths support the impression that the small Dominion suffered less. Such a judgment is, however, quite misleading, because the Second World War produced a much more profound effect on New Zealand society for a whole range of reasons.

First, the losses were still horrific and were worse in some districts than earlier if local men got caught in a disaster such as Crete or Cassino. Second, the threat of invasion and the experience of total war impacted much more directly upon women and children. The arrival of so many U.S. Marines both deepened and broadened that impact. Third, the huge effort of conscripting 194,000 men into the direct war effort also overstrained the New Zealand economy, and it took some time to move back into balance. Labor's tight management kept inflation under control, but maintenance of rationing and controls after the war led to distortions and built up deep resentment within the electorate.

Fourth, the soldiers themselves found the Second World War a broadening experience. Some developed a taste for good food, wine, theater, and opera in Italy and London. When they came home they, as much as their wives and girlfriends, wanted to make improvements. Unlike their fathers and uncles, they did not return to the exact way things were before the war. Certainly, they wanted domestic comfort, a family wage, and a nice house in the suburbs, but they also wanted many improvements and greater quality of life.

Finally, the failure of the Royal Navy to protect New Zealand forced the Dominion to reorient its foreign policy toward the United States and Asia. In 1942 New Zealand appointed its first ambassador to Washington, D.C., and sent none other than the deputy leader Walter Nash to begin the job of building closer bridges with the United States. In 1944 the Labor government (New Zealand appointed a bipartisan war cabinet in 1940, but Labor refused to establish a full coalition government as in 1915) also signed the Canberra Pact with the Australians to support one another in case of attack. In 1951, at the height of Cold War fears, this was easily extended to became the ANZUS Pact, a kind of gentlemen's agreement to come to one another's aid in times of crisis.

Despite this diplomatic shift, New Zealand remained as hopelessly dependent upon the British market as before the war. The volume of manufacturing output had been increased by over a third, but Britain still took over 90 percent of its remotest Dominion's exports. Covers of the *Journal of Agriculture* all stress the way in which the restructuring of postwar Britain held out bright prospects for New Zealand. Both government and opposition imagined that a food basket would fare well in a hungry world struggling to return to normal. Consequently, Labor once more tried to place returned soldiers on the land, admittedly with more care than Massey's government. This time Maori were included and, much as in the United States, many ex-servicemen of both races benefited from higher education that would otherwise have been denied. High prices paid for meat, butter, and wool under the revamped commandeer system buoyed the general sense of optimism. Unfortunately for the Labor government, this externally induced prosperity caused as much dissatisfaction within the urban electorates as it did in 1919.

Farmers once more had a good war, and they demanded the abolition of the guaranteed price scheme. They also replaced the rather dysfunctional Farmers' Union in 1944 with a better organized, modern-style pressure group called Federated Farmers. This organization helped farmers end guaranteed prices in 1946. Farmers, though, represented Labor's traditional adversaries. Much more serious was a growing militancy in the trade union movement, whose members felt that they had not shared in the prosperity induced by the war. Fraser's success as a statesman at the setting up of the United Nations meant little at home. Labor had essentially run out of ideas and had little new to offer. Nationalizing the Bank of New Zealand in 1945 held scant appeal, although the family allowance and cheap loans for young families introduced a year later proved sufficiently popular for Labor to win a narrow victory at the 1946 election.

It was the four Maori seats, all held by Ratana candidates since 1943, that kept Labor in power. Thereafter, the *New Zealand Herald* cartoonist Gordon Minhinnick always drew Fraser with four small Maori sitting on his shoulder. Labor had done more for Maori than any earlier government, and its Maori Social and Economic Advancement Act of 1945 shored up support. Dropping the word *native* in all official usage and replacing it with *Maori* also appealed to most Maori voters. Fraser personally oversaw the overhaul of the old Native Affairs Department and its replacement with the Maori Affairs Department in 1947 and won a reputation as the Pakaha leader most sympathetic to Maori needs. Fraser attributed this empathy to his upbringing among dispossessed crofters in the Scottish highlands. Only Gordon Coates among New Zealand prime ministers won anything like the same popularity with Maori. The undersecretary of Maori affairs from 1948, Tipi Ropiha, appointed welfare officers and Maori wardens who came to play an important role both in tribal areas and the cities as Maori began to move from remote pa to provincial towns.

THE DEMISE OF LABOR

Having scraped back into power unlike many wartime governments, Labor decided to ignore the farmers and headed a little to the left. This meant holding the economy under very tight control and experimenting with cooperative shops in the burgeoning suburbs. New Zealand now suffered from a chronic labor shortage and was forced to revive immigration. Migrants remained essentially Anglo-Celtic in origin, although a significant number of Dutch came along, with small numbers of refugees from various European countries such as Poland and Yugoslavia. This ethnic mix was quite different from neighboring Australia, which opened its doors to southern Europeans such as Italians and Greeks. Wages inevitably rose in such a situation, but disposable income could not be spent on either houses or consumer goods because of serious shortages of building materials and consumer goods. Frustration grew as the cautious Nash tried to hold down wages. Militant carpenters and wharf laborers, in particular, caused his government major headaches, and a serious showdown threatened throughout 1948.

What broke Labor's support, though, was Fraser's decision to introduce conscription in peacetime. As the Cold War deepened, British and American generals leaned on Fraser, and he capitulated. The old radical turned Cold War warrior held a referendum to secure democratic approval, but three to one support looked hollow when 37 percent—that is, Labor's traditional supporters—stayed away in disgust. This apparent betrayal alienated most of Labor's dwindling support, and National, led by the New Zealand-born businessman and First World War soldier Sid Holland, comfortably won the 1949 election by 46 seats to 34. National's campaign slogan, "Time for a Change," neatly caught the mood of the electorate.

In winning so comfortably, National, like Reform before it, also had to accept and maintain most of the earlier reforming government's initiatives. In short, National had to commit to maintaining the welfare state. Fraser could not believe the ingratitude of the electorate. His party had, after all, dragged the country out of the Depression and steered it through the trauma of total war. Fraser died soon after in December 1950, disillusioned and exhausted. Labor had now to regroup as National came to dominate New Zealand politics during the very prosperous years of the 1950s.

THE 1951 WATERFRONT STRIKE

Prosperity came as direct result of the Korean War. The troops assembled under the auspices of the United Nations, including 4,700 New Zealand soldiers and 1,300 sailors, needed warm coats to survive the severe Korean winters. New Zealand farmers gained by supplying wool to the uniform manufacturers and benefited from a huge hike in the price of wool. This boom ensured that New Zealand maintained its top-three world ranking in terms of living standards and did not experience painful postwar adjustments as in the early 1920s. Good times help any government, but Holland decided to cement his advantage by breaking the power of the more militant sections of the trade union movement in 1951.

Jock Barnes and Toby Hill, leaders of the New Zealand Waterfront Workers' Union (NZWWU), played into Holland's hands by talking of breaking away from the more moderate Federation of Labor (FOL). Patrick Fintan Walsh, president of the FOL, made things even easier for the new government when he forced the NZWWU out of the FOL in April 1950 because of its affiliation with the pro-Moscow World Federation of

Trade Unions. Cold War hysteria ran high at this time, and the majority of the electorate held deep suspicion of any organization with affiliation to communism. The NZWWU responded by forming an alternative Trade Union Congress (TUC) representing some 75,000 workers. The government watched, delighted, as the union movement split without its having to do a thing. Even so, the NZWWU still held considerable industrial muscle and was capable of putting up a stiff fight.

Throughout the rest of 1950 Barnes and Hill taunted government, port authorities, and the shipping companies by holding a series of lightning strikes over relatively trivial matters such as tea breaks and handling dirty cargoes. Government only averted a major showdown by appointing a royal commission of inquiry into the waterfront industry. By Christmas the NZWWU had alienated just about everybody, and the public held little sympathy for New Zealand's highest-paid workers.

Holland knew that he held the upper hand when the TUC rejected a 15 percent wage increase in February 1951. When Barnes ordered an overtime ban, the more consensual deputy prime minister, Keith Jacka Holyoake, tried to persuade the parties to return to arbitration. Holland, however, who returned from Washington, D.C., a few days later, would have nothing to do with reconciliation. He wanted to break the power of the NZWWU once and for all and so guarantee the free flow of exports from New Zealand's ports. Farmers naturally agreed with him, but so too did urban businessmen, clerical workers, and professionals. Holland, sensing the moment, deregistered the NZWWU on February 26 and declared the strike illegal. He also declared a state of emergency and introduced the draconian powers of the Public Safety Conservation Act of 1932. This legislation had been introduced to restore order after the Depression riots of early winter of 1932 and involved the loss of all civil liberties, including the right of free speech. No one could legitimately tell the NZWWU side of the story thereafter. Instead the beleaguered union members had to set up their own illegal presses and risk clashes with the police and arrest without trial if they tried to organize public rallies.

A few liberals expressed horror at the loss of civil liberties, but few others gave the NZWWU much support during the ensuing bitter 151-day strike. Servicemen loaded the boats with much less skill than the regular workers, and the economy continued to boom. Walter Nash, the new leader of Labor, did not help much when he stated that his party was neither for nor against the strike. He meant that Labor objected to the extremism of both sides and wanted a return to arbitration, but it sounded weak and lost him support from both the unions and the general public. As the months passed, waterfront workers' families began to suffer real hardship, although some of the wives gained new power and independence with their husbands stuck at home earning nothing. Women could at least take in washing, lodgers, and sewing and possibly find work. Eventually the workers capitulated on July 11.

The experience left deep scars on the memories of the unionists involved, and the 1951 waterfront strike has mythic importance among the left in New Zealand. Yet it is easy to exaggerate its significance for the simple reason that most New Zealanders opposed the strike. As far as the broader electorate was concerned, the waterfront workers were fighting for higher wages rather than for a noble cause. They rammed home this point in a snap election held on September 1 by voting the National government back into power by 20 seats with 54 percent of the low voter turnout. Some writers and intellectuals took up the task of converting grasping waterfront workers into proletarian heroes, but most other citizens remained unconvinced by this glorification. There is no doubt, however, that the strike was important in reducing the power of the union movement in New Zealand. National's decisive, if excessive, action helped the party gain a hold on the electorate down to the 1970s, only broken for one term in 1957 by Labor.

THE LAST GOOD YEARS, 1951–1967

The conservative mood revealed during the strike persisted well into the 1960s. The popular view of this period is that of the most boring time in the country's short history. Most people imagine or remember the 1950s in much the same light as 1950s America as portrayed in nostalgic situation comedies such as *Happy Days*. Yet this is a little misleading because plenty of change occurred during these apparently halcyon times. Certainly, many returned servicemen wanted to raise families of four or more children in quiet suburbs, but the boring fifties label tells us more about the expectations and judgments of the baby boom generation of the late 1960s.

For a start the 1950–1967 period saw considerable development of infrastructure and advances in technology. The National government was expert at building hydroelectric dams and roads as well as providing infrastructure for the new suburbs. The rapidly increasing population, which reached 2 million by 1952 and raced to 3 million by 1973, needed many more schools, and the well-paid labor force built them with enthusiasm. In many ways this era can be compared with the 1920s in terms of material development. Television arrived relatively late in 1960 to change family life forever, and the sales of radios, electric washing machines, and vacuum cleaners soared. Most New Zealand homes possessed electric refrigerators and telephones by the 1960s and soon incorporated the intrusive new medium of television, with over half a million sets having been sold by 1966. Motor vehicle sales also climbed to record levels. New Zealand turned back to Britain for its main supply of cars, despite their being far less suited to the tough driving conditions than larger and more powerful American cars. All this activity did little to reduce economic dependence on Britain, with over half of exports by value still going there as late as 1961. The visit of the new queen, Elizabeth II, in 1953–1954 only cemented sentimental ties with Britain.

Interestingly, all this development caused an increase of blue-collar jobs relative to white-collar jobs for the last time in New Zealand's history. The very narrow wage differential helped explain why many pupils did not stay in high school beyond 15 years of age.

The number of farms and farmers also expanded, reaching a record level of 92,000 and 74,000 respectively in 1955, before falling commodity prices forced consolidation of farm properties. Research and development kept agriculture internationally competitive by ensuring that New Zealand farmers were as efficient as any in the world. The so-called grasslands revolution, brought about by the aerial top dressing of superphosphate from 1949, saw sheep numbers rise steeply from 32 million in 1949 to 50 million by 1965. The South Island high country became productive once more, with the southern flock increasing from in 14.8 million in 1949 to 23 million in 1965 as against the North Island's 27 million. The giant forest of *Pinus radiata,* planted in the central North Island during the Depression of the 1930s, came into production from the early 1950s. Paper mills opened at the nearby towns of Kinleith near Tokoroa and Kawarau in 1953 and 1955 respectively.

The heavily protected manufacturing sector also took advantage of the growing demand for home appliances and began a tentative move into the export market. Over 200,000 people worked in manufacturing by 1970, but the sector still only earned 8 percent of export income. The majority of the factory workers were women, with 42 women participating in the paid workforce for every 100 men. A significant numbers of the workers were Maori, whose numbers had grown to nearly a quarter of a million by 1971. By 1971, 70 percent of Maori lived in cities as against a mere 10 percent in 1945. Over 45,000 Pacific Islanders, especially Western Samoans, had migrated to New Zealand by 1971, and many worked in factories.

This busy time also produced its fair share of social panics. One related to the discovery that juvenile delinquency and sexual promiscuity characterized the lives of many teenagers. The Mazengarb Report of 1954 condemned such behavior in the Hutt Valley on the outskirts of Wellington and blamed it on working mothers' not being at home when children came home from school. The bizarre murder of a teenage girl's mother in the Parker Hulme case of 1954, portrayed so brilliantly in Peter Jackson's film *Heavenly Creatures,* caused an uproar. Jackson's movie catches the stuffiness of Christchurch at the time.

Artists struggled to make much impact in the conformist society. Janet Frame's first novel *Owls Do Cry* appeared in 1957 to critical acclaim and the bemusement of the average New Zealand reader. Keith Sinclair's *A History of New Zealand,* a confident and rather nationalist book published by Penguin in 1959, won accolades and sold well. These little glimmers of cultural renaissance were offset by the marginalization of both fiction writing and painting at the bohemian edges of society.

Food remained stodgy and the wine, dubbed "purple death" by those unfortunate enough to experience it, remained virtually undrinkable. The culinary revolution that is such a feature of modern New Zealand had to wait for a raft of other social changes. Sports though, especially rugby, remained supreme. Visitors such as the American psychologist David Ausubel found the place unbearably dull and condemned it as a backwater in his controversial account, *The Fern and the Tiki.* Ausubel's 1960 publication reflected many of the prejudices of northeastern American intellectuals of the time, but he did recognize that Maori were being subjected to overt racial discrimination as they moved into the cities.

Even so, as the poet Brian Turner points out in his autobiography, these were good times for Pakeha family life as the country produced its healthiest and best-educated generation in a time of full employment. Rumors that the prime minister personally knew all seven unemployed persons caught the sense of security and self-satisfaction. The good times seemed set to last into the distant future. The stolid conformity also guaranteed that a major intergenerational clash would soon emerge. It took economic downturn, though, to unleash a profound sense of dissatisfaction with the status quo.

THE END OF THE GOLDEN WEATHER, 1967–1974

New Zealand's prosperous years threatened to end abruptly in 1957 when Britain tried to enter the European Economic Community. Commodity prices fell, and this downswing cost National the election in 1957. General Charles de Gaulle kept Britain out of the Common Market; Walter Nash and finance minister Arnold Nordmeyer took modest austerity measures; and things returned to normal. The so-called black budget of 1958 irritated the electorate, especially when these apparent killjoys increased the tax on beer and tobacco. The second Labor government achieved little, and National thereby easily overcame its shaky 2-seat majority and returned to power in 1960 by a comfortable 12 seats. National then held power for four further terms of office.

A much more serious collapse of commodity prices in 1967, however, brought Keith Holyoake's smooth, consensual style into question as New Zealand experienced a serious balance of payments deficit for the first time since the Great Depression of the 1930s. The economic historian C. B. Schedvin has shown that all primary producing countries suffered at this time when the relative value of their export staples collapsed. The world had recovered faster from war than New Zealand politicians and planners ever imagined. By the 1960s there was plenty of food for everyone, if only distribution systems could be reformed. Beef, wheat, and butter were now in chronic oversupply as American farming became more efficient and European farming recovered. The British economy itself did not help either, as its growth slowed in the face of fierce competition by the reconstructed German and Japanese economies and the superefficiency of Scandinavian competitors in producing high-quality manufactured goods. Demand for New Zealand's yellow butter and fatty, unattractively packaged frozen lamb understandably slowed. New Zealand had to suddenly find new products and new markets and overhaul its marketing strategies if it hoped to avoid stagnation and decay. This would, however, prove to be a Herculean task involving major restructuring to cope with the loss of guaranteed markets in a postcolonial world.

This end of the golden economic weather coincided with a veritable tidal wave of social changes as the period of 1967 to 1974 saw the old consensus and social order shudder under challenge from many movements demanding change. The year 1967 itself saw the abolition of the old imperial currency of pounds, shillings, and pence and its replacement by the American-style decimal system. Transfer to dollars and cents hiked inflationary pressures already undermining prosperity. The new minister of finance, Robert David Muldoon, who introduced decimal currency, also introduced very tight controls on the movement of money out of New Zealand, making overseas travel expensive and difficult. It just so happened that the peculiar institution of six o'clock closing was done away with in this year, unleashing a major shift in leisure patterns and paving the way for improvements in food and wine.

The God is dead controversy, which had caused much dissension and upset in Europe since the Second World War, finally found its way to sleepy New Zealand. The Presbyterian Church tore itself apart in public when conservatives tried the professor of theology at Know College, Lloyd Geering, for heresy. Geering had advocated that Christians could still practice their faith without believing in God. The professor escaped excommunication, but the Presbyterians lost their hold on their dwindling congregations.

Even more important, the growing anti-Vietnam War movement and antiestablishment youth culture finally began to have an impact at this time. Opposition to New Zealand's minimalist involvement (3,890 New Zealand troops served in Vietnam, with 37 being killed and 187 wounded, but the government did not introduce conscription as in the Australia) built to the point that the new Labor government pulled out the troops in 1972. Rock and revivalist folk music began to make a mark as the generations engaged in an unseemly war of words. Old soldiers expressed shock and disbelief at the sight of young men wearing long hair rather than the traditional short back and sides. Worse, the advent of the contraceptive pill in the late 1960s encouraged more promiscuous sexual behavior. By 1974 a major shift in the old puritanical mores had occurred. Institutions such as mixed flatting (flats shared by males and females) had become perfectly acceptable by then, whereas students had been expelled from Otago University for flatting with the other sex as recently as 1967. The counterculture flourished in some isolated locations, and rock music swept all before it. Private radio stations playing the new youth music emerged from 1968 and ended the monopoly of the old state-controlled system.

Second-wave feminism also made its entrance during this radical moment. Borrowing heavily from the international and especially the American movement, New Zealand women set up collectives in the main cities from which they set out to change the world. A woman's right to abortion became a key cause as elsewhere, as did better access to contraceptives; and so too did equal pay for equal work. Women had won this right within the civil service in 1960, but they had to wait until 1984 for it to be made universal. Even then, the National government abolished the right in 1992. Divorce law reform also followed, with fifty-fifty no-fault divorce being introduced in 1977. This movement whipped up huge controversy, but the rhetorical battle lost intensity as women systematically set about increasing their representation at every level of life. They had to fight until the 1990s, though, before they began to win more adequate representation in both national and local politics. Only in very recent years have New

Zealand women begun to secure the kinds of powerful positions in politics and big business equivalent to more progressive societies such as the Scandinavian countries.

Radical moments are usually stimulating times for artists, and the period from the late 1960s to the early 1970s saw significant advances in writing and painting. Maurice Shadbolt and Maurice Gee emerged as novelists of international caliber, while Don Binney, Phillip Trusttum, Robyn White, and a host of other painters reinvigorated both landscape and portrait painting. Maori writing also took off at this time with the emergence of Hone Tuwhare as a major poet, and Witi Ihimaera wrote the first novels to be published by a Maori. Maori painters and carvers such as Ralph Hotere and Cliff Whiting also began to make their mark, while Kiri Te Kanawa and Inia Te Wiata won international recognition in the difficult world of opera singing. At a more modest level, crafts such as pottery began to flourish, and professional theater companies spluttered to life in the four main cities.

9

Coping with a Decolonizing World, 1974–1984

The changes of the 1950s and 1960s would pale into insignificance beside the big shifts that took place as Britain joined the European Economic Market and the communications revolution unleashed the full force of globalization upon the fragile New Zealand economy.

MULDOONISM

Britain's joining the EEC in 1973 coincided with the first of two major oil shocks in 1974. The optimism of the early Kirk years began to fade as inflation raced out of control and New Zealand struggled to pay its large oil bill. Kirk's sudden death on August 31, 1974, only deepened the growing sense of anxiety, and the expansive mood soon gave way to a return to something of a fortress mentality. The National Party's astute new leader, R. D. Muldoon, sensed this shift in mood and made huge political gains. Kirk's replacement, the clever but unassuming economist Bill Rowling, proved no match for Muldoon's abrasive style, and National ousted Labor from power in 1975. Television advertisements devised by the American cartoon specialist Hanna-Barbera took advantage of the introduction of color television in 1974 by manipulating fears that British and Pacific Island immigrants were overrunning the country. An ebullient

Muldoon cashed in on fear of job losses, increasing crime, and accelerating change and exactly reversed the landslide of 1972. Whereas Labor won 55 seats to National's 32 in 1972, National won 55 to Labor's 32 in 1975.

The unofficial white New Zealand policy reappeared as immigration ground to a halt. Muldoon's populist nationalism tended to be inward-looking, in contrast to Kirk's extrovert nationalism. Consequently, New Zealand turned away from Asia and the Third World to entrench the gains of its European population. Muldoon made this clear in 1976 when he agreed to allow a rugby team to tour South Africa when that country still pursued a policy of apartheid, or separate development. This action caused a major boycott of the Montreal Olympics by the black African nations. New Zealand became something of the pariah of the British Commonwealth thereafter, until a change of government in 1984.

Muldoon also set out to undo Labor's few economic initiatives, most notably its new contributory superannuation or pension scheme. At great cost, Muldoon replaced it with a universal scheme paid out of general taxation to every citizen over 60, no matter how rich or poor. Such generosity proved unsustainable as the population began to age. Many New Zealanders soon regretted that Muldoon had persuaded them that Labor's sensible and sustainable system constituted some kind of backdoor nationalization of the country's resources. By 1984 the cost of superannuation, in fact, outstripped expenditures on health and education combined, forcing dramatic changes in the way the small country paid out its ever-increasing pensions.

In most other respects Muldoon's economic management remained orthodox in that he continued Labor's use of tariffs and subsidies to maintain high employment and high standards of living. The escalation of subsidies to farmers under the supplementary minimum price (SMP) scheme of 1978 supposedly aimed to restore prosperity to the countryside without devaluing the dollar, an alternative opposed by manufacturers and unions. Instead, subsidies for fertilizer and transport only encouraged refrigeration and trucking companies to raise their prices, while refrigeration workers and contractors demanded higher wages. Tax cuts and low-interest loans in addition to the subsidies did increase productivity as sheep numbers soared to a record 70 million by 1980, but only at considerable cost.

This traditional approach to stoking New Zealand's single-engine economy also proved rather ineffectual in a world little interested in eating fatty red meat and even fattier butter, which recent medical research had suggested induced heart disease. New Zealand had to attend to proper marketing of its products for the first time. This skill took some time to develop. Traditional producer boards struggled to make the change to competitive markets rather than a single, guaranteed British market, but eventually the Dairy Board led the way in the search for new markets and new products. Japan, the United States, and Australia began to challenge Britain as New Zealand's leading export market.

Muldoon must take more credit for encouraging the development of the ailing manufacturing sector and expanding the export of timber products. Tariffs and incentives saw manufacturing lift its share of export earnings from around 8 percent in 1972 to 22 percent by 1984. Manufacture of washing machines and dishwashers boomed as New Zealand industrialists began to take fuller advantage of a free trade agreement with Australia that was signed in 1966 and expanded considerably in 1983 into the Closer Economic Relations agreement or CER. Timber products also benefited from the CER and the expanding Japanese market. Export earnings from timber products topped $1 billion by 1984, and a new chipboard industry emerged in the Nelson area at the top of the South Island.

Interestingly, despite rapid growth of the tertiary education sector as the baby boomers poured into the universities, wage differentials remained lower than just about anywhere. Emissaries from communist countries who visited New Zealand were embarrassed by the fact that the gap between top salary and bottom wages was much lower than in the Soviet Union or its iron curtain satellites. Refrigeration workers could still earn more than schoolteachers and white-collar workers, but an increase from 30,000 tertiary students in 1971 to 160,000 in 1984 built pressure to change New Zealand's rather unusual order of remuneration. Significantly, the proportion of money spent on higher education also began to slide as student numbers escalated. According to James Belich's calculations, spending on education fell from a relatively high 17.5 percent of total government expenditure to 10.8 percent. This represented a miserable figure that dropped New Zealand from the upper levels of the Organization for Economic Co-operation and Development (OECD) rankings to the bottom end, below many developing countries as well as supposedly developed states.

Unfortunately, Muldoon's mix of pumping up the traditional grassland farming sector while encouraging some growth of manufacturing did not help ease the difficulties caused by another oil shock in 1979. The inconvenience of carless days rammed home the lesson that New Zealand needed to undertake some bolder economic changes if it hoped to pay its burgeoning debts and break ongoing economy dependency. According to his biographer Barry Gustafson, Muldoon dreamed up a solution pretty much on the fly when traveling around with his private secretary Bernie

Galvin. Galvin suggested that the slogan "Think Big" caught the magnitude of the task outlined after the second oil shock.

At the 1981 election Muldoon revealed a dramatic desire to make New Zealand into some kind of Japan at the bottom of the Pacific by encouraging greater self-sufficiency in energy and massive expansion in manufacturing activity. Growth would be based around the establishment of a special plant at Motonui in Taranaki to convert abundant natural gas into petrol (gasoline). Mobil would treat New Zealand as a guinea pig and develop a totally untried technology. In addition, Muldoon attempted to make New Zealand's abundant, cheap, and clean hydroelectricity available to overseas manufacturers by building more dams. The most controversial was the vast Clyde Dam in Central Otago. Its construction, like that of the Motonui plant, ran wildly over budget and escalated the national debt from a modest $1 billion in 1976 to $9 billion by 1984.

Infuriatingly for both Muldoon and subsequent governments, few overseas companies seemed interested in New Zealand's cheap hydroelectric power. One reason for their lack of enthusiasm related to high tax rates employed by Muldoon to protect jobs and maintain the welfare state. Tax rates on personal income rose as high as a staggering 66 cents on the dollar even on relatively modest incomes. Tax evasion soon became a major economic activity in its own right.

Muldoon also hoped to create some 410,000 new jobs by building a large fertilizer plant in south Taranaki to help boost farming output and by upgrading the steel mill at Glenbrook, south of Auckland. This mill made steel by extracting iron ore from the black sand beaches of the North Island's west coast. Even though this proved to be a very complex and expensive process, a market opened in China, and by 1984 production rose to 750,000 tonnes annually. Muldoon also hoped to establish a second aluminum smelter near Dunedin to supplement the large smelter at Bluff on the bottom of the South Island. The collapse of aluminum prices in the late 1970s, however, soon put an end to that alternative. Much to the relief of many Dunedin citizens, the mothballing of this project saved the only albatross colony near a city in the world, which sat directly opposite the proposed smelter site at Taiaroa Heads. This is the only such colony near human habitation in the world and attracts many tourists.

MAORI RESURGENCE

These bold but questionable economic strategies depended on the price of oil staying high. Falling oil prices from as early as 1982 soon brought the plan under serious scrutiny. This questioning made Think Big as divisive as many of Muldoon's other policies. The increasingly high-profile Maori protest movement, which emerged as cities grew, joined such unlikely allies as second-wave feminists and environmentalists in protesting Muldoon's increasingly dictatorial style.

Maori urban-centered protest, basing itself on the U.S. African American civil rights movement, attracted widespread media attention from 1969. Yet it is a mistake to talk of a Maori resurgence or renaissance, as such terms suggest that Maori protest was something new. In fact, it had begun almost as soon as the Treaty of Waitangi had been signed and never ceased thereafter. What these terms rather suggest is that Pakeha awareness of Maori grievances grew rapidly across this period as television, only introduced in 1960, and a growing urban presence made Maori more conspicuous.

Maori had suffered from overt racism as they moved into the cities, but organizations such as the Maori Women's Welfare League established in 1951 helped ease that adjustment. By the late 1960s, though, many younger Maori had grown impatient with the reasonableness and moderation of such organizations. They wanted more direct and immediate action to force redress of grievances. One such radical organization, called Nga Tamatoa, or the young warriors, emerged in Auckland in 1969 to challenge structural racism at every level. Its criticism of drunken student engineers for belittling the *haka,* or traditional war dance, really put an end to any notion that New Zealand had been blessed by good race relations. Maori protest gathered so much momentum by 1975 that a massive march against land loss, starting in the far north and ending in the capital of Wellington, occurred. Led by Dame Whina Cooper, a former leader of the Maori Women's Welfare League, this spectacular display of unity forced the ailing Labor government to set up the Waitangi Tribunal to advise on Maori land grievances.

Muldoon did little to enhance the powers of this body, and Maori antipathy built toward his government. Things came to a head in 1977 and 1978 when Muldoon responded to two particular protests in a heavy-handed manner. Maori at Kawhia, southwest of Auckland, complained bitterly that sacred burial sites taken for wartime purposes had never been returned. Instead this *tapu* land had been buried under a golf course. Muldoon tried to dismiss this grievance as mumbo-jumbo, but he underestimated the formidable Eva Rickard. She and her Ngati Toa people won back the disputed land as well as compensation for inappropriate use by the golf club in 1978.

Muldoon handled a much larger protest at Bastion Point in the heart of Auckland in 1978 much more severely. From 1977 Ngati Whatua, led by

Joe Hawke, occupied one of the most valuable sites in Auckland to protest land loss. On May 25, 1978, Muldoon used massed police supported by the Army to forcibly remove the protesters. This land then became available for a luxury housing development. An outraged Ngati Whatua eventually won compensation many years later, but in the meantime race relations sank to a low point as dawn raids on Pacific Island immigrants continued after the removal of Ngati Whatua from their ancestral lands. The former Labor minister of Maori affairs, Matiu Rata, added to the sense that Maori were becoming disillusioned with most of their traditional allies when he broke from Labor to form a separate Maori party in 1979. Known as Mana Motuhake (Maori sovereignty), his party challenged the alliance between Labor and the Ratana Church that went back nearly 50 years to 1932. Although Rata's party never gained a substantial number of votes, its emergence suggested that disaffection was growing within the Maori community.

Race relations problems reached something of flash point in 1981 when Muldoon decided that the South African rugby team (known as the Springboks) should tour New Zealand despite opposition of the police and many citizens. Nor did Commonwealth disapproval deter Muldoon. He gambled that conservative, provincial electorates, such as Invercargill, Central Otago, and Taranaki, which also happened to be benefiting from Think Big programs, would support this move.

The gamble paid off in electoral terms, with Muldoon narrowly winning the 1981 election even though Labor won more seats, but his decision tore the community in half. Generally, younger New Zealanders, both Pakeha and Maori, opposed the tour, whereas many older New Zealanders supported it, although grandmothers and heavily decorated returned serviceman such as Professor Angus Ross, a war hero, could also be seen amongst the protestors. Some Maori also supported the tour because rugby had always provided an avenue to acceptance by the wider community. Younger, tertiary-educated Maori, however, sided with oppressed black South Africans, and tempers ran high. After protestors forced the second match at Hamilton to be abandoned, only heavy police protection enabled the tour to continue. By the time of the final game in Auckland in late September, deep divisions had become very apparent. During that match a small plane rained pamphlets and flour over the playing surface; furious patrons joined the police in fighting the protestors after the match; and numerous arrests were made. The police eventually rescinded most convictions, but the tour had induced the greatest civil unrest in New Zealand since the wars of the 1860s. The rest of world looked on astonished as the heavily protected riot police belted helmeted protestors.

Despite the bitterness and violence, the tour left little easily discernable impact. Muldoon's gamble paid off in the short term, but the resentment unleashed by his handling of the tour undoubtedly helped oust him from power in 1984. One might have expected revolutionary cells to have developed, but instead Maori turned away from direct action to working through the courts and inside the system. Rugby certainly was briefly knocked off its pedestal, and soccer had a fleeting moment of glory in 1982 as the New Zealand team won its way to the World Cup. The emergence of a powerful new All Black team, which won the inaugural World Cup in Rugby in 1987, however, soon returned the games to their more traditional inequality. Suspicion of the police also lingered through the remainder of the century, but overall it is possible to argue that the 1981 tour did more to help the triumph of the African National Congress in South Africa than it did to improve race relations in New Zealand.

ARTISTS STRIKE BACK

This turbulent period inevitably produced some interesting cultural responses. At the more popular level, several pop groups emerged to challenge the rather closed nature of the old New Zealand order as personified by Muldoon. The most successful was Split Enz, whose bizarre stage act proved too radical for the United States and most other places outside Britain. Blam, Blam, Blam dented the notion that New Zealand remained God's own country with their tongue-in-cheek "There Is No Depression in New Zealand." Meanwhile, various Maori bands also emerged, combining reggae-style music with relaxed Pacific rhythms and protest lyrics. The most commercially successful of this style of band called itself Herbs.

At the level of so-called high culture, painting continued to develop in leaps and bounds, and crafts such as pottery and photography matured and grew. Maori Ralph Hotere emerged as major artist when he produced several memorable works opposing the erection of the Aramoana Aluminum smelter. Younger artists such as Bill Hammond and Patrick Hanley joined the elder statesman of New Zealand painting, Colin McCahon, in producing several powerful works as part of New Zealand artists' statement against nuclear weapons. In 1982 novelist Maurice Shadbolt wrote a very nationalistic play called *Once on Chunuk Bair* about the Gallipoli campaign, while Maurice Gee wrote the impressive *Plumb* trilogy between 1978 and 1983. The first volume of Janet Frame's eloquent autobiography, *To the Is-Land,* also appeared in 1982. Vincent Ward's bleak movie *Vigil* (1984) heralded a resurgence of New Zealand film making.

A CRUCIAL ELECTION

This burst of activity in part reflected a growing desire to break free from traditional strategic alliances, and the Labor Party came under increasing pressure to introduce an antinuclear policy, including the banning of any ship either carrying nuclear weapons or using nuclear propulsion. Labor's charismatic new leader, David Lange, elected in place of Bill Rowling in 1983, did not personally agree with many of these more radical policies, but Labor's activists forced acceptance upon the party. In adopting this stance Labor, with its young team of would-be ministers, offered a very real alternative to National at the 1984 election. Labor also pitched its appeal to those opposed to sporting contact with South Africa and accepted that government needed to make more concessions to the demands of second-wave feminism. Labor courted Maori by promising to increase the powers of the Waitangi Tribunal. Interestingly, despite its assiduous criticism of Muldoon's Think Big strategy, Labor never really offered a coherent economic policy to the electorate other than a promise to devalue the dollar and end Muldoon's rigid controls on imports, interest rates, and wages. Roger Douglas's radical, even revolutionary, change of direction came as something of surprise when unleashed shortly after the election.

Young and reinvigorated, Labor easily won the 1984 election by 19 seats (56 to 37, with Social Credit holding onto 2) against the tiring National government. National was not helped by the emergence of the libertarian New Zealand Party led by the flamboyant entrepreneur Bob Jones. Jones deliberately set out to win support for more of a free market approach and won 11 percent of the vote in a highly entertaining campaign. New Zealand's youngest cabinet ever, with an average age in the early forties rather than the traditional middle fifties, set about changing many features of New Zealand life with energy and enthusiasm. The cabinet represented young rather than aging New Zealand and heralded the most dramatic changes since the late 1930s, only this time many of the initiatives undid those of the first Labor government and dismantled large parts of the welfare state.

James Belich argues that New Zealand's loss of its imperial status after 1973–1974 was, in fact, more important than the sea change in policy that occurred after the election of the fourth Labor government in 1984. Many historians, including myself, question this interpretation. Certainly, having to cope in a postcolonial world without any guaranteed markets forced much rethinking about New Zealand's economic direction, but the changes between 1974 and 1984 seem rather modest when compared with those between 1984 and 1993. It is true that these changes probably would not have been so necessary had New Zealand somehow clung to its guaranteed British market, but despite the claims of many that the swing toward neoliberalism was inevitable and that there was no alternative, New Zealand could have followed a range of different strategies. The more important task of the historian, therefore, is to explain why New Zealand followed such a dramatically different path, ironically in the year chosen by British novelist George Orwell to mark the death of free society.

The change of direction occurred because of a particular conjunction of structural developments, demographic shifts, and changing ideological fashion. Escalating debt, a worsening balance of payments, and unemployment of 80,000, or Great Depression levels, seemed bad enough to many. The baby boomers who had seized power, however, wanted to go farther than simply patching up some more jobs. Instead, they aimed to make many changes to the restrictive welfare state that seemed to be stifling their ambitions as well as draining the public purse.

In addition, the old Keynesian/interventionist order had gone out of fashion in the United States and Britain. Keynes was out, and the long-out-of-favor Milton Friedman was in. The Chicago school knocked Harvard off its perch as Reaganomics and Thatchernomics turned the old order on its head in the United States and Britain. Economists trained in the new free market schools took over Treasury and university economics departments. They backed Roger Douglas and Labor's deputy leader, the constitutional lawyer Geoffrey Palmer, who had trained at Chicago. Lange himself confessed to being little interested in economics and turned his attention to foreign affairs, race relations, and social policy. Never again would a prime minister risk being minister of finance like Muldoon.

Lange's abrogation of fiscal responsibility and a lack of any kind of alternative forms of economic policy gave Douglas and the Treasury a virtual free hand to turn the world upside down and inside out. A few university economists protested, while Hugh Fletcher, managing director of New Zealand's biggest corporation, urged government to consider other alternatives, like those followed in Japan and Scandinavia. Douglas easily dismissed such alternatives because his approach seemed so fresh and different from anything tried before. He also won the approval of free market overseas journals such as *The Economist.*

New Zealand seemed to doing what such influential bodies as the International Monetary Fund and the World Bank wanted. Such approval held out appeal to the great majority of younger voters and carried considerable weight in a former colony where overseas experts have always been regarded with awe rather than skepticism. A financial crisis manipulated by Treasury also played into Douglas's hands when the governor of the Reserve Bank warned that New Zealand would have to default on payment of the interest on its overseas debts unless the dollar was revalued. Muldoon protested, but Lange and Douglas took the governor's advice, devalued by 20 percent, and immediately ended all of Muldoon's freezes on interest rates, prices, and wages. Inflation shot away; interest rates burgeoned; and wage demands ramped as these pent-up pressures were released. Double-digit inflation and interest rates did not deter New Zealand now that the country had determinedly set itself on a new course.

At a deeper level, this shift also related to ongoing globalization of the world economy stimulated by the communications revolution. Computers, improved telephone systems, and fax machines were fast shrinking the world. Douglas and his follows believed that New Zealand should take advantage of seeing the sun first in the world by freeing up its economy to foreign investors. He hoped that the computer and the speed with which capital could be moved would turn New Zealand into the financial hub of the South Pacific, a kind of Australasian tiger similar to booming Singapore.

10

Facing the Challenges of Globalization, 1984–2002

Having won the election comfortably, Lange, Douglas, and Palmer set about remaking New Zealand with enthusiasm and energy. Indeed, as Douglas later admitted, they deliberately moved so fast that their opponents and the voting public had no chance of catching up. Douglas concentrated on overhauling economic management and the welfare state, while Lange pursued a more independent foreign policy, and Palmer turned to constitutional reform. Assisted by other youthful enthusiasts like Richard Prebble, Stan Rodger, Michael Bassett, Ann Hercus, and Fran Wild, the fourth Labor government made sure that few aspects of New Zealand life escaped reform.

THE REFORMS OF ROGERNOMICS

Douglas had decided that New Zealand needed to become much more efficient to prosper. The best way, he believed, to achieve such efficiency was to convert one of the world's most regulated economies into one of the freest. Having brought various freezes to an abrupt end, he deregulated with enthusiasm. Subsidies to farmers and manufacturers disappeared in days rather than the traditional years. Despite holding a few initial talkfests, unlike Holyoake and Muldoon, he did not bother consulting with major pressure groups such as the Federation of Labor or Federated Farmers. Instead, he simply charged ahead. In 1985 he took the radical step of floating the New Zealand dollar in international currency markets rather than tying it to a rate fixed by the New Zealand Reserve Bank. Much to the surprise of most New Zealanders, the currency increased in value as money poured in to take advantage of high interest rates. Economic historian Brain Easton argues that this refusal to keep the dollar low slowed any kind of recovery, but Douglas never doubted his bold strategy.

The reforming minister of finance also encouraged New Zealanders to play the stock market for the first time in New Zealand's history. All kinds of people started trading in shares, and corporate raider companies such as Brierley Investments (that is, companies that bought and sold large parcels of shares in struggling companies all around the world) flourished until the international stock market crash of October 1987 brought that short-lived boom to a rather savage end. New entrepreneurial heroes such as Bruce Judge went bust overnight, and the likes of Brierley struggled thereafter.

Douglas also simplified the tax system in 1984, replacing New Zealand's steeply gradated taxes with a simple two-tier model, in which persons earning under $30,000 paid 24 cents on the dollar, rising to 30 cents on the dollar when they passed the $30,000 threshold. Douglas then added a goods and services tax, or GST, of 10 percent (raised to 12.5 percent in 1989) to every item sold and every service provided in the country. Douglas ignored pleas to exclude essentials such as food and clothing, and this new tax proved to be a big earner for the government. This change, nevertheless, horrified traditional Labor supporters because it was regressive rather than progressive. For the first time, those earning under $9,000 had to pay taxes.

Douglas's solution to helping low-paid families was rather to provide special income relief from the Department of Social Welfare. This shift represented a very different approach to operating the welfare state because Douglas aimed to target poverty rather than provide blanket assistance. He also alienated Gray Power by introducing a surcharge on Muldoon's expensive superannuation (pensions) and left it to others to strip back the state by corporatizing old-style departments and selling off activities he considered uneconomic—such as state forests, the Post Office Savings Bank, and Air New Zealand. High-powered chief executives who were paid large salaries replaced old-style department heads, while civil servants had their salaries reduced or lost their jobs altogether.

Richard Prebble, dubbed the mad dog by comedians, set about this process with great enthusiasm, reducing the old employment sponge of the Railways Department from 25,000 employees to a mean and lean 5,000. He also closed 423 post offices, many of which acted as community centers in small towns. In their place he divided the old post office into separate telecommunications, postal, and banking sections. He then sold Post Bank to an Australian trading bank in 1989 and Telecom to American investors in 1990. The standard of telecommunications improved spectacularly, but Telecom's sizable annual profits of around $600 million thereafter moved offshore, reducing government revenue by a significant amount. The Australian government learned from this mistake and restricted shareholding to Australian citizens when it privatized its telecommunications system in the 1990s.

Prebble also converted the state-owned national airline, Air New Zealand, into a corporation before selling it into private ownership in 1989. In addition, he allowed Ansett Australia into New Zealand to increase competition and improve services. New Zealand air travelers enjoyed the best domestic in-flight service in the world for the next decade, but such stiff competition in such a small market proved unsustainable. Unfortunately, Air New Zealand failed to win reciprocal rights into Australia, and although it outlasted Ansett the government had to buy 80 percent of it back in 2001 in a desperate rescue attempt.

By 1990 the fourth Labor government had sold off some $9 billion worth of state assets, including several large pine forests. This drastic action did reduce public debt a little and helped bring the balance of payments back into surplus for a brief time in 1990, but critics then and now suspect that the policy constituted a fire sale of the family silver. Any subsequent buy-back, as with Air New Zealand, will also be horrifically expensive, rendering these modest gains very questionable.

While Prebble slashed staffing levels, restructured, and sold state assets, Stan Rodger, former president of the Public Service Association, undid the 90-year-old industrial relations system so that unions would not resist the pace of change. Once compulsory conciliation and arbitration had been removed, New Zealand unions seemed to lose all will to resist. Consequently, they did not protest the rapid and dramatic changes like their Australian counterparts.

These drastic changes brought few short-term economic gains as unemployment soared to record levels of over 100,000, the national debt ballooned to $42 billion by 1987, inflation refused to abate, the balance of payments situation worsened, and New Zealand's OECD ranking stagnated at around 20. Government passed a new Reserve Bank Act in 1989 to empower the governor of the Reserve Bank to set interest rates independent of government in a desperate effort to limit inflation. This initiative came too late to reverse Labor's declining popularity, but it did succeed in pulling the country's inflation rate back into line with its major trading partners. In contrast to this success, Douglas and his team failed to develop new industries to supplement the traditional agricultural industries. Instead, farming reeled without the props of subsidies and tax breaks.

Farmers resented having the failed pig farmer but successful accountant Douglas portray farming as a sunset industry. Depression stalked the countryside as so-called yuppies (young, upwardly mobile professionals) wined and dined in the cities. Food and wine definitely improved along with entertainment as a café culture emerged, but the electorate began to doubt Douglas's claims that the country was only going through painful adjustment to the distortions caused by Muldoon's interventionist policies. Even so, suspicion of National remained so strong that voters gave Labor another chance at the 1987 election by a comfortable 19 seats.

Other members of the cabinet were trying to reform many more areas of New Zealand life. David Lange not only forced through antinuclear legislation, but set about reforming education. Lange's sharp wit did not amuse American diplomats, who were rankled by New Zealand's refusal to admit American or British ships into its ports. The antinuclear stance, though, proved popular with younger New Zealanders, whereas the educational reforms raised eyebrows even before they alienated teacher unions.

Hopes rose briefly that serious underfunding of education would end and that more enlightened policies would be introduced, much as in 1935. Lange soon dashed those high expectations when, instead of appointing a prominent educator to overhaul the system as Peter Fraser had with Clarence Beeby, he handed the investigation over to Brian Picot, operator of a chain of supermarkets. Suspicions deepened further when Lange appointed a bureaucrat who had overhauled forestry as director-general of education. Treasury had advised Lange that reform should not be captured by persons who worked in a field, and he took this advice at face value.

Picot recommended that, if New Zealand hoped to reform its education system to cope with the challenges of a rapidly changing world, schools and universities should be run more like businesses. He argued against the older orthodoxy that education constituted a public good that benefited the whole community. Instead, he suggested that it brought private gain because of the access it provided to high-paying jobs. He recommended, therefore, that the old-style boards of governors be replaced by boards of trustees that, for the first time, gave parents a direct say in the running of schools. According to Picot's working party, the old, locally based boards of education should also be replaced by a centralized Ministry of Education, with the new school boards representing local interest directly to government. A new centralized qualifications authority (NZQA) and an Educational Review Office (ERO) employing full-time bureaucrats would replace the old school inspectorate, which used to be run by top-ranking teachers who passed on their advice in a very hands-on manner to classroom teachers.

According to the Hawke Report, universities required similar reforms. So the old, centralized University Grants Committee, which made five-year grants to each university according to national need and projections of numbers, should be abolished, enabling universities to go head to head with one another in direct competition for students. University staff also expressed alarm at the recommendation that the setting of their salaries be removed from the jurisdiction of the Higher Salaries Commission (a body that ensured that judges, leading civil servants, and politicians were paid according to their market worth). This move signaled a deliberate attempt to lower the burgeoning university wage bill. This measure soon proved to be so successful that university salaries fell well below those paid in New Zealand's private sector, let alone in universities in Australia, Canada, the United Kingdom, or the United States. Labor increased fees moderately, but avoided large-scale up-front fees that Hawke argued were required to cover the cost of teaching rapidly increasing numbers in the tertiary sector as enrolments soared from just over 100,000 in 1981 to 165,000 by 1988.

The educational reforms, which Lange largely implemented under the fine-sounding rubric "Tomorrow's Schools," suggested that the new right was just as intent upon social engineering as the old left. Basically, Picot, Hawke, and others wanted a cultural change so that citizens approached education in a more entrepreneurial manner. To encourage such a shift, they literally changed the language relating to education overnight. Students suddenly became clients, staff were reconstructed as resources, while parents and the wider community acquired the status of stakeholders. Organizational structures increasingly resembled those of big business corporations. Chief executive officers replaced department heads, and institutions became more hierarchical. Universities adopted a more managerial approach, hiked the salaries of their vice chancellors (equivalent to American vice presidents), and appointed deputy vice chancellors and assistant vice chancellors to lengthen the chain of command. Economist Tim Hazeldine estimates that, whereas there was one manager per 22 workers in New Zealand during the 1960s, by the early 1990s there were four managers for every worker. Other commentators, whether critics of Rogernomics such as Bruce Jesson or supporters such as Colin James, agree that managers, accountants, and lawyers benefited most from these so-called reforms. At the same time, formerly powerful groups such as agricultural scientists lost much of their influence.

The expensive health system also attracted the attention of cost cutters and would continue to do so thereafter. Michael Bassett had tried to break the power of doctors and other health professionals in the early 1970s but failed. This time Labor called in another high-powered businessman to help. Alan Gibbs recommended that the well-paid should contribute more to covering health costs, advocated greater efficiencies, and demanded greater accountability from health care providers. Government accepted many of his recommendations, replacing the numerous old health boards with 14 larger, elected area health boards, which had to run their own budgets independently of the central ministry of health. In 1989 David Caygill and Helen Clark also increased the amount that those earning above set amounts had to pay toward their medical prescriptions and required such persons to pay for part of their hospital treatment. These compromises paved the way for much more draconian changes under the National governments of the 1990s.

Changes to welfare provision, education, and health services clashed somewhat with the more idealistic Royal Commission on Social Policy, which Lange also directed to report in 1988. This document advocated equity and level playing fields, or equal opportunity for all. Critics, and even Lange himself, doubted that more expensive education and health services would do much to make playing fields more level, so the prime minister called for a rest to give the public time to catch up with the giddy pace of reform. Lange also felt that it was time to reconsider some of the more drastic reforms, a point he underscored when he sacked Douglas as finance minister in December 1988 when Douglas suggested the introduction of a single, low-level flat tax. Before this loss of nerve, however, many other reforms had already occurred.

Michael Bassett had overhauled the unwieldy local government system by 1989. The abolition of New Zealand's federal system in 1876 produced a plethora of organizations including counties, town boards, road boards, harbor boards, pest destruction boards, noxious plant authorities, land drainage boards, river boards, maritime planning authorities, and united councils. Yet politicians never developed anything at the intermediary level to replace the old provincial councils. So Bassett simplified this cumbersome model. Since 1989, 14 regional councils, district councils, and city councils have supplemented the work of parliament and the centralized bureaucracy and absorbed the functions of the old boards. The number of territorial authorities was also reduced from 204 to 73, and special purpose authorities from 400 to 7. Bassett also did away with the catchment boards and the National Water and Soil Conservation Authority, which had controlled New Zealand's river systems with some success since 1941 and certainly reduced both flooding and erosion.

As minister of internal affairs, Bassett anticipated that a new Resource Management Act (RMA) would hand over all resource control to the regional councils or the Department of Conservation and Ministry of the Environment (founded in 1986 and 1987 respectively). The RMA was also meant to act as a check upon the kind of unfettered development undertaken by Muldoon. Bassett, however, did not hold onto power long enough to enact the RMA and left the introduction of that controversial measure to the National government in 1991. Both the Department of Conservation (DOC) and the Ministry for the Environment, meantime, took over the conservation tasks of the old New Zealand Forest Service, the Department of Lands and Survey, the Wildlife Service of the Department of Internal Affairs, and the Commission for the Environment. The idea driving these changes was that earlier organizations often performed contradictory roles, whereas the DOC and the new ministry could specialize in protecting the environment. They would be assisted in their work by a commissioner for the environment, who would supposedly act independently of government. His office could criticize policies that it considered damaging and unsustainable.

Labor could not afford to alienate the feminist vote that it had clearly attracted in 1984, so Ann Hercus immediately established a new Ministry of Women's Affairs. This new arm of the bureaucracy aimed to address women's special problems and acknowledged that, despite winning the vote so early, New Zealand women had fallen well behind their Scandinavian, German, and American counterparts. Men still held most chief executive positions in government, commerce, and education, and such male bastions as the military, boys' schools, and sporting clubs remained largely unaffected by second-wave feminism. Hercus made it clear that Labor hoped to address this imbalance by supporting the principle of equal pay for women introduced in 1972, and she committed her government to closing the gap in real wages between men and women (the average wage earned by women in 1990 still represented only 80 percent of the male average wage). National undermined this strategy in 1991 by throwing out the equal pay legislation. Even so, women began to make real advances into the professions, especially medicine, law, and dentistry, from this time and cemented some real gains. The election of Margaret

Wilson as the first women president of the Labor Party (following the example of National's Sue Wood in 1982) signaled an important shift in political life, as did the election of 10 women members of parliament.

Meantime, Fran Wild passed the controversial Homosexual Law Reform Act in 1986. This legislation made homosexual relationships legal for the first time in New Zealand's history. In many ways it represented the fourth Labor government's most successful piece of social engineering because noisy homophobia soon died away. Today New Zealand is more relaxed about the matter of sexual preference than most countries, although homosexual marriage is still not recognized in law.

The fourth Labor government also oversaw some big changes in dealings between the state and Maori. Maori themselves responded enthusiastically to greater empowerment of the Waitangi Tribunal by concentrating their efforts on presenting claims to the tribunal. Before 1985 the tribunal had little impact because it could not make retrospective judgments and acted largely as a rather inconsequential advisory body. Geoffrey Palmer changed all that when he granted the tribunal the power to make retrospective recommendations on settling grievances that went all the way back to 1840. Maori seized the chance with both hands, especially after the tribunal garnered even greater powers after 1987, when Palmer as attorney-general ruled that the property of state-owned enterprises (SOEs) also fell under the jurisdiction of the tribunal.

This decision proved more important than even Palmer realized because, although the tribunal could not (and still cannot) rule on privately owned land, the range of Crown resources subject to the tribunal's jurisdiction multiplied considerably after 1987. Large and well-organized tribes such as the South Island's Ngai Tahu and Tainui in the Waikato set to work researching and orchestrating claims. Few tangible outcomes occurred before the mid-1990s, however, apart from the return of Bastion Point to Ngati Whatua in 1989 and the granting of 10 percent of the fishing quota to Maori in 1988.

Labor also extended its general policy of decentralization and return of responsibility to the community by abolishing the old Department of Maori Affairs in 1989. The government established an Iwi Transition Agency to oversee the handover of power and funding to the tribes, while a new Ministry of Maori Affairs, or Manuta Maori, was constructed to devise policy. Critics such as Graeme Butterworth suggest that this move removed badly needed direct assistance to urban Maori (by 1991 over 80 percent of Maori lived in cities), but tribal leaders greeted the decision much more enthusiastically. Criticism of New Zealand race relations, made by Queen Elizabeth II and the Maori Anglican bishop Wharehuia

Vercoe at the 150th Waitangi celebration in February 1990, confirmed Maori leaders in their decision to establish an independent National Congress of Maori Tribes to act as a pressure group on government.

Maori also gained considerably in confidence at this time, and an obvious cultural resurgence swept the land. The Te Maori exhibition between 1984 and 1986, which received rave reviews as far away as New York and traveled the length and breadth of New Zealand, stimulated this cultural assertion. The enthusiastic overseas reception made many Pakeha curious. So, for the first time, many visited museums to view and appreciate the intricacy and beauty of traditional Maori art. Thereafter both the Maori language (Te Reo) and Maori ritual (such as *mihi* or traditional speeches of welcome and *waiata* or song) came to play a prominent part in any public ceremony, ensuring that New Zealand presented a more bicultural face to the world. The new Labor government helped by incorporating Maori ritual in the opening of parliament from its inauguration in August 1984.

Preschool language nests, or Kohanga Reo, mushroomed to help revitalize both language and culture. The language was in danger, but concerted effort by many Maori helped to save it, even if rather late in the day. Government tried to help, too, by making Maori into the official language of New Zealand along with English in 1987 and by setting up a Maori Language Commission. Only about 50,000 Maori still commanded fluency in the language, and most members of this group were over 55 years old. As Maori language commissioner, Professor Timiti Karetu had much work to do to rescue one of the world's many vulnerable languages. The results of his efforts and the efforts of others such as Dr. Pita Sharples were presented to the world during the spectacular opening ceremony of the Auckland Commonwealth Games in 1990. Maori clearly had made big gains in terms of cultural confidence.

On the other hand, Maori still languished on the margins of society in terms of health, educational achievement, and crime, and many battles lay ahead in terms of closing the gap with the European sections of the community. One hundred and fifty years after signing the Treaty of Waitangi, far fewer Maori than any other group won entrance to tertiary education, while over half of the prison population was of Maori descent. Maori women suffered from the highest levels of lung cancer in the world, and Maori life expectancy languished several years behind that of persons of European descent. This gap reflected the concentration of Maori in more dangerous blue-collar jobs, as well as inadequate housing. Maori infant mortality had fallen to a respectable 20 per 1,000, but that was still well above the national average of 12 infant deaths per 1,000 births. Maori rates of cot death, or sudden infant death syndrome, remained more than twice as high as for any other group. Diabetes also threatened to become endemic. Each of these alarming statistics related once again to inadequate housing, poor diet, and problems with the delivery of health care. Far too many Maori children also grew up in homes devoid of fathers.

Pacific Islanders suffered from a very similar set of problems, but their strong church congregations provided much-needed stability as they adjusted to New Zealand life. Single-parent households remained relatively uncommon in the Western Samoan, Tongan, Fijian, Tokulean, and Cook Island communities. These groups had also established their own specialist language newspapers and supportive community groups since the 1970s and had won considerable success in both Rugby Union and Rugby League play. On the positive side, Pacific Islanders, like Maori, had adjusted to urban living with extraordinary speed in little over one generation.

Geoffrey Palmer hoped to embed the growing importance of the Treaty of Waitangi into law by passing a Bill of Rights that gave the treaty full legal recognition. He failed, however, to do this, so that the Treaty of Waitangi still floats as a rather vague moral agreement that has never been enshrined in either New Zealand or international law. Palmer did pass a Bill of Rights, but it represented a mere shadow of the original legislation. As a result, constitutional matters still assume a much less important place in New Zealand than they do in the United States. Palmer also enacted some principles of the Treaty of Waitangi, but these are so vague and so little understood that their influence has been negligible.

Such an extraordinary burst of change took its toll on the government as well as on the electorate. From early 1989 the Labor government imploded. Having sacked Douglas (who was followed out of the cabinet almost immediately by Richard Prebble), Lange himself decided to hand over leadership to Palmer on August 8, 1989. Lange cited health problems, but it seemed that he had lost faith in the new right agenda and market liberalization. Soon after he retired, Douglas returned to the cabinet in October. The government shifted right once more, corporatizing New Zealand Steel, Coal Corp, State Insurance, and Post Bank; selling off Telecom; raising GST (goods and services tax) to 12.5 percent; introducing prescription charges for medicine and hospital stays; and selling off more state forests. Douglas's return proved too much for Jim Anderton, the president who rebuilt Labor as a mass democratic party in the early 1980s. Anderton deserted a government he condemned for selling out on traditional Labor principles and founded a more orthodox socialist party called New Labor.

The colorless Palmer seemed unable to control Douglas, and as the government's standing plunged in the polls, a desperate party removed

Palmer and replaced him with the more charismatic Mike Moore in September 1990. The change came too late to repair the damage with the traditional constituency as unemployment continued to climb to over 7 percent of the workforce. Unskilled workers, both Maori and Pakeha, had been hit particularly hard, and big gaps had opened up between prosperous Auckland and Wellington and the rest of the country. Timber workers and employees of clothing factories had been especially affected by the sale of assets and the lowering of tariffs. Their anger spread to the middle classes, who resented ever-increasing charges resulting from the cessation of free state services as government departments turned to operating on a user-pays basis.

Many in the education and research sectors also felt alarm at the rundown of research and development as user pays brought inquiry-led research to an end. All research after 1984 was supposed to be for specific purposes and expected to produce measurable outcomes. Many scientists became unhappy with the constant demand to turn a profit. Some headed overseas, particularly to Australia. Labor had also done little for the arts apart from Michael Bassett's success in making monies available for writing history. Growing arrogance also made the government unpopular with just about everybody. It came as no surprise, therefore, when National easily won the 1990 election by 67 seats to 30 (New Labor won the seat of Sydenham).

What came as a surprise were the policies pursued by Jim Bolger's government. Bolger had presented himself as a moderate who would consolidate on the changes made by Labor, slow the dizzy pace of change, and reconstruct a decent society. The electorate desperately wanted some solidity and responded warmly to this message. Instead, Bolger gave finance minister Ruth Richardson a free hand. Far from slowing down, she pushed down the accelerator to finish the job begun by Roger Douglas. This acceleration should have come as no surprise to anyone who listened to her election speeches, but most voters had been taken in by farmer Bolger's quiet calm. Even Bolger himself may have been surprised, but he did little to stop her. Another three-year burst of liberalization and free market reform followed as Richardson set out to build what she called the "enterprise society."

RUTHANASIA AND THE ACCELERATION OF REFORM, 1990–1993

Richardson startled both the media and the public when she ordered the minister of social welfare, Jenny Shipley, to cut welfare benefits before

Christmas. This decisive action signaled a full-scale attack upon the welfare state, which would escalate despite the howls of beneficiaries, the unemployed, and the ragged remnant of the union movement. Like Douglas in 1984, the new minister of finance also engaged Treasury to paint a very bleak picture of New Zealand's economic condition. Her reading of the statistics suggested that the country was living far beyond its means and drowning in debt. According to Richardson, only massive slashing of government expenditures and an extension of Douglas's reforms could save the day. She also argued that there was no alternative. ("There is no alternative" soon became a slogan and earned the acronym TINA.) Even so, most of the electorate took this outburst as rhetorical posturing, assuming that National would soon return to its more pragmatic ways. Such judgment soon proved false because few voters or commentators realized that ideologues had seized control of this normally centrist party.

This determination to extend the reforms of Douglas became clear in her first budget of July 1991. Dubbed the "mother of all budgets" by Richardson herself, it made clear the government's determination to slash spending. Most obviously, she reduced benefits by over a billion dollars, supposedly to break the cycle of dependency. Instead, this withdrawal of purchasing power hurt small businesses and fostered the growth of an alarmingly criminal underclass, the very group New Zealand had tried to eliminate ever since the Wakefield experiments of the 1840s.

Meantime, in May, Bolger himself and the former champion of Think Big, Bill Birch, set out to break the already weak union movement by passing an Employment Contracts Act. This legislation made unionism voluntary, supposedly to enable employers greater flexibility in setting wages. It also encouraged the negotiation of individual contracts rather than national awards in an effort to increase productivity. In addition, it did away with equal pay for women. Unfortunately, this rather drastic measure proved as unsuccessful as Labor's reforms in increasing New Zealand's lamentably low levels of productivity. Richardson also slashed the controversial accident compensation fund introduced by Labor in 1974 on a no-fault basis. This scheme had always been dogged by abuse, but it did free the country from the huge costs of medical litigation that have caused so many problems in the United States. Unemployment soared to over 200,000, or about 11 percent of the workforce, a post-Depression record. On the positive side, the Reserve Bank Act did its job by holding inflation to 2 percent, putting New Zealand back on level terms with its major trading partners.

Growing public unease did not slow Richardson. Instead, in 1992 education minister Lockwood Smith, despite claiming during the election that

National would never increase university fees, introduced a new system of up-front fees to be paid by loans provided at market rates of interest. The Australian alternative of graduate tax after training had been considered but rejected because it would not raise funds fast enough to cover booming enrollments. Government went farther than Labor in handing control of these loans over to trading banks. Given that interest rates ran at over 10 percent at this time and that debt accumulated from day one at college, students protested in increasingly voluble ways. The government replied that, as the Hawke Report had suggested, tertiary education enabled individuals to make large personal gains. What was the difference, asked Bolger and Shipley, between a young farmer or a professional starting out? Both had to take loans and risks if they hoped to prosper. According to this thinking, highly paid professions such as medicine and dentistry would return the highest remuneration, so these students should pay the highest fees. Consequently, fees for these subjects rose from Labor's $1,000 to $10,000 for medicine and an extraordinary $23,000 for dentistry.

New Zealand parents were caught unawares by this drastic change and had made no provision for such costs. Most students, therefore, had to take the loans and live with the escalating debts. Not surprisingly, New Zealand students largely disappeared from the dental school to have their places taken by wealthy Asians, while medicine also became more dominated by Asian students. Maori and Pacific Islanders found it harder than ever to attend, although the central importance of treaty claims saw a substantial increase in the number of Maori taking law. Universities themselves also had to become much more competitive and businesslike. University councils tightened their budgets, except for advertising and the provision of much more generous packages for vice chancellors and higher-level managers. Supposedly luxury subjects such as Russian soon fell victim to this reorientation toward a more businesslike approach.

Outside the universities, government infuriated state house owners by raising their rents to market levels. Special buyback deals did not make up for the huge hike in rents. A new party calling itself the Alliance, made up of a coalition of the remnants of New Labor, Mana Motuhake, the Greens, and the Democrats, emerged to champion the interest of this burgeoning underclass. The worsening plight of Maori brought forth protests from the minister of Maori affairs, Winston Peters, who had set up a Ministry of Maori Development or Te Puni Koriki in 1991 and had done away with the Iwi Transition Agency two years ahead of schedule.

Peters's flamboyant style and sometimes unorthodox methods proved too much for Bolger, and he sacked Peters as minister of Maori affairs in

October 1991. Before Peters was summarily ejected from membership in the National Party a year later, other Maori leaders managed to secure the Sealord Deal in 1992. Under this agreement Ngai Tahu won monopoly over the South Island's coasts, a decision that brought forth howls of protest from other Maori tribes as well as from many Pakeha fishermen. Peters responded to his dismissal by moving off to form his own New Zealand First Party in 1993.

Asset sales continued apace, despite the diversions caused by the clash between Bolger and Peters. The ailing Bank of New Zealand was sold to the National Bank of Australia in 1991, handing almost total control of New Zealand's trading bank to overseas interests. Government also sold New Zealand Timberlands, a giant, state-backed forestry enterprise, and Muldoon's Taranaki Petroleum to overseas interests in 1992.

The most controversial reforms of all related to the big-spending health sector because they affected the entire population rather than particular groups such as students or state house owners. Richardson appointed a special task force to investigate how costs could be cut and services maintained, or even improved. The task force reported in 1991 and suggested radical overhaul. In particular, it wanted much greater accountability (another buzz word of this period) in the system. By dividing administration of the system between funders (Regional Health Authorities) and providers (Crown Health Enterprises, or CHEs), taxpayers would know exactly how much was spent on what.

Government also increased fees for doctors' visits, medicines, and hospital stays in an attempt to encourage the middle classes to take out medical insurance and receive treatment in the private system. The appointment of prominent businessmen such as Ron Trotter and Peter Troughton as CEOs of the CHEs suggested that privatization was definitely on the government's agenda. Public spending now accounted for 77 percent of total health spending as against a high of 88 percent in 1981. (In the United States around 40 percent of health spending comes from government.) Unfortunately for the reforms, spending continued to escalate, despite the flight of many into the private sector. By 1996 New Zealand still spent a higher percentage of its gross domestic product on health than Sweden or the United Kingdom. On the other hand, the government made some provision for lower-income earners by introducing a community services card that provided cheaper care for those below specified income levels.

The National government applied its health reform model to research and development as well by abolishing the old Department of Scientific and Industrial Research established in 1926. It was replaced with several competing Crown Research Institutes (CRIs) that would have to contest funding every year. Guaranteed long-term funding became a thing of the past as scientists diverted their energies to grant applications. Some complained that they no longer had any time to do research, or any certainty that they could commit to long-term projects. Yet another large group left the country, and Australia benefited directly once more.

Few state assets were left to sell by 1993, but National still managed to sell the ailing New Zealand Railway Corporation to the Wisconsin Central Transport Company for a measly $328 million. Critics then and now consider this to have been a virtual fire sale of a major strategic asset, especially in a world confronting an energy crisis. These critics find support for their argument in the difficulty Wisconsin Central has had in turning a profit, especially as Wisconsin Central has withdrawn to the point where a government buyback at greatly enhanced value is almost a necessity.

Despite the extension of Labor's reforms in many areas of New Zealand life, National failed to change the antinuclear policy. Ministers found it difficult, especially in terms of improving trade relations with the United States, but any mention of modification brought forth powerful condemnation from the electorate. New Zealand, though, did assist in the United Nations–led Gulf War in 1991 by supplying medics and naval support.

The celebration of a centenary of women's suffrage in 1993 caused National some embarrassment as the government had done away with equal pay. The party tried to win back women voters by appointing Sylvia Cartwright as New Zealand's first woman high court judge. Social liberals had little else to celebrate, though, as National slashed funding for the arts. On the other hand, the Privacy Act passed in 1993 did help protect individuals against prying media and state agencies, and lovers of the arts took much pleasure in the success of Jane Campion's movie *The Piano,* which won an Oscar for best supporting female actor.

Luckily for National, the achievement of a small budget surplus in 1993 enabled the party to persuade a doubtful electorate that the pain had started to produce some gain. This unexpected good news and the disorganized state of the Labor opposition enabled the party to scrape back into power by five seats. Significantly, the electorate signaled its dissatisfaction with the relentless pace of reform when 53 percent voted in the new mixed member proportional (MMP) electoral system. This West German system did away with the old first-past-the-post system, ostensibly to allow parties to be represented according to the percentage of the vote they won. In the past, small parties that had often won a significant vote were not represented. Parties with smaller votes could also be elected into power if they won more seats.

MMP ensured that tiny extremist parties could not be represented, as representation required a 5 percent threshold, but electoral seats were now reduced from 97 to 60, with another 60 going to list MPs, elected according to the size of party votes. In other words, parliament would now be much bigger than ever before, but supposedly also more representative of the wider society because groups other than middle-aged white men had a greater chance of winning enough votes to take their place in the House of Representatives. This happened despite expensive media campaigns organized against MMP by big business, which feared that political instability would result from such a drastic change in the electoral system. Big business also feared that that the neoliberal reforms would be slowed under MMP. This reading proved more accurate than an outbreak of instability because many New Zealanders felt that only such a change would slow the new right juggernaut.

The period 1984–1993, then, witnessed such an extraordinary burst of reform that it constituted a veritable revolution in New Zealand history. Critics then, now, and no doubt in the future will argue about the efficacy of these reforms, but there is general consensus that a sea change occurred, which meant that New Zealand would never be the same again. New Zealand politicians rejected the comfortable welfare model, swung the tiller of the ship of state hard to the right, and set forth on a very different direction. The costs were high as the reforms tore large holes in the existing social fabric. Unemployment decimated many communities. In the remote east coast of the North Island and areas like the far north, rates of Maori unemployment climbed to Third World levels at around 80 percent of the workforce.

Things have improved a little since, but government policy inflicted severe damage. Both theft and violent crime flourished in these kinds of places, as did a large-scale marijuana industry. Urban areas of cheaper housing, especially those dominated by large Maori and Pacific Island communities, such as Otara in South Auckland and Porirua north of Wellington, also witnessed frightening leaps in criminal behavior. Families spilt apart; health worsened; and single-parent families became ever more common. Factory and forestry workers, just like car assembly workers, found themselves on the scrap heap, and many never retrained or regained work.

Yet this formerly tight, rather dull society also opened up and became more tolerant and dynamic. New energy began to pulse out of the deprived areas in particular. Public debt also dropped significantly, only to be replaced by a huge leap in private indebtedness. New Zealand became technologically sophisticated, as the gap between rich and poor widened to nineteenth-century levels. Average earnings lagged behind the rate of inflation as families continued to struggle with high interest rates and escalating house prices. Real wages consequently fell throughout the 1990s. By 1993 the old problem of low productivity had not been solved, nor had any large-scale industries appeared to supplement agriculture, despite huge encouragement given to businesses and entrepreneurs. It seemed that the enterprise society could not be built over night.

Bureaucracy still remained a problem despite rolling back the state, because it now flourished in the private rather than the public sector. Welfare dependency had not lessened, and new government agencies seemed to have grown as large as the old ones they replaced. Certainly, the Ministry of Education, for example, employed less staff than the old boards of education, but once commentators remembered to add in the Qualifications Authority and Education Review Office, savings seem minimal. Declining real wages for ordinary New Zealanders, meantime, encouraged further out-migration to Australia, and, like most small countries, New Zealand seemed to be suffering from a chronic brain drain as its most talented left in droves. In short, the big reforms looked spectacular and helped create a superficially more modern and sophisticated society, but they achieved far less than architects such as Douglas, Prebble, Richardson, and Treasury economists had hoped.

THE SLOW SWING BACK TO THE CENTER, 1993–1999

Astute politician that he was, Prime Minister Jim Bolger removed the unpopular Richardson from the finance portfolio and replaced her with Muldoon's former lieutenant, Bill Birch. Yet, at first, it seemed that National had taken little heed of electoral protest in the 1993 election. Education minister Lockwood Smith increased tertiary student fees and so incensed students that they occupied registry buildings on several campuses. Smith also brought considerable advantage to private schools by integrating them into the state system on extremely favorable terms. He tried to encourage schools to adopt a bulk funding system whereby boards of trustees rather than central government controlled teachers' salaries. Some schools accepted the terms offered by government, but the majority of parents and teachers condemned these offers as bribes and supported the status quo. The Postprimary Teachers' Association went farther in condemning bulk funding as ideologically driven and struck several times in opposition.

Jenny Shipley, as minister of health, similarly pushed on with her reforms of health administration despite the constant protests of health professionals. Things looked bad for the government by 1995 as economic recovery failed to materialize and the country earned the dubious distinction of having the highest rate of suicide among young males in the world.

Yet amid the gloom, National, under the astute direction of Douglas Graham, managed to negotiate two major deals with large tribes. The Tainui settlement of 1995 included a formal apology from government for *raupatu* or land confiscation in addition to a cash settlement of $187 million as compensation for past grievances. Ngai Tahu, led by the charismatic Tipene O'Regan, secured the same level of compensation in 1996, won the right to lease out large tracts of high country to runholders, and saw passage of the Runanga o Ngai Tahu Act. This legislation established a separate legal identity for the tribe so that it had to sink or swim under its own control. In Maori terms, they had achieved *tino rangatiratanga* (big chieftainship or control over one's destiny) at the tribal level at least. O'Regan argued that the tribe constituted the most perfect form of collective capitalism. So far, smart investment decisions, sale of less productive assets, and careful management have defied the tribe's critics to the point that it is now one of the biggest and wealthiest corporate entities in the South Island. Green activists, however, remain skeptical of the tribe's claims that it will manage the environment better than central government.

These two successful settlements made the direct protest actions of Wanganui Maori at Motua Gardens and the burning of a historic school near Kaitaia in the far north appear senseless and unjustifiably negative. The contrast between negotiated settlement within the law and radical action outside the law worked to the government's advantage. So too did the success of the powerful movie version of Alan Duff's *Once Were Warriors,* which suggested that Maori should now get on with the job of sorting out their problems by themselves.

A small economic upturn in 1996, including a fall in unemployment to around 7 percent of the workforce, or about the OECD average, also helped the government's cause. The government sweetened the gains by offering small tax cuts. New Zealand's sailors helped too by winning the prestigious America's Cup in 1995, and the All Blacks played with great flair despite coming in second in the 1995 Rugby World Cup.

Yet National struggled at the 1996 election because Labor's new leader, Helen Clark, who replaced Mike Moore in a messy coup in 1993, performed far above expectations at the 1996 election. Special coaching in how to handle the media helped, but so too did the presentation of policies that distinguished Labor from National. By targeting National's failures in education and health and talking of a more moderate third way, like that promoted by Britain's Tony Blair, Labor saved itself from possible oblivion. Winston Peters's New Zealand First Party also won a powerful support base among an unlikely coalition of Maori and white pensioners championed by their Gray Power pressure group. Peters whipped up fear of rising levels of Asian migration and won a healthy 13 percent of the vote. Significantly, his young Maori candidates won all 5 of the Maori seats from Labor. Under the new MMP system, this gave him 17 seats in the new parliament. Roger Douglas's and Richard Prebble's new party, known as the Association of Consumers and Taxpayers, or ACT, drew another 8 percent of votes away from National. On the left Jim Anderton's Alliance Party also did well, winning 10 percent of the vote and 13 seats against Labor's 28 percent of the vote and 37 seats.

In short, the worst fears of the opponents of MMP seemed to have been borne out because this constituted a hung parliament. Winston Peters eventually overcame the impasse because he held the balance of power. After three months of negotiation, he eventually decided to form a government with his old party, National. Labor refused to accept his suggestion that he assume the new role of treasurer, a position above that of minister of finance, which had been developed a little earlier in Australia. As many anticipated, Peters returned to his ideological home by creating a right-of-center coalition.

Even so, Peters tried to ring some concessions from National to benefit his Maori and pensioner supporters. The new kingmaker won considerable sympathy from several elements in a very different looking parliament. Maori had won a record 15 places and were represented in all parties, while women also achieved their highest level of representation, rising from under a quarter to nearly a third of parliamentarians. Many of this new group wanted cheaper health delivery and better access to education, but National conceded little apart from making doctors' visits free for small children from poor families and removing the surcharge on superannuation (pensions) in 1998.

The impetuous behavior of some of Peters's inexperienced new ministers did not help. Tau Henare's and Tuku Morgan's attempts to set up a Maori television channel soon degenerated into scandal and farce as the media clamored over gross overexpenditure on fashionable underpants. Such frippery weakened Peters's hold on Bolger and weakened his ability to restrict new right policies. By 1998 National had sold off $6 million worth of state assets, including the Housing and Forestry Corporations, and ended car assembly in New Zealand. This measure put at least 1,500 Pacific Islanders out of work and hurt several related downstream industries.

Jenny Shipley replaced Bolger in a bloodless coup on December 8, 1997, to become New Zealand's first woman prime minister. She found Peters more difficult to handle than did Bolger, and the coalition broke up in August 1998. Shipley only stayed in power because of the support of one maverick Alliance MP, Alamein Kopu. Peter Dunne, the sole survivor of the United Party, which emerged in 1996, also pledged to support the government. ACT generally also voted with National, especially when the government moved away from the center toward the right. Tau Henare formed his own Mauri Pacific Party in 1998, but remained minister of Maori affairs, insisting that he could achieve more for Maori by serving in government than by joining the opposition.

Remarkably, this rather fragile coalition government survived the serious Asian financial crisis of 1997–1998. It did little more than survive, though, as economic indicators worsened. Debt soared to over $100 billion as New Zealand slumped to twentieth in the OECD tables, below such maligned interventionist states as Australia, the Netherlands, Ireland, and all the Scandinavian countries. By early 1999 New Zealand faced a serious balance of payments crisis as it became clear that the country continued to live well beyond its means. The tax cuts had only encouraged consumer expenditure on imported luxury goods and overseas holidays. They had not enhanced savings or encouraged new enterprise. No new industries had emerged to supplement agriculture, and growth stagnated at a disappointing 2.6 percent as against the 4 percent OECD average. Productivity only increased by a paltry 1 percent per annum over this period, when reunified Germany managed 4 or more percent annual increases. Unemployment refused to drop below 7 percent of the workforce. Lower government revenue also forced up tertiary fees and a growing list of user-pays services.

Some new right excess in 1999 also damaged the government's waning reputation, especially John Luxton's suggestion that selling electricity was exactly the same as selling baked beans. Public condemnation of such inanity did not stop his colleague, Max Bradford, from replacing the old nationally organized Electricity Corporation with several new power companies. These competitors would supposedly force down the cost of power and improve services, but there is little evidence so far of either goal's having been achieved. Indeed, the electorate greeted this change skeptically because New Zealand's biggest city, Auckland, had experienced long blackouts in 1995 and nearly ran out of clean drinking water the following year. Both the media and Labor blamed both problems on excessive deregulation.

A growing section of the community also became increasingly alarmed at ongoing damage to the environment and the seeming inability of either government or the Resource Management Act to slow development. Large-scale protest against degradation had first emerged in opposition to the raising of beautiful Lake Manapouri for hydroelectricity from as early as 1967. The success of this protest led to the formation of the Values Party in 1972, but Labor soon absorbed this group. Growing concern over such global issues as the hole in the ozone layer, as well as an older desire to adopt a more organic approach to food production, persuaded green activists to form a Green Party, which joined Jim Anderton's Alliance for the 1993 election. Tension between the somewhat domineering Jim Anderton and the Greens' able coleaders Jenette FitzSimmons and Rod Donald persuaded the Greens to spilt and go it alone for the 1999 election. The Greens' determination to bring New Zealand's clean and green image more into line with reality, and their opposition to unfettered global trade, touched a chord with many younger voters. The party's fortunes rose sufficiently in the polls during the 1999 campaign to suggest that it might win a few seats.

Scandal erupted throughout 1999 to embarrass the government. Apparent conflict of interest forced Murry McCully to resign as minister of tourism. The decision of the new welfare department, known as Work and Income New Zealand, or WINZ, to entertain its managers in grand style at a luxury resort proved far more damaging. Both the media and Labor condemned this as gross extravagance and a waste of taxpayers' money. A public outcry followed, and the chief executive, Christine Rankin, was forced to resign by the new Labor government.

Labor then had a relatively easy job in winning the 1999 election, although the party had first to convince the electorate that it would offer clear-cut alternatives to National. Some voters also wanted guarantees that Labor could work with the Alliance and avoid the destabilizing splits of the first MMP coalition. Clark and Anderton responded to this fear by drawing up a carefully worded agreement and by demonstrating their good will in attending the conferences of each other's party. Labor continued to talk of third ways and greater state assistance to industry and regional development. The Labor candidates also made it clear that they would reintroduce compulsory unionism after repelling the Employment Contracts Act, and they guaranteed that they would not introduce bulk funding in schools. Elected regional health boards would also be reestablished, so ending the funder/provider system as operated by the RHA and

CHEs. Otherwise, their policies did not look especially different than National's, apart from a promise to raise the top tax rate to 40 cents on the dollar for those earning over $60,000. In return, Labor made vague promises concerning reduced tertiary fees and freezing of loan interest.

A pledge card in which Labor committed itself to seven modest reforms seemed to appeal to an electorate weary of ambitious schemes for radical change, and Labor won comfortably with 39 percent of the vote and 49 seats. This proved sufficient to form a government because the Alliance won 7.7 percent of the vote and 10 seats, and the Greens with 5.2 percent of the vote and 7 seats pledged their support. New Zealand First, meantime, collapsed to 4.3 percent of the vote, only hanging on to 5 seats because of Peters's success in retaining the Tauranga seat. His party's problems saw the traditional Maori vote return all 5 seats to Labor. John Tamihere also won the general seat of Hauraki and emerged as a new champion of urban as opposed to tribal Maori.

THE TRIUMPH OF THE CENTER, 1999–2003

Clark's first government proved to be thoroughly pragmatic and determinedly centrist. It did pretty much everything it said it would, which wasn't a lot. Nevertheless, this satisfied an electorate tired of unwelcome surprises, and Labor was returned comfortably in 2002. Clark and finance minister Dr. Michael Cullen, a university historian rather than an accountant by training, though, had to weather a six-month storm from big business. The Round Table, a pressure group that emerged in 1984 to promote the interests of big business, gave the new government a particularly hard time, especially over the abolition of the Employment Contracts Act. The media, which had absorbed a generally new right view of the world, joined in this interrogation by querying whether New Zealand should, or could, go back to more old-fashioned ways of doing things. But Clark and Cullen stuck to their guns, ably supported by Deputy Prime Minister Jim Anderton, and duly abolished the Employment Contracts Act.

The introduction of so-called good faith bargaining did not collapse the economy, and only angry secondary-school teachers and disgruntled university academics engaged in strike action. In fact, Cullen behaved in a very cautious and orthodox manner. His government was also lucky that world commodity prices picked up, especially for dairy products.

Tourism also flourished on the low value of the New Zealand dollar and benefited directly from the success of Peter Jackson's *The Lord of the Rings: The Fellowship of the Ring* movie. Critics argued about the acting and scripting, but all agreed that New Zealand provided a stunning backdrop to the epic fantasy journey. The tourist boom helped persuade the public that the government did the right thing in injecting $800 million to save Air New Zealand after the crisis induced by terrorist attacks in New York on September 11, 2001. Tourists soon overcame their shock and turned their attention to safe destinations like New Zealand. Sheep and beef farmers also benefited directly from the mad cow disease or BSE scare in Britain. Farming and tourism between them thrived to the point that unemployment dropped below 6 percent, public debt declined, growth soared to over 4 percent of GDP, and the balance of payments showed a small surplus in 2002. New Zealand had not been this prosperous since the early 1970s.

Little changed during this time of economic recovery except in foreign policy, where Clark annoyed both her Australian and American allies by shutting down the combat wing of the New Zealand Air Force and rejecting a special offer of F-16 bombers. Instead, she increased spending on the New Zealand Army to assist with peacekeeping in such trouble spots as Kosovo and East Timor. The change remains controversial, but probably it is realistic in terms of what a tiny country of 4 million can afford. Charm offensives directed at both Australia and the United States have repaired some of the ill will generated by the radical restructuring of the armed forces, but New Zealand's insistence that the United Nations oversee the removal of Saddam Hussein and the reconstruction of Iraq may have more serious trade repercussions.

Clark's government also pumped more money into the arts as she took a close personal interest in promoting a greater awareness of New Zealand's history in general and military history in particular. An extra $86 million seemed like a lot, but it soon proved to be a drop in the bucket, and most artists continue to struggle in contemporary New Zealand. Limited funding does not stop the best—such as Maori soprano Deborah Wai Kapohe, bass Jonhathon Lemalu of Western Samoan descent, Che Fue, a pop musician also of Western Samoan descent, and the Malaysian-Maori pop singer Bic Runga—from breaking through, but most painters, writers, and musicians merely subsist. Even so Maurice Gee, Witi Ihimaera, Patricia Grace, and a host of younger novelists still produce plenty of books, while painters such as Ralph Hotere and Graham Sydney sustain international reputations. New Zealand's children's writers such as Margaret Mahy and Lynley Dodd sell the most books, especially in the overseas market. New Zealand also continues to produce a steady stream of solid poetry from the likes of Hone Tuwhare, Brian Turner, and Elizabeth Smithers as well as numerous younger poets such as David Eggleton and Greg O'Brien. This small country also produces much excellent nonfiction, including history books, which reflects the fact that New Zealanders remain the biggest book buyers per capita anywhere on the globe. Scientists, especially those in the biological areas, also continue to make significant international contributions.

But no single artist or intellectual has produced anything like the international impact of filmmaker Peter Jackson, a man who got to the top despite, rather than because of, grudging government support. His greatest success has been in attracting vast amounts of American and international investment to underwrite the *Lord of the Rings* trilogy and in the affirmation of winning 11 Oscars for *The Return of the King*. Other filmmakers such as Jane Campion and Nicy Caro are helping to put New Zealand on the map, and Lee Tamahori directed the latest James Bond movie. Russell Crowe, half Australian and half New Zealander, has also had obvious success, but breaking into the international scene remains a huge problem for people from this small, isolated country with their strange, flat dialect.

Labor cruised through the early part of 2002 but ran into trouble with Green Party allies over the question of genetically modified organisms (GMOs). Labor had agreed to a ban on all GMO research in the field until October 2003, whereas the Greens wanted it extended for several years. Labor's case-by-case approach angered the Greens, and accusations flew during the election campaign that GMOs had already been accidentally released in New Zealand. The genetic engineering issue generated so much heat that the Greens refused to guarantee support to a new Labor-led government.

The collapse of both the Alliance and National in the polls, despite the appointment of Bill English to replace Jenny Shipley, made this less of a problem than it otherwise might have been. The unexpected surge in popularity for the socially conservative United Futures Party, which combined United with the old Christian Heritage Party, also worked to Labor's advantage. So Labor won with relative comfort in the 2002 election, with 41.4 percent of the vote and 52 seats. United Futures won a surprising 6.8 percent of the vote and 8 seats, and Jim Anderton's new Progressive Coalition Party, with its 2 seats, guaranteed Labor the right to hold office. Anderton deserted the old Alliance Party, and it collapsed so badly that it failed to win a seat. The disgruntled Greens won a disappointing 6.5 percent of the vote and 9 seats, but the party promised to supply support so that the government could survive comfortably with 71 seats. National, meantime, crashed to a record low of 21.1 percent of the vote and a miserable 27 seats. New Zealand First fared rather better as Winston Peters produced another masterly campaign to win 10.6 percent of the vote and

13 seats. Support for ACT remained relatively static at 7.1 percent of the votes and 9 seats. Richard Prebble, though, failed to regain his electoral seat, which he lost to Labor's Marian Hobbes in 1999.

Since the election, falling commodity prices, a strengthening New Zealand dollar, the war in Iraq, and the SARS epidemic have dampened down the economic recovery. Tourism and meat sales in particular are suffering as tourists refuse to risk traveling and food connoisseurs refuse to eat out at restaurants in such apparently dangerous times. Another severe drought, a mere two years since the last one in 2001, is also threatening power cuts. Rivers and lakes are also suffering from chronic pollution brought about by the dairy boom.

AN UNCERTAIN FUTURE IN A GLOBALIZED WORLD

New Zealand now sits at an important crossroad in its history. It remains hopelessly vulnerable to the vagaries of prices for agricultural products until it can find another engine for its economy. Visiting Scandinavians express amazement that the country maintains a relatively high standard of living without adding much to its farming base. Tourism, too, remains a fickle business, heavily dependent upon fashion and the level of international anxiety. The country faces hard choices in terms of abuse of its beautiful but fragile environment. Intensive dairying dependent on irrigation is possibly unsustainable.

Then there is the matter of GMOs. Should the country take the organic route favored by Europeans, or intervene more in natural processes like the Americans? New Zealand has a long and proud tradition of agricultural science and considerable expertise in biotechnology, not to mention powerful vested interests committed to following this path. Huge risks are involved in going either way as the potential market seems likely to half whatever the country decides.

New Zealand also needs to make better use of its well-educated, highly skilled, and creative population. Other small countries such as Ireland and Finland seemed to be finding ways of developing new industries, and New Zealand must learn from their example. New Zealand is also trying hard to retain a multilateral position in foreign affairs, believing that this approach probably works best for small countries, but such a principled standard may threaten its trading opportunities.

At home, more needs to be done to redress problems of poverty and crime. An epidemic of diabetes threatens as increasingly sedentary youth have become locked in front of computer screens and have failed to take advantage of the great outdoors. Women have made real advances, breaking into the medical and legal professions and currently holding all the top posts in the land. Yet there is still a long way to go in terms of achieving more equitable divorce settlements, securing higher managerial positions, winning professorships, and attaining freedom from domestic and social violence.

Finally, there is the matter of race relations. The Waitangi Tribunal process has brought some redress to certain tribal groups, but the lot of many urban Maori has been little improved. Disparities of wealth, health status, and educational achievement remain alarmingly wide. Yet by 2040 Maori will comprise over a quarter of the population and Pacific Islanders around 10 percent. Asians will possibly make up as much as 15 percent of the population, with persons of European origin becoming a slight minority. New Zealand's future, therefore, will be shaped as much by the dynamic and young Polynesian section and the high-achieving Asians as its will by its aging European population. This greater racial and cultural mix might also produce a better combination of skills to cope with the challenges of globalization. This new polyglot country will need the extraordinary capacity of its indigenous people to cope with change, the ingenuity of its European settlers, and the entrepreneurial skills of its more recent Asian arrivals to prosper as a healthy democracy in the twenty-first century.

Notable People in the History of New Zealand

Atkinson, Jane Maria (1824–1914). Matriarch and pioneer. Jane was the matriarch of a large and influential clan of settlers in Taranaki whom she dubbed the "mob." A radical and a Unitarian who never fitted easily into polite English society, she thrived in the freer atmosphere of New Zealand. She loved the great outdoors, reputedly being the first white woman to climb Mount Taranaki. She enjoyed being useful in the myriad of ways so essential to successful pioneering. After marrying Arthur Atkinson, nine years her junior, in 1854 she supported him in farming, politics, and the law. She only had one child—Arthur—but worked to develop both Nelson Boys' and Girls' Colleges after moving to Nelson in 1868. Despite the rather more conservative views of her Richmond and Hursthouse relations, she supported temperance and women's suffrage. As she aged, she played an increasingly crucial role in holding together her large, three-generation family.

Ballance, John (1839–1893). Journalist, intellectual, politician. This Northern Irish radical led the Liberal Party to victory in 1890 and steered the reforming government through its first term of office. Disillusioned by both Ireland and England and his failure to develop a career in either Belfast or Birmingham, Ballance migrated to New Zealand in 1866. After a somewhat jingoistic start fighting Maori, he settled into a career in journalism and politics based in the river port town of Wanganui. Through his newspapers, the *Wanganui Herald* and *Yeoman,* he advocated the yeomen ideal, that is, a country based on small family farms rather than great estates. Ballance also wanted to improve the lot of urban workers, but despite being influenced by such land radicals as John Stuart Mill and Henry George, his commitment to the ideal of self-help prevented him from becoming a socialist. He entered parliament as MP for Rangitikei in 1875 and served as colonial treasurer in the Grey ministry from 1878 to 1879. As minister of lands in the Stout-Vogel government he provided some help to stepping-stone farmers in 1886 and 1887. In July 1889 he won leadership of the opposition and slowly built a coalition of skilled workingmen, small-town merchants, and small farmers who eventually emerged as the Liberal Party in early 1891. As the first Liberal and second free-thinking premier (Sir Robert Stout was also a self-confessed agnostic), Ballance introduced both a land tax and a modest income tax in 1891. More importantly, he appealed successfully to the Privy Council in London to break the stranglehold of the Legislative Council or upper house. After appointing such humble men as printers and boilermakers to this body, the Liberal reform program proceeded much more smoothly. Ballance was very able but very cautious and resisted attempts to give women the vote despite his wife Ellen's being a prominent suffragist. The historian is left with the feeling that he was somewhat lucky to die when he did because it took tougher politicians such as John McKenzie and Richard Seddon to make hard changes in 1893–1894.

Clark, Helen (1950–). Politician. New Zealand's second woman prime minister and easily the most dominant political figure in the early part of the twenty-first century, was born into a conservative farming family in the Waikato, south of Auckland. After taking a degree in political science, she became a staunch advocate of social justice and social democracy. Much to the horror of her parents, she threw herself into Labor Party affairs from a young age. She served on the executive committee of the New Zealand Labor Party in 1978 and won the Mt. Albert electorate in Auckland in 1981, which she has retained ever since. She rose to the rank of deputy prime minister in 1989 and held the portfolios of Health, Conservation, Housing, and Labor in the fourth Labor government. She won leadership of the party in late 1993 after Mike Moore lost the election. Despite some poor polling and being written off by most political commentators, she performed well during the 1996 election and held onto the leadership. Eventually, she got her chance in 1999 and has proved to be a tough and pragmatic politician. She has held Labor and its coalition partners together, won over big business and pursued an independent foreign policy without totally alienating the United States. Although she has disappointed her more left wing supporters, she remains easily New Zealand's most popular political leader. Unless some great catastrophe occurs she seems likely to lead Labor to a third term of government in 2005. Genetic engineering and potentially divisive racial issues exacerbated by the government's attempts to improve the lot of Maori constitute the greatest threats to her government. Given her calm demeanor and solid track record, she should cope with such difficulties, but as many historians and political scientists have remarked a week is a long time in politics.

Coates, Joseph Gordon (1878–1943). Farmer and politician. The first New Zealand–born prime minister was an extremely able but somewhat unlucky politician. Gordon (as he was popularly known) Coates was born into one of the few wealthy farming families in North Auckland. His father Edward assumed a leadership role in the small Matakohe community on the Kaipara harbor, and Gordon took over his mantle in 1905 when he joined the Otamatea County Council. Gordon also played a prominent role in the local militia and went on to serve as a major in the First World War. Before then he won the Kaipara seat in 1911, which he held for the rest of his life. He was elected as a Liberal but crossed the floor of parliament in 1912 to join William Massey's new government. After returning as a war hero with the Military Cross and Bar, the good-looking Coates assumed a prominent role within the Reform government. In 1920 he was appointed as minister of public works. Coates set about building thousands of miles of formed roads with enthusiasm and created the basis of New Zealand's modern roading system. He also completed the Midland, East Coast, and North Auckland main trunk railway lines and pushed ahead with the construction of hydroelectric dams. During this time he worked closely with both Apirana Ngata and Princess Te Puea as native minister and assisted them in establishing a Maori Arts and Craft Center at Rotorua in 1926. Coates's energy and efficiency made him the obvious successor to Massey, and he went on to win the 1925 election with ease. This was New Zealand's first modern election, and although the slogan "Coats off with Coates" seems naive today, it represented an important shift in New Zealand politics. Coates revealed his progressive side by establishing the Department of Scientific and Industrial Research along with the Dairy Research Institute in 1926. He also established Massey Agricultural College in the same year and overhauled the older Lincoln Agricultural College. His efforts to establish a dairy board to improve the marketing of butter and cheese in Britain, however, proved less successful, and his popularity waned as New Zealand slid into depression throughout 1927. By 1928 Coates had alienated the more conservative business wing of his party along with many smaller farmers. These groups moved their support to the United Party led by the geriatric Joseph Ward in 1928. Ward won a close-run election by accidentally reading that he would borrow £70 million immediately, instead of over 10 years, and Coates was forced into opposition. With the arrival of full-scale depression, however, Reform rejoined United in a coalition government in September 1931. Coates took on the role of minister of public works with responsibility for employment. This made him very unpopular when unemployment soared to record levels. The electorate did not realize that, once he became minister of finance in 1933, his decision to devalue the New Zealand pound by removing it from parity with Sterling and his setting up of the Reserve Bank in the same year proved crucial in New Zealand's rapid recovery after 1935. Coates was swept aside by Labor with his coalition partners in 1935, but soon turned his energies to forming a new mass-based conservative party known as National in 1936. Coates's depression taint ruled him out as leader of the new party, and in 1940 he joined the war cabinet as a member of the executive council. Coates got on well with Labor's wartime leader Peter Fraser and made a very real contribution to the war effort. He traveled to the United States, Canada, Australia, and Fiji organizing war supplies and stayed with the war cabinet even when National withdrew its cooperation in late 1942. He died in his office in May 1943 mourned by all sides of the political spectrum. As his biographer Michael Bassett suggests, he linked the older, looser world of Liberal politics with the greater state interventionism of the mid-twentieth century. Coates was unlucky in that his prodigious abilities did not always fit very well within the broader contexts in which he acted out his political career.

Cockayne, Leonard (1855–1934). Botanist, ecologist, and intellectual. New Zealand's most famous botanist and one of the pioneers of ecology was born and raised near Sheffield in the north of England. He migrated to Australia in 1877 and eventually to New Zealand in 1880. Although he never finished his formal qualifications as a botanist in England, he developed a deep love of the countryside and considerable powers of observation. After teaching for a while, Cockayne developed a horticultural property near Christchurch when money inherited on his father's death ended his need to earn a salary. An experimental garden he established in sand dunes soon won the interest of other important New Zealand scientists such as G. M. Thomson, but also attracted German scientists such as Karl von Goebel, who visited New Zealand in 1898. This networking ensured that many of his famous books on New Zealand plants were published in Germany and read by a truly international audience. From 1903 Cockayne traveled widely over the whole of New Zealand and south to the sub-Antarctic islands on various government commissions. This extensive fieldwork enabled him to compile comprehensive studies of New Zealand flora. He also served on the forestry commission in 1913 and investigated problems with high-country tussocks in 1913 and 1920. His constant research attuned him to the complex ecology of plant habitats, and he developed the theory of natural hybridization of species as the driving force of evolution. His work also helped disprove Charles Darwin's theory of displacement by demonstrating that New Zealand plants were just as vigorous as those of the Northern Hemisphere, provided they could grow in environments to which they had adapted. Many papers on this subject, in addition to several classic books such as *New*

Zealand Plants and Their Story published in 1910 and the *Vegetation of New Zealand* published in 1921, won Cockayne the Royal Society of London's Darwin medal in 1928. The esteem reflected in this achievement saw Cockayne elected president of several leading scientific bodies, and he played a key role in persuading the government to establish the Department of Scientific and Industrial Research in 1926. This self-taught man rose to become New Zealand's most influential scientist before the famous physicist Ernest Rutherford. Cockayne's only son, Alfred Hyde, also became a powerful and important agricultural scientist, although like the next two generations of scientists Alfred lost sight of his father's warnings regarding the need to treat New Zealand's fragile ecosystems with great care.

Cook, James (1728—1779). Explorer, navigator, cartographer, and astute observer. This master navigator rediscovered New Zealand for Britain and Europe in 1769 and greatly expanded knowledge of a country first rediscovered by Dutchman Abel Tasman in 1642. Along with botanist Joseph Banks and several other scientists and artists, Cook made New Zealand much better known to the intelligentsia of the day and promoted it as an ideal place for British colonization. He circumnavigated and mapped New Zealand in 1769–1770 and returned two more times on more adventurous voyages of discovery. Between 1772 and 1775 he proved conclusively that the fabled great south land did not exist as he probed the edges of the frozen continent of Antarctica. Then he returned in 1776 in pursuit of the supposed northwest passage between the Americas and Europe. Hawaiians killed him in 1779 when he became embroiled in a local religious dispute and overused kidnapping of local leaders as a means of securing the return of stolen goods. This curious self-made man could not resist playing the ethnographer and perished doing what he loved best—observing the world around him. He remains an iconographic figure in New Zealand, with his image represented on banknotes, stamps, and brewery emblems. Even Maori view him with begrudging admiration, and he has not been subjected to the same critical revisionism as among Hawaiian radicals.

Cooper, Dame Whina (1885–1994). Tribal leader, national Maori women's leader, mother of the nation. This remarkable Maori leader, whose long life spanned two centuries, was born into a chiefly and deeply Catholic family at Pangaru in the remote northwest of New Zealand. She emerged as leader of her Hokianga people from as early as 1914 by protesting the attempt of local Pakeha farmers to drain mudflats rich in traditional sources of food. For a time she worked quietly on land development and ran a cooperative store for her people. She then faced a period of ostracism from her own community for marrying a man without the permission of her elders. They eventually forgave her, and she put herself back to work developing farming in the Hokianga and improving health services.

Ngata's land schemes helped her in this task, but after the death of her first husband, Richard Gilbert, she shocked her supporters once again by taking up a with a married man named William Cooper. She removed herself into self-imposed exile for seven years before returning and rising to national prominence in 1951 when she helped establish the Maori Women's Welfare League. This organization aimed to help Maori women make the difficult adjustment from rural to urban living, something Whina herself had to learn to do once she moved to Auckland in 1951. The league had much success, winning the respect of both Maori and Pakeha communities and elevated the *mana* of Whina and its other leaders. Then in 1975 Whina gained national prominence by leading a land march from the far north to the capital of Wellington. Although she struggled to control more youthful and radical elements, the march persuaded the third Labor government to establish the Waitangi Tribunal to address Maori land grievances. From this time on, Whina became the elder stateswoman of New Zealand politics. The press and Prime Minister Muldoon lauded her as mother of the nation, but she remained a much more controversial figure in the Maori world. The Methodist parts of her own clan and tribe always remained distrustful of her Catholicism, while young radicals felt that she sold out to the Pakeha establishment. Many others found her impossibly domineering. Nevertheless, no other Maori leader achieved such prominence in both the Maori and Pakeha communities in the twentieth century.

Deans, Jane (1823–1911). Matriarch, pioneer, sheep farmer, gardener. Jane McIlraith emigrated from Ayrshire, Scotland, in 1852 after marrying John Deans who returned from 12 years of pioneering in New Zealand. They arrived at Riccarton, then on the outskirts of Christchurch, in 1853, only for John to die from tuberculosis in 1854. Jane now devoted herself to raising her son John; and with her three half brothers, who emigrated in 1856, she ran both the small Riccarton farm and a much bigger inland run at Homebush. She went on to become the matriarch of an important Canterbury dynasty as John Junior raised 12 children to adulthood. She also played an active role in promoting the growth of the Presbyterian Church in Anglican Canterbury, but she is most remembered for the trees she planted at Riccarton and for saving a block of native bush on the edge of the growing city.

Douglas, Roger (1937–). Accountant and radical politician. The politician who did more than any other individual to push New Zealand in a more free market direction grew up in a staunch Labor household. His father Norm was a Labor MP, and his brother Malcolm briefly held the Hunua seat. Roger himself held the Manukau seat for Labor between 1969 and 1978 before moving to Manurewa in 1978. He won a reputation for getting things done when he set up New Zealand's second television channel in

1974 and introduced color television to the nation. He remained something of a maverick when Labor was in opposition, and Bill Rowling demoted him when Douglas produced a very different economic strategy for Labor in 1982. With Rowling's departure as leader in 1983, Douglas seized his chance and became Labor's finance spokesman. Labor never really spelled out any particular economic policy during the 1984 election campaign, and new leader David Lange gave him a free hand. Unbeknown to the electorate, Douglas had worked closely with Treasury and big business to implement a drastic program of liberalization. A constitutional crisis induced by Muldoon's refusal to devalue the currency gave Douglas his chance to push reform even harder, and he seized it with enthusiasm. New Zealand not only devalued but opened up its economy more than most other countries. Subsidies were ended overnight, tariffs removed, and the dollar floated. Douglas also simplified the taxation system, sold off state assets, and corporatized state departments. User pays became the norm, and even official language changed, with department heads becoming CEOs while students became clients and parents stakeholders. Eventually Douglas went too far for Lange when he talked of introducing a flat tax system, and Lange dismissed him as minister of finance in December 1989. Lange himself resigned soon after, and Douglas returned to sell off the Bank of New Zealand and Telecom. After Labor's disastrous 1990 election defeat, Douglas moved on to form the free market ACT (Association of Taxpayers' and Consumers') Party with the other Labor maverick, Richard Prebble, in 1994. He remains an unrepentant apologist for his reforms, arguing that they would have worked better had he been allowed to push them farther. The electorate has become deeply cynical about such claims, but there is no argument that despite being a poor speaker and not being charismatic Roger Douglas remains one of the most important revolutionaries in New Zealand history.

Fletcher, Hugh (1947–). Big businessman, leader in management. This son of the magnate of New Zealand's largest building firm went on to become the head of New Zealand's largest corporation. In many ways New Zealand's first modern-style big businessman, Hugh Fletcher took a masters of business administration at Stanford before returning to build Fletcher Challenge Limited into the first multinational corporation to operate out of New Zealand since the Union Steamship Company in the early 1900s. Hugh merged his father's Fletcher Holdings with Challenge Corporation in 1981, thereby combining the traditional agricultural financing and provisioning of a stock and station agency with a major construction enterprise. He then extended the company's activities to include fishing, timber processing, steel manufacturing, and financing in Canada, the United States, and Asia. Despite his obvious commitment to private enterprise, Fletcher preferred the Japanese model of close cooperation between government and corporations rather than Douglas's more free market approach. Even though he lost this debate, Fletcher remains a respected business commentator and by continuing as a director has helped the corporation weather the storms of environmental protest over cutting policies pursued in Canada. He and his corporation have also remained committed to New Zealand and continue to provide leadership in management practice and support for the arts. His wife, Sian Elias, became the first woman to serve as chief justice in New Zealand in 1999.

Frame, Janet (1924–2004). Novelist, short-story writer, and poet. New Zealand's most internationally acclaimed novelist was born into something of an unlucky and eccentric family in Dunedin. Although they were not exactly poor, they did not manage money well, and the whole family struggled because her brother suffered from the then untreatable disease of epilepsy. The freakish drowning of two sisters also helps explain Janet's initial problems with mental illness. She was only saved from a lobotomy at the last minute by her former lecturer in psychology, John Money, who later went on to become a controversial sexologist. Initially diagnosed as schizophrenic, Janet was subjected to electric shock treatment and isolation before wiser therapists realized that she was simply eccentric and original. She emerged from the mental hospital to write *Owls Do Cry* in 1957, a startlingly original critique of complacent New Zealand middle-class society. She went on to write 10 other highly acclaimed novels. Several relate to her time in mental institutions. Frame is also a fine poet, and the novels feature inventive use of language. In many ways her highly symbolic and allegorical stories, rich in symbolism and heavy in irony, are almost the opposite of Frank Sargeson's terse social realism. In 1982 she turned to autobiography and wrote three delightful accounts of her unusual life: *To the Is-Land, An Angel at My Table,* and the *Envoy from Mirror City.* Jane Champion made these into an excellent movie entitled *An Angel at My Table.* This creative burst won her honorary membership in the American Academy of Arts and Letters. With her status raised by Michael King's fine biography, she became the elder stateswoman of New Zealand literature. Although she has not published for some time, she remained the New Zealand writer most likely to win the Nobel Prize because of her extraordinary courage, linguistic skill, and very unusual vision of the world. She died in early 2004.

Fraser, Peter (1884–1950). Wharf laborer, unionist, politician, and intellectual. The man who rivals Seddon and Massey as New Zealand's greatest prime minister was born at Fearn in the northeastern Scottish highlands, only a few miles from the birthplace of the Liberal land reformer John McKenzie. Despite being forced to leave school early, he became a deep reader from an early age. Bad eyesight forced him to give up an apprenticeship as a carpenter, and he tried his luck in London in 1908. There he fell under the influence of socialist doctrines and joined the Independent Labor Party. In 1910 he immigrated to New Zealand and worked first as a general laborer, then on the Auckland wharves. Fraser soon became involved in union activity. Like Savage, he joined the Red Feds in 1912 and rose to serve on its executive council. He played a leading role in both the 1912 gold miners' strike in Waihi and the 1913 wharf laborers' strike. After the 1913 strikers had been defeated, Fraser moved to Wellington and worked for greater unity within the labor movement. His chance came in July 1916, when the Labor Party emerged in opposition to conscription and he was elected to the executive council. The government imprisoned Fraser and other Labor leaders for 12 months on grounds of sedition. On his release he edited Labor's newspaper, the *Maoriland Worker,* before winning a by-election for Wellington Central in late 1918. Fraser showed great personal courage during the influenza pandemic that immediately followed his election and won much popular support. He also served on the Wellington City Council from 1919 to 1923, where he made quite an impact. In 1919 he married Janet Munro, who became acted as an enthusiastic lieutenant throughout his long political career. Fraser soon became Labor's most effective debater and moved policy away from Marxist extremism. He had no time for communism and made sure that Labor dropped its unpopular usehold, or compulsory leasehold, land policy in 1927. In 1933 he became deputy leader to Savage and worked hard to secure electoral victory in 1935. As a well-read Scot Fraser held a passionate believe in the importance of education, and he worked hard to make quality education available to all New Zealanders. He not only appointed the talented young educationalist Clarence Beeby director-general of education, but also hosted an international conference of educational experts in 1937 to advise New Zealand on how to overhaul its clearly outdated system. Fraser also believed strongly in collective security and backed Savage in criticizing Britain for not working with the League of Nations against Mussolini's invasion of Abyssinia (Ethiopia). He failed, though, to overcome the opposition of the powerful British Medical Association to free visits to the doctor. When Savage died, Fraser took over as wartime leader and proved tough and able in this arduous task. At the war's end he also played a key role in ensuring that small nations such as New Zealand played a full role in the United Nations. His success overseas, though, disguised the fact that ongoing austerity measures instituted by his orthodox finance minister, Walter Nash, were becoming very unpopular. Then Fraser seemed to lose all touch with the electorate when he introduced conscription in peacetime in August 1949. An almost inevitable defeat followed at the December election. He died a year later, exhausted and bitter at what he perceived as a betrayal by an ungrateful electorate. Nevertheless, his reputation as one of the key architects of both the welfare state and a more independent foreign policy lives on, and his biographer, Michael Bassett, argues persuasively that he was the most able of New Zealand's three outstanding prime ministers. After all, he had to lead New Zealand through its first experience of total war and the threat of invasion rather than a distant war in Europe or South Africa.

Grey, George (1812–1898). Governor, premier, intellectual, politician. Grey, twice governor (1845–1853 and 1861–1868), and premier from 1877 to 1879, bestrode nineteenth-century New Zealand like a colossus. No other individual exercised so much influence in the fledgling colony. The posthumous son of an Anglo-Irish soldier, he too received a military education at Sandhurst. After falling under the influence of both classical writers and German romantics, he set out to make his mark in the colonies. Grey's experiments in race relations in New Zealand, South Africa, and South Australia soon turned sour when native peoples forcibly resisted his authoritarian and frequently patronizing policies. Nevertheless, he sincerely believed that Maori, Zulu, and Aborigines would benefit from being dragged into modernity, even if by force. Grey's dislike of large-scale sheep farming soon gave way to a pragmatic acceptance once wool proved the only reliable export earner. He would be delighted to see the diverse forms of land use in twenty-first century New Zealand because he imagined this land as a Mediterranean paradise of orchards, vineyards, and olive groves. He also helped set up the reforming Liberal Party in New Zealand after failing to join the ranks of the English Liberals. A lifelong correspondent with such intellectual giants as John Stuart Mill and Charles Darwin, he returned late in life to London to mend his long-ruptured marriage. He died as one of the grand old men of British imperialism.

Hillary, Edmund (1919–). Apiarist, mountaineer, and national icon. This self-effacing beekeeper has risen to become the most respected living New Zealander. The first man to climb Mount Everest with the Sherpa Tenzing in 1953, Hillary became both a national and Commonwealth hero at a young age. His reputation also spread to the United States. Since conquering Everest, Hillary returned his thanks to the Sherpa people of Nepal by building schools and directing aid projects. He also continued his adventures, crossing the Antarctic by tractor in 1958 and jet-boating up the Ganges River. He served between 1985 and 1989 as New Zealand ambassador to India and developed a close friendship with Indian Prime Minister Indira Gandhi. Recently, he received international acclaim along with other survivors of the 1953 climb. He maintains a busy schedule of speaking and fundraising around the world. He is loved above all else for his humility, sound common sense, and practical provision of charity to others less fortunate than himself.

Holyoake, Keith Jacka (1904–1983). Farmer and politician. One of New Zealand's longest serving and most astute prime ministers grew up on a poor tobacco farm near Motueka at the top of the South Island. Despite his plummy-sounding voice, he left school at 12, his elocution lessons serving as compensation from his mother. Despite his latter reputation for being ill educated, the self-taught Holyoake was well-read like many of his Labor opponents. He first won election to parliament at the 1932 Motueka by-election and quickly rose through the ranks of the National Party after its formation in 1936. Holyoake also played a prominent role in the New Zealand Farmer's Union and helped overhaul this somewhat antiquated organization into Federated Farmers in 1944. Thereafter, the rather ineffectual union became a powerful pressure group. After being defeated in 1938 Holyoake returned as MP for Pahiatua in 1943. He then worked his way to become second in command in the National Party when it won the 1949 election. Holyoake served with distinction as minister of agriculture and adopted a more consensual style than the more abrasive prime minister Sid Holland. When Holland died in 1957, Holyoake took over as prime minister but narrowly lost to Labor a few weeks later at the election. He returned as prime minister in 1960 and held this post down to his resignation in 1971. Holyoake ran a very open kind of government, consulting constantly with allies such as Federated Farmers and the Employers' Federation as well as with potential rivals such as the Federation of Labor and the Public Service Association. He also gave free rein to more liberal colleagues such as Tom Shand and Les Gandar as well his more conservative supporters. He held New Zealand together through the difficult years of the late 1960s as the baby boom generation protested ever more raucously about the Vietnam War and the conformist nature of New Zealand society. Holyoake only committed troops to Vietnam with great reluctance, and his pragmatism proved electorally successful. His successor Jack Marshall lost the 1972 election before Robert Muldoon won back power in 1975. Holyoake served as a backbencher in Muldoon's government before the aggressive Muldoon removed Holyoake's moderating influence by promoting him to the role of governor-general in 1977. Holyoake was the first partisan politician to be appointed to this post, and his elevation remains controversial to this day. His rather pompous persona prevented him from winning wide popularity, but he won respect as one of the most astute controllers of parliament in New Zealand's history. Some historians believe that his steady-as-she-goes policies suited New Zealand well as it adjusted painfully to Britain's inevitable move into the European Economic Community. Agricultural scientists such as Levy and McMeekan basically ran New Zealand during this era, with accountants, lawyers, and managers assuming less prominent roles. Some historians judge this social and political order favorably. Others, though, feel that harder and more radical changes were required. The jury is still out until we know whether New Zealand has been successful in making the transformation to a more balanced and modern economy.

Hongi Hika (1772–1828). Powerful tribal leader, warlord, and patron of the missionaries. This fearsome Nga Puhi warlord altered the balance of power between the tribes by pioneering the use of the musket in the early 1820s. After the heavy defeat of his tribe by neighboring Ngati Whatua in 1807,

Hongi worked to build alliances and gain access to muskets in order to avenge his tribe and his brothers, killed in 1807. He traveled to England with the missionary Thomas Kendall in 1820, met King George IV, and acquired over 300 muskets. His firearms enabled him to overwhelm not only Ngati Whatua but also the Ngati Paoa and Ngati Maru tribes south of Auckland. He raided as far south as the Hawke's Bay and took many slaves. His warriors also fathered many children in their travels and so bound most tribes of the east coast of the North Island to Nga Puhi. Some kind of balance had been established by the late 1820s as various tribes learned how to counter the musket. Hongi, meantime, became ensnared in an inter-*hapu* conflict and died of a gunshot wound in 1828. Although he never attacked any European, grew wheat successfully, and drank tea rather than alcohol, the musket wars he unleashed killed at least 10,000 Maori and devastated parts of the North Island. Most importantly, he forced Ngati Whatua and Ngati Paoa out of the Auckland isthmus, leaving the area open to rapid European settlement.

Hyde, Robin (Iris Wilkinson) (1906–1939). Novelist, short-story writer, and poet. This important if short-lived writer was born in South Africa, but raised in a working-class family in Wellington. Having shown considerable flair with composition at Wellington Girls' High Schools, Iris went into journalism. She soon learned that it was easiest to get her stories and poems published if she wrote under a male pseudonym, so she became Robin Hyde. Her bohemian lifestyle, especially losing one son out of wedlock and fostering out her second son fathered by a married man, shocked her contemporaries. She was largely ostracized from polite society and rejected by her family. Intermittent bouts of depression and stays in mental institutions did not help her career. Her outsider perspective, though, provided many insights into mainstream society, and her work has stood the test of time better than that of most of her contemporaries. Male writers and critics largely pushed her out of the canon in the 1950s and 1960s, but she has gained a new currency in more recent times. Her most important book is probably the autobiographical *The Godwits Fly,* but her novels based around the life of Private Douglas Stark—*Passport to Hell* and *Nor the Years Condemn*— are also now regarded as wartime classics. The experimental and playful *Wednesday's Children* represents the first attempt by a New Zealand writer at magic realism. She left her son with his foster parents and departed for a trip to China and Europe in 1938, but she struggled to find acceptance in London, and overwhelmed by her problems committed suicide at the very young age of 33. Hyde can be compared in some ways with Sylvia Plath in that she was too unconventional for the rather conformist society of her time and yet gained creative impetus and deep insights from her sense of alienation.

Jackson, Peter (1961–). Filmmaker. Peter Jackson is easily the most important New Zealander in the twenty-first century thus far. Jackson's *The*

Lord of the Rings trilogy, which won 11 Oscars for the third film in the trilogy and was shot and made in New Zealand, has done more to put the small country on the world map than any promotional campaign. Tourists are flocking to see New Zealand for themselves, and cutting-edge facilities for film production are now available in Wellington. Jackson began making cult splatter movies for art theaters, but gained recognition for his excellent *Heavenly Creatures* in 1994. *Time* magazine rated it one of the movies of the year, and this accolade won Jackson the right to make the popular fantasy epic into a big budget production. Through his remarkable organizational skills, Jackson made the three *The Lord of the Rings* movies simultaneously and kept them somewhere near budget. The weak New Zealand dollar and tax breaks helped, and the government might actually make more tax breaks available for further large-scale productions. Whatever else happens in filmmaking, New Zealand's international profile has been raised to unprecedented levels by the energy, drive, and vision of this filmmaker and the skill of his scriptwriter wife, Fran Walsh.

Kirk, Norman (1925–1974). Semi-skilled worker, politician, and intellectual. The big, soft-spoken man, who countered Muldoon's aggressive style better than any of his contemporaries, was born into humble circumstances in the small town of Waimate in South Canterbury. Norm's cabinet-maker father was also an active member of the Salvation Army, and Kirk remained a religious man all his life, ending close to Roman Catholicism. Norm, too, had a hard depression, leaving school at 13 and working as a boiler operator in dairy factories and later at a tire factory in Christchurch. Despite his lack of formal education, Kirk was a vociferous reader with a strong sense of social justice. He became active in local body politics after World War II and served as mayor of Kaiapoi from 1953 to 1958. In 1957 he won the Lyttelton seat for Labor and rose to become president of the party in 1964. The following year he took over as party leader from the aging Arnold Nordmeyer. In 1969 he changed to the Sydenham electorate and represented it until his premature death. In 1972 Kirk's persistence paid off when he easily won the election. He tried hard to steer a new course in foreign policy, pushing New Zealand toward Asia and the Third World rather than maintaining the traditional relationship with Britain and the United States. This shift involved sending a frigate to Mururoa Atoll in the Pacific to protest French atmospheric nuclear testing. Several Third World leaders such as Julius Nyerere of Tanzania visited New Zealand for the first time, and a very successful Commonwealth Games followed in Christchurch in 1974. Kirk also promoted such social democratic policies as introducing no-fault accident compensation and state financial support for unmarried mothers. Unfortunately, the oil shock of 1974 led to rapid inflation and undid much of his good work. Kirk's weight began to trouble him, and he suffered heart problems throughout early 1974. When he died suddenly in August 1974, he left Labor bereft. No other Labor politician was his equal as a leader, and all lacked his drive and vision. The able but rather colorless Bill Rowling failed to inspire the electorate and lost badly to the aggressive Muldoon in 1975. Kirk was a man of principal and vision, but his untimely death makes it hard to assess his true worth. He remains something of a J.F.K. type of figure in New Zealand in that his passionate rhetoric has inspired later generations, but he did not serve long enough for history to judge his real ability.

Kupe (?). Mythical eastern Polynesian discoverer of New Zealand. One tradition has it that he found New Zealand after chasing a giant squid that had been breaking his fishing nets. The ethnographer Percy Smith calculated that he arrived in 925 A.D., but this now seems too early. Prehistorians currently opt for an arrival date of around 1180 A.D.

Levy, Bruce (1892–1985). Grassland scientist. This scientist, who did more than any other individual to convert New Zealand into Britain's far-flung, but highly efficient, grassland farm, was the son of a nurseryman. He started out as cadet in the Department of Agriculture before moving on to take a B.Sc. degree at Victoria University of Wellington. Once he passed his degree and published his seminal *Grasslands of New Zealand* in 1923, he rose rapidly through the ranks to become, in 1928, director of the Plant Research Division of the new Department of Scientific and Industrial Research (DSIR), located in Palmerston North. In 1936 he moved on to direct the new Grasslands Division of the DSIR, located next to the Plant Research Division. Working closely with the famous British grassland scientists R. G. Stapeldon and William Davies, he pushed New Zealand even more firmly in the direction of becoming the most highly specialized stock farm within the British Empire. Initially he expressed a more balanced view of ecology and New Zealand's development, but by the second edition of his book in 1951 Levy had little time for trees, cities, or anything else that stopped the extension of stock farming. As far as he was concerned, the North Island should just become one giant farm with mountains and a pine forest in the middle. His practical advice to farmers to use the dung and urine method of pasture rejuvenation certainly saw spectacular increases in productivity and sheep numbers. Top dressing, carried out by airplanes that dropped superphosphate (a mixture of guano and sulfuric acid) over the hill country of New Zealand from 1949, also saw spectacular increases in sheep numbers. Whereas New Zealand carried a modest 30 million sheep in 1949, that figure had risen to 70 million by 1980. This increase occurred most spectacularly in the South Island, whose sheep carrying capacity had fallen behind that of the North Island from the turn of the century. Levy rejoiced at this increase but dreamed of improving pasture so that it could carry over 100 million sheep. He can take much credit for this so-called grasslands revolution, but he gave little thought to its environmental consequences (today, New Zealand's 40 million sheep, 10 million cattle, and 2 million deer produce as much organic waste as 150 million people!), or to the possibility that the market for fatty red meat might become saturated. Consequently, sheep numbers fell sharply after his death once New Zealand lost its guaranteed British market, and the search for new products and new markets accelerated along with the quest for more sustainable forms of farming.

Massey, William Ferguson (1856–1925). Farmer and politician. This important farmer and politician, who helped conservatives adjust to the realities of a more democratic kind of politics, was the son of small farmer in Northern Ireland. He followed his family to New Zealand in 1870. After working as a laborer on the Longbeach estate, famous for the progressive approach of its owner John Grigg, Massey moved onto a leasehold farm in 1877 at Mangere, now the site of Auckland's international airport. He eventually freeholded the property and rose to become a local notable. As chairman of the Mangere Farmers' Club he networked with many business and farming leaders and won their nomination for the Waitemata seat, which he won in a by-election in 1894. Massey suffered through many long years in a weak opposition but served conscientiously and learned many lessons from the dominant Liberal premier Richard Seddon. From 1905 Massey built the Reform League as an extraparliamentary party from the grassroots up and copied Seddon's populist style by stumping the country from one end to the other. Eventually the Reform League developed into the Reform Party in 1909, and Massey won the support of increasingly prosperous small farmers and businessmen. These citizens feared that their hard-won gains might be ripped away by the socialistic excesses of the labor movement and the left wing of the Liberal government. Massey played on those fears and also gained from the rapid growth of the Auckland region in comparison with the rest of the country. The Liberals had always been dominated by South Islanders and never secured much traction in the dairy farming districts around the burgeoning port city. Massey finally won power in July 1912 when five Liberals crossed the floor to join his Reform Party. Massey kept his pledge of offering leasehold farmers the right of freeholding their properties at original valuation and won credit for both his firm handling of the 1913 wharf strike and his efficient administration. He proved a tough wartime leader and managed a difficult coalition government with considerable skill. Despite much contemporary criticism and the opprobrium of some nationalistic historians, he managed to pursue New Zealand's national interest to a surprising extent given the contingencies of war and the power of the imperial government. He won the so-called khaki election of 1919 by stressing the importance of patriotism and held onto power until his death in 1925. Despite sometimes behaving like an Ulster bigot toward the Roman Catholic minority, Massey was surprisingly well read, and he implemented many more progressive reforms in the 1920s than most historians acknowledge. Perhaps the most important was setting up the Meat Board in 1922 to regain control of New Zealand exports from shipping companies and English importers. Massey also encouraged the massive development program in areas like roading and the provision of hydroelectric power. New Zealand became a much more comfortable place to live thanks to his foresight and that of his successor Gordon Coates. When Massey died he had become New Zealand's second-longest-serving prime minister, a tribute to his hard work, astute leadership skills, tenacity, and cool head in a crisis. Equally important, the once stiff and gruff farmer Bill learnt to adopt some of the successful populist style of Richard Seddon, an adjustment vital to his survival in a mass democracy.

McKenzie, John (1839–1901). Land reformer, farmer, and populist politician. The six foot four inch, 18 stone son of a tenant farmer in the Scottish highlands became the most important land reformer in nineteenth-century New Zealand after immigrating to Otago in 1860. Although his family was never evicted during the highland clearances, McKenzie witnessed the Glencalvy clearance as a small boy and never forgot the experience. He determined thereafter that such injustices would not be repeated in New Zealand. After entering politics as a provincial councilor in 1871, he devoted his career to removing the problem of land monopoly. He did not have a particularly successful career as a backbencher but relished the opportunity offered when he became minister of lands in the Liberal government in 1891. McKenzie tried experiments with several different kinds of leasehold, including the notorious lease-in-perpetuity, or 999-year lease without revaluation, but these experiments proved less important than the provision of quality control and practical assistance through the Department of Agriculture, which he set up in 1892. Cheap credit provided via the Advances to Settlers' Office, established in 1894 and set up by his close ally the Colonial Treasurer Joe Ward, also proved hugely beneficial to small farmers. In combination these efforts helped New Zealand farming restructure and become much more efficient and modern. McKenzie also decided that viable, medium-sized farms would provide a solid base for the development of grassland farming, rather than the tiny, uneconomic plots of the Scottish highlands or Ireland. Debate still rages over the efficacy of his reforms because rising prices for frozen meat and butter persuaded many big companies and families with large holdings to unfreeze their assets by selling to a safe buyer in the form of the state. The practice of partible division, whereby estate owners divided their properties among all their children, also encouraged sales. In short, many great estates, including the famous 84,000-acre Cheviot estate, were broken up from the inside rather than by government pressure. Nevertheless, McKenzie's efforts ensured that family farming not only triumphed, but flourished. Unfortunately, in an endeavor to get hold of cheaper land for dairy farming in the North Island, he bought up most of the remaining farmable land owned by Maori. This purchase at rock-bottom prices thereby shut Maori out from sharing in the new prosperity. Like most contemporary British settlers, he did not believe that Maori were capable of using land as effectively as white settlers. In the process he bequeathed long-term problems to the nation as Maori were forced to subsist a low standards of living until they later moved to the cities. So in attempting to right one historical injustice, he and his government compounded the mistakes of a earlier governments and worsened a problem that New Zealand is still struggling to resolve.

McMeeken, Campbell Percy (1908–1972). Agricultural scientist. New Zealand's most influential agricultural scientist after the Second World War was a bright student from Taranaki who won a scholarship to the newly established Massey Agricultural College in 1928. His ability set him off from his peers, and he won a junior lectureship in animal husbandry in 1932. He moved from Massey to the University of Edinburgh before moving on to Cambridge, where he won a doctorate for his pioneer work in animal genetics. He returned to Massey but soon after took up new professorship of animal husbandry at Lincoln. He never fitted in very well with the conservative nature of Lincoln, so he moved in 1943 to become the director of the Ruakura Research Station near Hamilton. Here he led path-breaking work on how to increase the productivity of sheep, pigs, and especially dairy cattle. This large, ebullient man with an ability to address farmers in the field in highly colorful language was a champion of rural interests. Pig McMeekan, as he was affectionately known, became something of national hero. He used his high profile to advocate the necessity of keeping New Zealand agriculture ahead of its international competition by integrating scientific research and development as an integral part of the farming industry. Unfortunately, he was a rather disorganized administrator, and his own scientists eventually maneuvered him out of Ruakura. Having failed to win the plum job of director-general of agriculture, he moved instead to the World Bank between 1960 and 1965. He worked as an independent researcher thereafter, warning New Zealand to avoid the dangers of running down its agriculture, a process he dubbed "Uruguayisation." Before he drowned in a boating accident, he had become acutely aware that New Zealand's high standard of living could not be sustained without making some big and hard changes to the economy. Had he lived longer, however, he would not have approved of Roger Douglas's attempts to treat agriculture as a sunset industry in the late 1980s.

Moncrieff, Perrine (1893–1979). Naturalist, ornithologist, and conservationist. The rather eccentric woman who established the Abel Tasman National Park, much beloved of tourists, was born in London. Her medical doctor father died four years later, but she was brought up by the comfortably-off Millias family, including her naturalist uncle John Guillas Millias. During frequent holidays in the Scottish highlands and Europe, Perrine, encouraged by her uncle, developed a love of nature. After marrying a retired military officer in 1914, she lived in Scotland and Canada before immigrating to New Zealand in 1921. She became a founding member of the New Zealand Native Bird Protection Society in 1923, but her lack of formal training always limited her acceptance by other scientists. Nevertheless, her *New Zealand Birds and How to Identify Them,* first published in 1925, proved popular and ran to five editions. On the death of her elder son in 1925, Perrine devoted her life to saving birds and helped convert Lake Rotoroa and Farewell Spit into sanctuaries. She also worked tirelessly to establish the Abel Tasman National Park in 1942. Thereafter, she worked assiduously to promote the conservation cause. Her efforts began to bear fruit as major conservation movements emerged from the 1960s, culminating in the formation of the Green Party in the 1990s. One historian has described her as a kind of "proto eco-feminist," and all New Zealanders salute her for saving a lovely stretch of coast and forest for the enjoyment of future generations.

Muldoon, Robert David (1921–1992). Accountant and populist politician. Like several of New Zealand's most prominent political leaders, Rob Muldoon grew up in relative poverty. After his father succumbed to tertiary syphilis contracted during the First World War, his mother Amie struggled to raise Rob through the hard years of the Great Depression. Although his mother was an excellent manager who ensured that her only son was well fed, Muldoon never forgot his harsh childhood and always set out to champion what he called the "ordinary bloke." His maternal grandmother exerted a left-wing influence, and Muldoon always remained an admirer of Labor's maverick John A. Lee. But this socialist influence was counterbalanced by his mother's wealthy businessman brother, who persuaded Rob to become an accountant and join the National Party. Rob had a rather undistinguished war, rising to sergeant in New Zealand, but serving as a private in New Caledonia. After the war, though, the bright young accountant made his mark in the resurgent National Party. After serving as president of the Auckland Young Nationals, Muldoon won the Mount Albert seat in 1954, Waitemata in 1957, and Tamaki in 1960, which he continued to represent for the rest of his political career. He rose to become minister of finance in 1967. Muldoon introduced austerity measures to reduce the sudden deficit and won a reputation as a strong-willed and determined politician. After National's heavy defeat at the 1972 election, Muldoon ousted Jack Marshall in an unpleasant coup and went on to win the 1975 election handsomely. He ran a very effective if questionable election campaign that played on the electorate's fears of backdoor nationalization, increasing immigration, and racial violence. The first thing he did was to can Labor's sensible contributory superannuation system and replace it with a universal pension paid out to everyone over 60. This new scheme was funded directly out of general taxation, and the country struggled to sustain it. Having slowed immigration, Muldoon tried to bolster the struggling farming industry by introducing hefty subsidies known as supplementary minimum prices or SMPs. These inducements to increase productivity, however, only raised the cost of freight and refrigeration workers' wages, so Muldoon turned instead to the so-called Think Big strategy in a desperate attempt to diversify New Zealand's export base. This scheme involved the erection of giant energy plants in Taranaki to make New Zealand more self-sufficient in the event of further oil price hikes like that of 1979. In fact, the natural gas to petroleum plant proved hugely expensive, and the national debt soared. Muldoon responded by tightening government control of the economy. He clung to power in 1981 only by allowing the tour by the South African rugby team to proceed despite widespread protest. This action won him vital provincial seats. Finally, on the auspicious date of July 14, 1984, the Labor Party, led by the ebullient and charismatic David Lange, won back power. Muldoon's populist genius has been compared with Seddon's, but his abrasive style, which so dominated New Zealand politics in the late 1970s and early 1980s, alienated many voters. His obsession with trying to control every part of the New Zealand economy by holding the post of minister of finance as well as that of prime minister also helps explain why New Zealand moved rapidly to free up its economy from 1984. Muldoon lingered on as a politician until bad health forced him into begrudging and bitter retirement in 1981. He remains a controversial figure, admired for his courage but condemned for his bullying and sensitivity to criticism. For these reasons, he can be judged an important but not great prime minister.

Ngata, Apirana Turupa (1974–1950). Tribal leader, national leader, politician, and intellectual. This extraordinary man, who stood tall in both Maori and Pakeha worlds, was the son of the high-born chief of the powerful Ngati Porou tribe of the east coast of the North Island. Under the patronage of his great uncle, the influential Kupapa (friendly chief) Rapata (or Ropata) Wahawaha, Ngata secured a place at the Anglican boarding school of Te Aute in the Hawke's Bay. Here he fell under the influence of the charismatic headmaster John Thorton, who preached an assimilationist message but also urged his pupils to take up the mission of ameliorating the condition of their race. Ngata went on to Canterbury College of the University of New Zealand, where he graduated with a B.A. at the very young age of 19. He then moved on to Auckland, graduating LLB in 1896 and becoming the first Maori to complete a degree. He returned to the east coast and helped set up the Te Aute College Students' Association, or Young Maori Party, in 1897. He also worked with his other patron, Sir James Carroll, minister of native affairs from 1899 to 1912, to improve Maori health and develop Maori farming. In 1905 he won the eastern Maori seat from the Wi Pere and remained loyal to the Liberals down to his defeat by Labor in 1943. Ngata worked closely with Sir Robert Stout on the Stout-Ngata Commission between 1907 and 1909 to encourage Maori to incorporate their land holdings into trusts so that sufficient land could be retained for farming. At the same time, he never forgot his Maori heritage and worked hard to save Maori arts and crafts, dance, song, myth, and oral tradition. He worked closely with the brilliant young Maori anthropologist Te Rangi Hiroa (Sir Peter Buck, who ended up as professor of anthropology at Yale) in this endeavor and helped establish a carving school at Rotorua in 1927. Ngata supported the First World War effort in the hope of winning concessions for Maori but achieved little other than the belated release of some cheap credit in 1926. He became minister of native affairs in the Ward ministry in 1928 and worked hard on land development schemes, but resigned in 1934 after a commission of inquiry alleged that he favored his own tribe. Thereafter he worked with "Princess" Te Puea of Tainui to build Maori unity and never relented in his collecting of song, dance, and story. Once again he recruited enthusiastically to support the Second World War effort and helped organize the centennial celebrations. After his defeat by Labor in 1943, Ngata concentrated on helping his own Ngati Porou people and served as president of the Council of the Polynesian Society from 1938 to 1950. In 1948 the government awarded him an honorary doctorate of literature. He died as a man honored by both races despite his awkward and unfair dismissal as a minister in 1934. His place in the pantheon of great New Zealanders remains secure, thanks to a fine biography by the Maori historian and activist Ranginui Walker.

O'Regan, Tipene (1939–). Tribal leader and intellectual. The most effective and prominent tribal leader of the 1980s and 1990s grew up in a family with strong links to the left in New Zealand as well as to the South Island's Ngai Tahu tribe. Tipene's grandfather, John Patrick, was a land nationalizer who acted as the lawyer for the notoriously militant Federation of Labor during the waterfront strike of 1913. His father, Rolland, was also a prominent doctor, but it was his mother Rena Ruhia Bradshaw's Ngai Tahu links that became more important in shaping his life's work. After a relatively quite life as a wharf laborer and Teachers' College lecturer, O'Regan emerged in the early 1980s to lead the Ngai Tahu claim for redress of the sale of the South Island for very little money in the 1840s and 1850s. *Te Kemare* or the Claim, as it was known, had been pursued by his people since 1849. O'Regan's skill as chief negotiator finally saw it triumph in 1996 when the government passed the Runanga o Ngai Tahu Act to give the large tribe the right to control its own destiny. A package of $170 million contained in the deal, in addition to increased fishing rights and the return of some high-country leasehold land, enabled the tribe to secure its economic base. Under O'Regan's careful direction, the Ngai Tahu corporation has invested its monies wisely and can now claim to be one of the wealthiest and most powerful corporate bodies in the South Island. This charismatic man and wonderful orator handed over the chief executive's job recently to Tahu Potiki, but still keeps a close eye on proceedings. During his time as leader O'Regan also won respect as a significant historian in his own right. His very able daughter, Hana, carries on the traditions of combining sharp scholarship and careful research with oratorical flair and fluency in Maori to advance the cause of her people.

Potts, T. H. (1824–1888). Conservationist, naturalist, explorer, and politician. Thomas Potts was New Zealand's first serious conservationist who was most unusual in bringing the High Church Anglican tradition of stewardship of the environment with him to New Zealand. The son of a wealthy gun maker Potts immigrated to Canterbury in 1854 and tried his hand at extensive sheep farming. He acquired the lease of some 81,000 acres and left the running of these properties to hired managers. He bought a farm of 255 acres at Governor's Bay on Banks Peninsula near Christchurch, where he raised his 13 children and created spectacular gardens. Potts served for a time on the Canterbury Provincial Council and then as an MP between 1866 and 1870. He attempted to conserve native tress from as early as 1866 and engaged in intensive study of the natural history of the South Island. He became a champion of the conservation of native birds and argued that offshore islands should be developed as sanctuaries for endangered species, something that only happened in the 1890s. He lost his fortune in the depression of the 1880s and died a pauper, but his efforts as a pioneer conservationist have enhanced his reputation as an early eco-hero in recent years.

Reeves, William Pember (1857–1932). Politician, intellectual, historian. The most intellectually self-conscious member of the reforming Liberal government was born into a wealthy and privileged Canterbury family in 1857. His father William was not only a substantial landholder but also edited the *Lyttelton Times*. William made it to Oxford, but his health deteriorated and he retreated to New Zealand to recuperate. After working in the open to regain his strength, he qualified as a lawyer and then turned to journalism. By 1885 he took over as editor of his father's weekly paper—the *Canterbury Times*—and promoted various radical reforms. A self-confessed Fabian socialist, Reeves believed that gradual change enacted through legislation could engineer social improvement. He won the chance to prove his ideas at the 1887 election and somehow managed to edit the *Lyttelton Times* as well from 1889. He became the minister of labor in the

Liberal government in 1891. His most famous reform related to industrial relations. Despite strong employer opposition, he introduced compulsory conciliation and arbitration under his 1894 legislation and saved the fragile trade union movement as a result. This system, whereby both parties in a dispute took their grievances to a court for arbitration, lasted down to the 1970s and removed strikes until 1906. Reeves's other ideas, especially his attempt to control the hours and conditions of family businesses, soon proved too radical for Seddon and the electorate, however. So he was promoted to agent-general in London in 1896. There Reeves promoted New Zealand assiduously as the social laboratory of the world, winning the interest of several leading British, French, and American radicals as a result. In 1898 he wrote New Zealand's first serious history, *The Long White Cloud,* which remains a classic account of the whiggish view of history in which intelligent legislation improves the lot of everyone. *State Experiments: Australia and New Zealand* followed in 1902, and it still remains one of the best comparative histories of the two countries. Thereafter, Reeves served as director of the London School of Economics from 1908 to 1919. His lack of an academic background meant that he did not succeed in this role, and so he saw out his day as chairman of the board of directors of the National Bank of New Zealand, which had its headquarters in London. Even though he lived outside New Zealand for much of his life, he remained passionately committed to the country of his birth and laid down a view of the country's development for later historians to critique and challenge.

Sargeson, Frank (1903–1982). Short-story writer, novelist, and literary patron. This son of the Hamilton town clerk went on to become New Zealand's most famous short-story writer. Norris Frank Davey developed a dislike for the stifling puritanical code from adolescence. He particularly disliked what he called the "impure" puritanism of his mother, or the obsession with being seen to do the right thing. He spent his life as an outsider looking in. Homosexuality was illegal in the world in which he lived, and he spent his life hiding his true identity, even changing his name to Sargeson (after his mother's brother) in 1931. After qualifying as a solicitor he made a brief visit to Britain in 1927–1928. He returned to New Zealand to write several famous short stories, including "The Making of a New Zealander," which won second prize in the centenary competition of 1940. Heavily influenced by the American Sherwood Anderson, Sargeson concentrated on social realism. His greatest accomplishment was catching the rhythm of New Zealand speech in his sparse sentences. All earlier writers, including the much acclaimed Katherine Mansfield, had their New Zealand characters talk like Cockneys. This is quite misleading, and Sargeson steered the reader toward a more accurate representation of how New Zealand English sounds. He lived very frugally and derived some belated relief from the Literary Fund established in 1946. As he grew older Sargeson became a patron of younger writers, including Janet Frame.

He exercised a great deal of influence over the direction of New Zealand writing in the 1950s and 1960s. In the 1970s he produced a delightful trilogy of autobiographies entitled *Once Is Enough, More Than Enough,* and *Never Enough!* He could not stop new voices from emerging, however, as social realism gave way to a range of approaches from the 1970s. Some critics condemn his stories of down and outs and losers (Oliver Duff called him the "hobo's laureate") as being unrelentingly bleak and one-dimensional. But all agree that he made a huge contribution in the search for a style of writing that distinguished New Zealand literature from its English, American, and Australian equivalents.

Savage, Michael Joseph (1872–1940). Barrel washer, unionist, and politician. New Zealand's most loved prime minister was born to Irish Catholic parents in the poverty-stricken northeastern corner of Victoria, Australia. This was the country that produced bush rangers like Ned Kelly, and Savage determined early in adulthood that poverty should be conquered in less violent ways. After holding down a series of tough laboring jobs, he fell under the influence of the American radicals Henry George and Edward Bellamy as well as of the British socialist Tom Mann. Savage migrated to New Zealand in 1907 and, after engaging in the tough work of flax cutting, settled in Auckland where he worked as a cellar man for the Captain Cook Brewery. He soon became deeply involved in the union movement and joined the militant Federation of Labor, or Red Feds, in 1910. After standing unsuccessfully for various socialist parties he helped form the Labor Party in 1916 and won the Auckland west seat in 1919. He also served with distinction on the Auckland Hospital and Charitable Aid Board. In 1922 Savage became deputy leader of Labor and won a reputation for reliability and hard work. He never married and committed himself to the Labor Party. When the more militant Labor leader Harry Holland died in 1933, Savage took on the mantle of leadership and won strong support in the city electorates. His mild, nonthreatening nature also won the support of middle-of-the-road voters, and he led Labor to triumph in 1935. Once in power Savage showed himself to be a very astute politician who ensured a landslide in the 1938 election by announcing that the government would introduce a welfare state in 1939. He also pushed New Zealand foreign policy into a more independent direction because he never liked, nor trusted, the British. At the peak of his powers Savage developed cancer, which reduced his effectiveness through 1939. Nevertheless, he continued to work very hard and battled on gamely. Unfortunately, the very able but tactless John A. Lee criticized him at this point, and Labor made the mistake of dismissing one of its most able members. Savage's funeral evoked huge outpourings of grief, and his photograph can still be found in the best rooms of many elderly New Zealanders. Although he hated privilege and literally gave away all his spare clothes to the unemployed, Savage was extremely well read, highly intelligent, and much tougher than his benign public persona suggested. He died too soon to be ranked as a great prime minister, but no other leader has been so adored by the public, nor has any other assumed so much iconographic significance.

Seddon, Richard John (1845–1906). Storekeeper, bush lawyer, and populist politician. The large and ebullient son of Lancashire and Scottish schoolteachers went on to become arguably New Zealand's most effective prime minister. After forgoing a career as a skilled artisan in the metal trades in St. Helens, Seddon moved to the Victorian gold rushes in 1863. He stayed there briefly, working in the railway workshops and marrying before immigrating to the west coast of New Zealand in 1866. After a brief stint in hydraulic mining building dams and races, Seddon became a storekeeper, publican, and miners' advocate at Kumara. There he developed a power base among the egalitarian gold miners, rising to become mayor in 1877. Like McKenzie, Seddon's career as a backbencher after his entry to parliament in 1879 was not especially distinguished, except as a champion of the mining industry, but he impressed as minister of public works in the new Liberal government. When Ballance became ill, Seddon took over the job of premier and then won it against the challenge from Sir Robert Stout, who had been out of the house. A brilliant populist politician with a fierce commitment to democracy, Seddon won the hearts and minds of the electorate so completely that he remained premier down to his death in 1906. Affectionately known as King Dick, he trumpeted every Liberal success to the world and helped win New Zealand's reputation as the social laboratory of the world. He also was an ardent imperialist who declared war on the Boers before the British government in 1899, annexed the Cook Islands in 1901, and promoted New Zealand's interests unashamedly at imperial conferences and royal jubilees. Essentially a pragmatist, Seddon contributed little to the Liberal reform program other than ensuring that difficult legislation passed into law. He did have a humanitarian streak, though, and took great pleasure from making secondary education available to academically able children from 1903. He also championed the introduction of a very miserly old age pension in 1898 and had hospitals built for working-class mothers in 1905. Although he fancied his ability to get on well with Maori, he did little for their welfare apart from granting a modicum of self-government in 1900. Seddon also expressed vehemently racist prejudice towards the Chinese and other Asians, whom he saw as threats to the high living standards achieved in what he called "God's own country." Such prejudice only added to his electoral appeal, and he became a kind of benevolent dictator before his death, serving as minister of practically everything. No other New Zealand politician would ever dominate his cabinet or manipulate the electorate to such great effect as this antipodean Andrew Jackson.

Sheppard, Kate (1847–1934). Woman's suffragist, temperance advocate, and intellectual. This charismatic leader of the women's suffrage movement immigrated to Christchurch in 1869 with her mother, sister, and two brothers. Her Scottish parents imbued in her the Presbyterian belief that gender relations should be made more equitable. She soon married in 1871 (her merchant husband, Walter Allen Sheppard, remains a shadowy figure, but he possessed considerable means), and she turned her comfortable economic situation to advantage by advocating greater equality for women and supporting the temperance movement. A foundation member of the Women's Christian Temperance Movement (WCTU) in 1885, Kate was appointed national superintendent of the franchise and legislation department of the WCTU in 1887. From then on she lobbied politicians and newspaper editors to considerable effect. A great organizer as well as a most persuasive woman, she pulled together three large petitions. The last gathered 30,000 signatures in 1893, representing a quarter of the adult women of New Zealand. Her relentless pressure paid off when two legislative councilors called Seddon's bluff and supported the Electoral Bill, which enfranchised New Zealand women on September 19, 1893. Thereafter Kate continued to play a leading role in both the WCTU and the National Council of Women (NCW), formed in 1896. She served for three years as president of the NCW. Kate also edited the *White Ribbon*, the periodical of the WCTU, until 1903. She concentrated her efforts on improving the lot of women and children within families, but always remained far more radical than the majority of first-wave feminists. For example, she believed that the state should either pay women a wage for performing the multitude of tasks required of wives and mothers or force husbands to pass over half their pay. Even in the 1920s, although she expressed delight at women's right to stand for parliament from 1919, she still realized that many more reforms were required before women could become truly equal citizens. Health problems from 1903 reduced her influence, but she traveled widely, promoting the cause of women's suffrage in Britain, Europe, and Canada. Her energy, vision, and effective lobbying won tangible gains for her contemporaries as well as for future generations of New Zealand women.

Snell, Peter (1938–). Athlete and sports scientist. New Zealand's most famous athlete grew up in Auckland and like Robert Muldoon received his education at Mt. Albert Grammar School. He trained under the controversial coach Arthur Lydiard with a group of high-achieving middle distance runners. He went on to win a gold medal in the 800 meters at the 1960 Rome Olympics and a remarkable double gold in the 800 and 1,500 meters in Tokyo in 1964. No other middle distance runner has so dominated his contemporary rivals. He continued his devotion to athletics by training as an exercise physiologist at Davis University in California. Since then he has moved on to direct the Human Performance Unit at the University of Texas in Dallas. Snell has become something of an icon because of his humility, which endeared him to a culture that prizes humility as a virtue, and his determination, which made him into the greatest athlete of a sports-loving nation.

Tawhiao (?–1894). Pan-tribal leader and priest. Tukaroto Matautaera Potatau Te Wherowhero was the son of the first wife of the Ngati Mahuta ariki, or supreme chief, Te Wherowhero. Tawhaio was raised as a man of peace, first under traditional Maori religious instruction and, later, as a Christian. Always more of priest than a warrior, he committed himself to the role of Maori king when his father died in 1860. The Taranaki prophet Te Ua Haumene bestowed the name Tawhiao upon him in 1864. After that Tawhiao adapted the Pai Marire faith into his own religion, which he named *tariao* or "morning star." This rather mystical religion helped sustain the Kingites through these difficult years. Comparing his people to the ancient Jews exiled in Canaan, Tawhaio turned to pacifism and renounced all war. He secured a permanent peace with the government in 1881, which enabled the opening up of the so-called King Country for the building of the main trunk railway. Believing that he would never receive justice in New Zealand, Tawhiao visited England in 1884. Although he failed to meet Queen Victoria, he did arrange an interview with Lord Derby, secretary of state for the colonies. Tawhaio argued that the settler government had breached the Treaty of Waitangi and asked for a royal commission of inquiry into the land confiscations. The New Zealand government fudged this challenge by claiming that only the imperial government could deal with complaints relating to the period before 1865, so the visit achieved little. In the late 1880s he created his own parliament, or Te Kahanganui, but this institution only operated effectively once he returned to his ancestral home of Ngaruawahia in 1892. There in 1893 he banned all Pakeha from New Zealand. Although he failed to unite Maori, he did at least keep the King Movement going, and he inspired his influential granddaughter, Princess Te Puea, to revive aspects of his faith as well as to invigorate the movement in the 1920s.

Te Kanawa, Kiri (1944–). Opera singer. New Zealand's best-known classical singer was raised by European foster parents. They recognized her extraordinary talent and sent Kiri to St. Mary's Convent in Auckland to study with the famous singing coach, Sister Mary Leo. Kiri subsequently won all the major New Zealand and Australian opera competitions before moving on to train in London. Since then she has sung in many famous opera companies around the world. Her greatest moment came when she sang at the wedding of Prince Charles and Princess Diana in 1981. Although now in the twilight of her career, her combination of striking looks, hard work, and success have inspired a whole new generation of exciting singers from Maori and Pacific Island backgrounds, as well as young Pakeha. Kiri showed that if you are good enough you can conquer the world.

(Watch for Samoan bass Jonathan Lemalu, Maori soprano Deborah Wai Kapohe, and the red-haired soprano Anna Leas.)

Te Puea Herangi (1883–1952). Tribal leader and prophet. Te Puea, who grew into one of most influential Maori leaders of the twentieth century, was born near Pirongia in the King Country. Initially she experienced some problems in being accepted by the Kingitanga hierarchy because her part-English father, Te Tahuna Herangi, was not accepted as a suitable husband for King Tawhiao's daughter, Tiahuia. Te Puea's paternal grandfather, William Searancke, was in fact a very well-educated English surveyor rather than a German as later Pakeha critics claimed. Te Puea inherited her ability and intelligence from him as well as from her Kingitanga side. Eventually Tawhiao accepted his granddaughter into the family, and Tawhiao's successor, King Mahuta, picked her out as the most able member of her generation. Te Puea got her chance to prove her uncle right in when in 1911 she backed his campaign to replace Henare Kaihau as MP for the western Maori seat with the American-educated doctor Maui Pomare. Then, during the First World War, she opposed recruitment of Tainui men for military service. She strengthened her opposition by reviving the Pai Mairire religion so beloved of Tawhiao and adopted an essentially pacifist stance. Te Puea added further to her growing *mana* when she worked tirelessly, without the slightest thought for her own safety, throughout the devastating influenza pandemic of 1918–1919. Once the flu had passed, she set out to build a new *marae* at Ngaruawahia, known as Turangawaewae, as a focus of unity for her people. Much to the amazement of both Maori and European critics, she completed the structure by 1921 and moved on to develop farming to sustain her people's recovery from land loss and marginalization. She cooperated closely with both Apirana Ngata and Gordon Coates in pursuit of this goal and succeeded in bringing some prosperity to her people. A traveling cultural group known as Te Pou o Mangatawhiri helped raise money for improvements to the *marae* buildings. She also tried to bring greater unity to the Maori people by holding *hui* (large gatherings) with other tribes, but things turned sour in 1929 when Ngata's eldest son and wife died from dysentery while attending a *hui* to celebrate the opening of a great house known as Mahinarangi. Eventually, relations with Ngati Porou improved, and Te Puea began to accept some assistance from Peter Fraser and the Labor government in developing agricultural skills and providing more European-style education for her people. Te Puea also revived both canoe carving and racing but boycotted the Waitangi celebrations in 1940 in protest against the failure of the government to provide adequate compensation for the land confiscations of the 1860s. She also did not support recruitment for the Maori Battalion in the Second World War, and Tainui men did not serve in anything like the concentrations of other tribes. After

1945 Te Puea turned to developing her tribe's land further with the help of a £5,000 annual annuity from the Labor government and continued to try to revive such traditional activities as canoe racing. She won over Peter Fraser, as she had earlier won the support of Coates, and achieved much for her people. She remained a tough leader to the end, banning both smoking and alcohol from her *marae,* and she never stopped working seven day weeks until her death. Te Puea led by example and restored hope for a people decimated by war, poverty, and disease. Her efforts rank with those of the greatest New Zealand leaders, although she would never have liked the title of Princess imposed upon her by Europeans ignorant of Maori social organization. She died fully aware that many changes remained to be made before Maori could achieve any kind of meaningful partnership with Pakeha.

Te Rauparaha (?–1849). Tribal leader, warrior, builder of alliances. This astute but minor Ngati Toa chief completely changed the Maori settlement patterns of the North Island during a major migration he led in the 1820s. His small tribe, based on the coast at Kawhia, could no longer withstand constant attack by larger inland tribes, so Te Rauparaha led his entire tribe south to escape constant harassment. He also took some of his Ngati Raukawa relations with him, along with Ati Awa allies he made in Taranaki. After overrunning several small tribes including Muaupoko and Rangitane, he eventually settled at Kapiti Island on the southwestern corner of the North Island. Ngati Raukawa, meantime, settled at Otaki, and Ati Awa at Waikanae. Te Rauparaha made a good living from whaling and supplying other whalers with flax but soon began to raid the South Island. In 1830 he hid in the hold of a ship captained by a European and kidnapped and killed the leading Ngai Tahu chief, Te Maiharanui. Major conflict with Ngai Tahu ensued over the next few years, with Ngati Toa winning major victories until Ngai Tahu turned things around in 1836, when they wiped out the last Ngati Toa raiding party. Thereafter, an uneasy peace ensued. Te Rauparaha next turned his attention to the top of the South Island. Even though he signed the Treaty of Waitangi, he protested British efforts to take his land around the Wairau River in Marlborough. An attempted arrest turned sour in 1843, and Te Rauparaha and his more warlike nephew, Te Rangihaeata, killed some 22 settlers in revenge for the death of Te Rangihaeata's wife. Te Rauparaha thereafter retreated to Kapiti, only to be kidnapped by Governor Grey in 1848. After living under house arrest in Auckland, he returned with his *mana,* or authority, in tatters, and he died in 1849. His cunning and unerring survival instinct nevertheless changed the balance of power within the Maori world, slowed the European settlement of the southern North Island, and earned the undying distrust of Ngai Tahu.

Te Whiti O Rongomai (?–1907). Tribal leader, prophet, and pacifist. The leader of pacifist resistance in Taranaki, Te Whiti o Rongomai infuriated the colonial government but inspired his followers to resist British domination down to his death in 1907. The son of a high-born Ati Awa chief, he was deeply influenced by the Lutheran missionary Johann Riemenschneider as a young man. During the early 1860s he also fell under the influence of the prophet Te Ua Haumene. Then from the mid-1860s he worked with his cousin Tohu Kakahi to establish a viable community at Parihaka near New Plymouth. After the failure of Titokowaru's military resistance in 1869, Te Whiti counseled peace and began to use the techniques of nonviolent resistance long before Mahatma Gandhi did. In particular, his followers ploughed up confiscated land that they believed had been wrongly taken by the settler government. In a shameful incident on November 5, 1881, John Bryce invaded the peaceful community with 1,589 armed men. Te Whiti, Tohu, and many followers were sentenced without proper trial and sent to jails in the South Island. Upon their return in 1883 the leaders modernized Parihaka by overhauling its sanitation systems, building new villa-style houses, and even introducing electric lighting. Further periodic arrests followed, along with stints in prison in 1886 and 1897. Each time Te Whiti returned he upgraded the settlement, which irritated the settler government even more. In 1895 Premier Seddon visited but made the mistake of trying to produce more elaborate metaphors than this master orator. Seddon retreated in humiliation. Unfortunately, Te Whiti and Tohu fell out in the 1890s, and two divisive factions soon undermined the effectiveness of this resistance. After Te Whiti's and Tohu's deaths in 1907, the settlement largely collapsed, but the charismatic prophet left behind an example that has inspired Maori resisters ever since.

Vogel, Julius (1835–1899). Journalist, entrepreneur, politician. Vogel was man of grand visions who tried to expand the New Zealand economy spectacularly in the 1870s. He left his family of Jewish merchants in London after brief training as a mining engineer to try his luck in the Victorian gold rushes in Australia in 1852. After failing as a retailer and assayer he turned to journalism as a means of earning a livelihood. He moved on to Dunedin in 1861, where he set up New Zealand's first daily newspaper, the *Otago Daily Times,* which survives to this day. An ambitious and able man, he soon made his mark in politics, working his way up through the Otago Provincial Council and service as an MP for the Goldfields electorate to become colonial treasurer in 1869. In this role he promoted a large loan of £10 million (which eventually rose to £20 million) to build infrastructure and bring in large numbers of immigrants. Vogel believed that such large-scale expenditure was required to develop the colony and end any hope of further Maori resistance. The policy proved popular, and he won the premiership between 1873 and 1876. He was subsequently blamed for New Zealand's problems during the depression of the 1880s, but the colony would have stagnated without his daring loan. Vogel also led the move to abolish the provincial system in 1876 because he found it much easier to raise funds on the London market as a larger entity called New Zealand rather than as a little-known province. After 1876 he served until 1880 as agent-general (forerunner of the high commissioner) in London and became embroiled in many speculative money-making ventures. One known as the New Zealand Agricultural Company went so badly that he returned to politics to save it and served as colonial treasurer under Robert Stout between 1884 and 1887. Thereafter he faded into obscurity and returned to England. He remained a devoted supporter of both the British Empire and women's suffrage. He even wrote a novel in 1889 entitled *Anno Domini 2000; or Woman's Destiny,* in which he imagined what the world would be like when women got the vote in the twenty-first century! He also tried to conserve forests against chopping and burning in 1874, but largely failed as a conservationist.

Wakefield, Edward Gibbon (1796–1862). Advocate of colonization, political economist, lobbyist, promoter. Wakefield was the somewhat erratic dreamer and schemer who first promoted New Zealand as an ideal site for an experiment in colonization. The difficult eldest child of a radical family, Edward ended up eloping with an underage heiress, Eliza Pattle, in 1816. After she died tragically in childbirth in 1820, he tried marrying up again to an underage heiress in 1826. Ellen Turner's family objected, and Wakefield spent three years in Newgate Prison, dreaming about how colonization might be carried out more successfully than in Australia or America. His "Letter from Sydney" published in 1829 outlined his schemes. In this and larger works, such as *England and America* (1833), he argued that the wild frontier of America and Australia could be avoided if the price of land was set sufficiently high to debar laborers from immediately becoming landowners. Wakefield also insisted that migrants be carefully chosen and that women and children should equal adult male immigrants. Civilization rather than crudity would thereby be encouraged. His dubious behavior scared off officialdom, and after his unsuccessful attempt at colonizing South Australia between 1834 and 1836 the Colonial Office refused a charter to settle New Zealand. Wakefield then converted the association into a private company and sent his brother and son off to buy land in late 1839. Settlements following his principles were founded at Wellington (1840), Wanganui and New Plymouth (1841), Nelson (1842), Otago (1848), and Canterbury (1850). Only Canterbury really flourished because it attracted capital and wealthier immigrants. A chronic shortage of capital undermined the other settlements, as did absentee ownership and inadequate preparation. Wakefield came to live in New Zealand in 1853, only to see extensive sheep raising replace his favored wheat farming as the engine of the colonial economy. Settlers now scattered far and wide rather than concentrating in civilized towns as Wakefield had hoped. Ill health soon sidelined his influence, and he died a bitterly disappointed man in 1862. Little remains of his experiments other than the deep-seated New Zealand belief that the free settlers who migrated to these struggling settlements came from vastly superior stock than did the convicts who settled Australia.

Williams, Henry (1792–1867). Missionary leader, author of the Treaty of Waitangi. Henry Williams was probably the most important of the missionaries, even though he was not an expert linguist like his younger brother William. After his arrival in 1823, this Church Missionary Society (Church of England) leader set out to break dependency on the warlord Hongi Hika. He succeeded by shifting emphasis toward civilizing Maori before attempting to Christianize them. Slowly he began to win their support. The tough former naval midshipman won the respect of Maori and played a key role in drafting the Treaty of Waitangi. Many chiefs signed only because of his advocacy. This man of modest, lower-middle-class origins never got on well with the new bishop, the aristocratic George Augustus Selwyn, who arrived in 1842. Soon after, Williams also fell out with Governor George Grey, who arrived in 1845. This loss of support ended any hope Williams had of building some kind of theocracy. William's 11 children, for whom he gained substantial landholdings, enabled this large family to become something of a dynasty that exercised an important influence in New Zealand life into the twentieth century as clerics, politicians, and farmers.

Wiremu Tamihana Tarapipi Te Waharoa (1805?–1866). Tribal leader, warrior, pan tribalist, intellectual. King maker, Christian, and man of principle, Wiremu Tamihana remains one of the most remarkable individuals in New Zealand history. As the second son of the leading Ngati Haua (one of the Waikato tribes and part of the Tainui Confederation) chief Te Waharoa, Tamihana held considerable inherited *mana*. He built on his inherited leadership rights by acting as the key player in crowning Te Wherowhero as the first Maori king in 1858. Always a reluctant warrior who stopped the constant raiding of nearby enemy tribes from the mid-1830s, Wiremu converted to Christianity in 1839. He spent the 1840s developing farming in the Matatmata district and built schools, flour mills, and churches. During the 1850s he promoted the King Movement to maintain Maori control over their land and destiny. He also believed that Maori had to implement their own variant of law as promised under clause 71 of the 1852 constitution because European law seemed unable to stop Maori killing Maori. He also set up a newspaper, *Te Hokioi e Rere Atu Na*, to communicate the Kingite perspective to other Maori and worked hard to cement relations with neighboring Ngati Maniopoto. Wiremu brokered a peace to end the Taranaki war on April 8, 1861, and always argued that it was the settler government and the governors who had breached the treaty rather than the King Movement. He tried hard to keep the peace but was outmaneuvered by wily Governor Grey and other settlers politicians who refused to listen to his reasoned arguments. After assisting Maori resistance during the wars, Tamihana again secured a peace on May 27, 1865. His people's lands were ravaged by confiscation, and he protested against both this injustice and the label of rebel imposed upon his people. No reparation occurred until 1995, but Wiremu Tamihana started the long fight for redress by always working to secure full partnership with the new settler government.

Glossary: Maori Names and Terms

Ahi ka. Literally, keeping the fires burning on the land; a Maori system of claiming rights to land through regular reoccupation.

Ariki. Paramount chief.

Atua. Spirit.

Haka. Chant of defiance accompanied by warlike dance.

Hapu. Group of extended families or clan.

Harakeke. New Zealand flax *(Phormium tenax).*

Hine-ahu-one. First woman created out of the earth.

Iwi. Tribe.

Kahanganui. Parliament or great council.

Kahikatea. Tall, soft-wooded native tree of the podocarp family *(Dacrycarpus dacrydioides),* which dominated the wetlands but was heavily milled to make butter boxes, among other things.

Kainga. Village, often of a single *hapu.*

Karakia. Prayer or incantation.

Kaumatua. Elder, family head.

Kauri. A native conifer tree *(Agathis australis)*, among the largest in the world, which produces excellent timber suitable for both house building and boat building and resin that can be used in industrial processes such as varnish manufacture.

Kawanatanga. Governance.

Kereru. Native pigeon *(Hemiphaga novaeseelandiae)*.

Kingitanga. Maori king movement.

Kotahitanga. Unity.

Kowhai. Native tree (*Sophora* spp.) famous for its yellow flower.

Kumara. Sweet potato brought to New Zealand from Polynesia *(Ipomoea batatas)*.

Mahoe. Small native tree *(Melicytus ramiflorus)*.

Makutu. Sorcery.

Mana. Prestige and status reflected in genealogy, attachment to place and achievement, generosity, caregiving or compassion.

Mana whenua. Right of an *iwi, hapu,* or *whanau* to claim land through genealogy, occupation and use, or conquest.

Manuka. Shrub with small leaves and usually white flowers, though colored forms are widely cultivated *(Leptospermum scoparium)*.

Mapou (pronounced with a long *a*) or **Matipo.** Small native tree sometimes cultivated for its reddish stems and foliage *(Myrsine australis)*.

Marae. Open space in front of meeting house, used for assembly.

Matai or **black pine.** A native tree of the podocarp family *(Prumnopitys taxifolia)*.

Mauri. Life force or vital essence of an individual, species, or place.

Miro. A native tree of the podocarp family *(Prumnopitys ferruginea)*.

Moa. Extinct native ratites (flightless birds) ranging from small to even larger than modern-day ostrich and emu (*Dinornithiformes* spp.).

Moriori. Separate tribe of Maori who lived on the Chatham Islands from the fifteenth century, rather than an earlier non-Polynesian stratum of people in New Zealand as imagined by the early twentieth-century ethnographers Percy Smith and Elsdon Best.

Muriwhenua. Northern area of North Auckland, with which the Rarawa, Te Aupouri, Ngati Kahu, Ngati Kuri, and Ngati Takoto tribes are associated.

Ngati Toa. *Iwi* (tribe) from the Kawhia area that migrated south to Kapiti Island and Otaki in the 1820s under the leadership of the chief Te Rauparaha, and also ventured into the north of the South Island in the early 1830s and clashed with the major South Island tribe of Ngai Tahu.

Nikau. New Zealand palm tree *(Rhopalostylis sapida),* literally frond on coconut palm tree.

Pa. A fortified place.

Paepae. Special place; horizontal beam on the *marae* from which speeches are made.

Pai marire. Good and peaceful religion founded in the early 1860s by Te Ua Haumene in Taranaki and revived by Princess Te Puea of Tainui and the Kingitanga in the 1920s.

Pakeha. Person of non-Maori descent who arrived after Maori, usually but not always European.

Papatuanuku. Earth mother.

Paua. Black-lipped, iridescent-green, univalve shellfish (*Haliotis* spp.).

Poi. A dance performed with poi, that is, a light ball on a string.

Rahui. Prohibition on harvesting of food supplies, normally enforced in the interests of resource management and conservation.

Rangatiratanga. Full, chiefly authority.

Ranginui. Sky father.

Rimu or **red pine.** Native podocarp tree *(Dacrydium cupressinum),* which produces top-quality timber ideally suited to furniture making.

Rohe. Territorial area claimed by an *iwi, hapu,* or *whanau,* including all resource rights.

Ruaumoko. God of earthquakes and volcanoes.

Tane mahuta. God of the forest.

Tangaroa. God of the sea.

Tangata whenua. People of the land; in other words, all Maori rather than the *iwi* or *hapu* occupying a *rohe,* who are known as *manawhenua.*

Tangi. Death ceremonial; cry or lament.

Taniwha. Water monster; often a guardian.

Tapu. Under restriction (sacred). Once a food resource, such as an eel weir or a tree housing nesting birds, was declared *tapu,* it could not be touched other than by especially designated persons. More commonly declared under a *rahui*.

Taro. Edible root plant (*Colocasia* spp.) brought from Polynesia and grown in the northern parts of the North Island.

Tawa. Native tree *(Beilschmiedia tawa)*.

Täwhirimatea. God of wind and atmospheric events.

Te Ao. The world of light.

Te Hiku o Te Ika. The tail of the fish of Maui or North Island.

Te Ika a Maui. The fish of the demi-god Maui or North Island.

Te Po. Primeval darkness before creation.

Ti. Native cabbage tree *(Cordyline australis);* an imported variant (*Cordyline terminalis*) was cultivated along with *Cordyline australis*.

Tiki. Stylized human image made from wood, stone, or bone.

Toetoe. Robust New Zealand tussock grass (*Cortaderia* spp.), closely related to the pampas grasses of South America.

Tohunga. Expert, specialist (in canoe building, memorizing *whakapapa*, poet, historian), often religious or seerlike with a capacity to see into the future.

Totara. Tall native podocarp trees *(Podocarpus totara* and *P. hallii)* having resistant wood, prized for carving, and once used for fence posts.

Tuatara. Ancient and long-lived native lizard *(Sphenodon punctatus)*.

Tui. Native bird *(Prosthemadera novaeseelandiae)*.

Tupuna. Ancestors.

Tutu. Native grass poisonous to stock *(Coriaria arborea)*.

Utu. Redressing an imbalance in relationships to maintain harmony, rather than simple revenge as claimed by some Pakeha.

Waitaha. Early South Island tribe.

Waka. Canoe, or a group of tribes based on common descent from occupants of one of the early migratory canoes.

Weka. Small, flightless native bird (*Gallirallus* spp.).

Whakapapa. Genealogy.

Whanau. Extended family.

Whanaungatanga. The primacy of kinship bonds in determining action and in settling rights and status.

Whare. House.

Bibliographic Essay

There are several useful general histories of New Zealand including Keith Sinclair, *A History of New Zealand* (Auckland, 1990), first published in 1959, provides a confident, nationalist, and masculinist perspective. James Belich's two volumes, *Making Peoples* and *Paradise Reforged* (Auckland, 1996 and 2001), are lively, provocative, and up-to-date. Geoffrey Rice, ed., *The Oxford History of New Zealand* 2nd ed. (Auckland, 1992), is a scholarly and comprehensive multiauthor volume. Tom Brooking with Paul Enright, *Milestones: Turning Points in New Zealand History,* 2nd ed. (Palmerston North, 1999), is heavily illustrated and geared toward high school seniors. Different perspectives can also be gained from Eric Pawson and Tom Brooking, eds., *Environmental Histories of New Zealand* (Melbourne, 2002), and Malcolm McKinnon, ed., *The Historical Atlas of New Zealand* (Wellington, 1997). For military history Ian McGibbon, ed., *The Oxford Companion to New Zealand Military History* (Auckland, 2000), is indispensable. Michael King's and Erik Olssen's new general histories are awaited with keen anticipation. The Web site of the History Group of the Ministry of Culture and Heritage also will enable students to keep up with current developments in New Zealand historical writing; see http://www.nzhistory.net.nz.

For information on people see the four volumes of the *Dictionary of New Zealand Biography,* Vol. 1 edited by W. H. Oliver and the rest edited by

Claudia Orange Wellington (Bridget Williams Books/Department of Internal Affairs, 1990, 1993, 1996, 1998, and 2000). On New Zealand literature see Terry Sturm, ed., *The Oxford History of New Zealand Literature in English* (Auckland, 1991), 2nd ed. 1998; and Nelson Wattie and Roger Robinson, eds., *The Oxford Companion to New Zealand Literature* (Auckland; 1998). The best introduction to painting remains Gordon Brown and Hamish Keith, *An Introduction to New Zealand Painting, 1839–1967* (Auckland, 1969).

On pre-European New Zealand see Atholl Anderson, "A Fragile Plenty: Pre-European Maori and the New Zealand Environment" in *Environmental Histories of New Zealand*, ed. E. Pawson and T. Brooking, 35–51, and Janet Davidson, *The Prehistory of New Zealand* (Auckland, 1984) for archaeological accounts. David R. Simmons, *The Great New Zealand Myth* (Wellington, 1976), contains a fascinating examination of the story of the Great Fleet myth. James Belich, *Making Peoples: A History of the New Zealanders from Polynesian Settlement to the End of the Nineteenth Century* (Auckland, 1996), contains easily the fullest synthesis on the various theories concerning pre-European New Zealand yet published. Margaret Orbell, *The Illustrated Encyclopedia of Maori Myth and Legend* (Christchurch, 1995) provides an up-to-date if somewhat universalized coverage of the world of Maori myth and story. Te Rangi Hiroa (Sir Peter Buck), *Vikings of the Sunrise* (Philadelphia, 1938), and his *The Coming of the Maori* (Wellington, 1949) remain the classic studies. On Maori cultural beliefs and conceptions see Cleve Barlow, *Tikanga Whakaaro: Key Concepts in Maori Culture* (Auckland, 1991), and for the extraordinary story of European explanations of Maori origins see Kerry Howe, *The Quest for Origins: Who Discovered and Settled New Zealand and the Pacific Islands* (Auckland, 2002).

On exploration and discovery see J. C. Beaglehole, *The Exploration of the Pacific* (London, 1966), which is classic and indispensable. Andrew Sharp, *The Voyages of Abel Janszoon Tasman* (Oxford, 1968), and Oliver E. Allan, *The Seafarers: The Pacific Navigators* (Alexander, VA, 1980) are helpful, and J. E. Herries, ed., *Abel Janszoon Tasman's Journal* (Los Angeles, 1965), gives something of the feel of Tasman's voyage, while Anne Salmond, *Two Worlds: First Meetings between Maori and Europeans, 1642–1772* (Auckland, 1991), establishes the cultural contexts in which these early encounters took place and is essential reading on early culture contact. J. C. Beaglehole, *The Life of Captain James Cook* (Stanford, 1974), remains the authoritative biography on the master mariner, and J. C. Beaglehole, ed., *The Journals of Captain James Cook on His Voyages of Discovery* (Cambridge, 1955–69), are indispensable. Vol. I, *The Voyage of the Endeavour 1768–1771*, is particularly relevant to New Zealand. Anne Salmond, *Between Worlds:*

Early Exchanges between Maori and Europeans, 1773–1815 (Auckland, 1997), unpacks this encounter and that of other European explorers in interesting ways.

On sealing and whaling see A. Charles and Neil C. Begg, *The World of John Boultlbee, Including an Account of Sealing in Australia and New Zealand* (Christchurch, 1979); Jim McAloon, "Resource Frontiers, Environment and Settler Capitalism," in *Environmental Histories of New Zealand*, ed. Pawson and Brooking, 52–68; and Harry Morton, *The Whale's Wake* (Dunedin, 1982).

There are many useful articles on missionaries in the *New Zealand Journal of History* and several major theses, but there is no one comprehensive study. The most helpful books are Judith Binney, *The Legacy of Guilt: A Life of Thomas Kendall* (Auckland, 1968), and J.M.R. Owens, *Prophets in the Wilderness: The Wesleyan Mission to New Zealand, 1819–27* (Auckland, 1974). Warren E. Limbrick, ed., *Bishop Selwyn in New Zealand 1841–68* (Palmerston North, 1983), also contains some useful essays.

On the musket wars see Jeffrey Sissons, Wiremu Wi Hongi, and Pat Hohepa, *The Puriri Trees Are Laughing: A: Political History of Nga Puhi in the Inland Bay of Islands* (Auckland, 1987), for a Nga Puhi perspective. Ormond Wilson, *From Hongi Hika to Hone Heke: A Quarter Century of Upheaval* (Dunedin, 1985), and G. S. Parsonson, "Hong Hika," *Historical News*, October 1981, provide lively overviews. Judy Corballis, *Tapu*, is a faction novel with fresh insights into this story, and Ron Crosby, *The Musket Wars: A History of Inter-Iwi Conflict 1806–1845* (Auckland, 1999), provides the most comprehensive overview of these disruptive years. A new book is Angela Ballara, *Taua: "Musket Wars," "Land Wars" on Tikanga? War in Maori Society in the Early Nineteenth Century* (Auckland, 2003), provides an updated overview.

On Te Rauparaha see Patricia Burns, *Te Rauparaha: A New Perspective* (Wellington, 1980), for an orthodox biography, and Ray Grover, *Cork of War: Ngati Toa and the British Mission. A Historical Narrative* (Dunedin, 1982), for an interesting faction novel. Harry Evison, *Te Wai Pounamu the Green Stone Island: A History of the Southern Maori during the European Colonisation of New Zealand* (Christchurch, 1993), provides a Ngai Tahu corrective.

There is now a small industry in books relating to the Treaty of Waitangi and the British annexation of New Zealand, but the most useful book on annexation remains Peter Adams, *Fatal Necessity: British Intervention in New Zealand 1830–1847* (Auckland, 1977). T. Lindsay Buick, *The Treaty of Waitangi* (London: Thomas Avery & Sons, 1914) still contains the best account of the story of the treaty. Claudia Orange, *The Treaty of Waitangi*

(Wellington, 1987), is the best single source. D. F. McKenzie, *Oral Culture, Literacy and Print in Early New Zealand: the Treaty of Waitangi* (Wellington, 1985), is a provocative essay. Ruth Ross, "Te Tiriti and Waitangi: Texts and Translations," *New Zealand Journal of History* 6, no. 2 (1972): 129–57, stands as a landmark revisionist piece. Alan Ward, *A Show of Justice: Racial "Amalgamation" in Nineteenth Century New Zealand* (Auckland, 1973, 2nd ed. 1994), and *An Unsettled History: Treaty Claims in New Zealand Today* (Wellington, 1999), provide an important context, as does Ian Wards, *The Shadow of the Land: A Study of British Policy and Racial Conflict in New Zealand, 1832–1852* (Wellington, 1968).

The most helpful of the newer books are I. H. Kawharu, ed., *Waitangi: Maori and Pakeha Perspectives on the Treaty of Waitangi* (Auckland, 1989), and William Renwick, ed., *Sovereignty and Indigenous Rights: The Treaty of Waitangi in International Context* (Wellington, 1991). W. H. Oliver, in *Histories, Power and Loss: Uses of the Past, a New Zealand Commentary,* ed. Andrew Sharp and Paul McHugh, 9–30 (Wellington, 2001), is a salutary reminder of the dangers of letting current political agendas distort good historical practice.

F. E. Maning, *Old New Zealand: A Tale of the Good Old Times* (Auckland, 1973), remains a classic account by a contemporary. Michael King, *Moriori: A People Rediscovered* (Auckland, 1989), tells the story of a long-forgotten episode in our history—the conquest of Moriori by the northern sections of Ati Awa from Taranaki.

Until very recently there was no good biography of Edward Gibbon Wakefield, nor a modern study of the New Zealand Company but Philip Temple, *A Sort of Conscience: The Wakefields* (Auckland, 2002), makes up for that lack, as does *Edward Gibbon Wakefield and the Colonial Dream: A Reconsideration* (Wellington, 1997). Erik Olssen, "Mr Wakefield and New Zealand as an Experiment in Post-Enlightenment Experimental Practice," *New Zealand Journal of History* 31, no. 2 (1997): 197–218, is a most important revisionist article that helps reinstate Wakefield to some extent. John Miller, *Early Victorian New Zealand: A Study of Racial Tension and Social Attitudes, 1839–1852* (London, 1958), and Michael Turnbull, *The New Zealand Bubble: The Wakefield Theory in Practice* (Wellington, 1959), remain useful pieces of earlier debunking.

On the Wakefield settlements see David Hamer and Roberta Nicholls, eds., *The Making of Wellington 1800–1914* (Wellington, 1990); Miller, *Early Victorian New Zealand,* for Wellington and Wanganui; and E. J. Wakefield, *Adventure in New Zealand, from 1839–1844: With Some Account of the Beginning of the British Colonization of the Islands,* 2 vols. (London, 1845), for a lively contemporary account. On Nelson see Ruth Allan, *Nelson: A History of Early Settlement* (Wellington, 1965), and Jim McAloon, *Nelson: A Regional History* (Nelson, 1997). On Otago see Tom Brooking, *And Captain of Their Souls: An Interpretative Essay upon the Life and Times of Captain William Cargill* (Dunedin, 1984), A. H. McLintock, *The History of Otago. The Origins and Growth of a Wakefield Class Settlement* (Dunedin, 1949), and Erik Olssen, *A History of Otago* (Dunedin, 1984). On Canterbury see James Hight and C. R. Straubel, eds., *A History of Canterbury, Vol. 1, to 1854* (Christchurch, 1957), and John Cookson and Graeme Dunstall, eds., *Southern Capital: Christchurch towards a City Biography* (Christchurch, 2000).

On early Auckland see Russell Stone, *Young Logan Campbell* (Auckland, 1982), and *Tamaki-makau-rau: The Sale of Auckland* (Auckland, 2002); and G. W. A. Bush, *Decently and in Order: The Government of the City of Auckland 1840–1971* (Auckland, 1970).

On pastoralism see Steven Eldred-Grigg, *A Southern Gentry: New Zealanders Who Inherited the Earth* (Wellington, 1980); A. G. Bagnall, *Wairarapa: An Historical Excursion* (Masterton, 1976); and Peter Holland, Kevin O'Connor, and Alex Wearing, "Remaking the Grasslands of the Open Country," in *Environmental Histories of New Zealand*, ed. Pawson and Brooking, 69–83.

On early political and constitutional developments see Raewyn Dalziel, "The Politics of Settlement," in *The Oxford History of New Zealand*, 2nd ed., ed. G. Rice, 87–111 (Auckland, 1992) and D. G. Herron, "Provincialism and Centralism, 1853–1858," in *Studies of a Small Democracy: Essays in Honour of Willis Airey*, ed. R. M. Chapman and Keith Sinclair (Auckland, 1963). Ned Bohan, *Edward Stafford: New Zealand's First Statesman* (Christchurch, 1994), is also helpful on this period.

To understand how the South Island was alienated for so little money see Harry Evison's magisterial study, *Te Wai Pounamu*.

The gold rushes await a new synthesis, but meantime consult the plates in the *Historical Atlas of New Zealand* and see Philip Ross May, *The West Coast Goldrushes* (Christchurch, 1962); Erik Olssen, *A History of Otago*, Erik Olssen and Tom Field, *Relics of the Goldfields* (Dunedin, 1973); J.H.M. Salmon, *A History of Goldmining in New Zealand* (Wellington, 1963); and Terry Hearn, "Mining the Quarry" in *Environmental Histories of New Zealand*, ed. Pawson and Brooking, 84–99.

The most important recent work on the New Zealand Wars/Wars of Rangatiratanga is James Belich, *The New Zealand Wars and the Victorian Interpretation of Racial Conflict* (Auckland, 1986). James Cowan's two-volume *The New Zealand Wars: A History of the Maori Campaigns and the Pioneering Period* (Wellington, 1922–23), reissued in 1986, contains much useful information on the military side of the conflict. Also see B. J. Dalton, *War and Politics in New Zealand 1855–1870* (Sydney, 1967), and Alan Ward, *A Show of Justice*.

For the causes of the Taranaki wars see Keith Sinclair, *The Origins of the Maori Wars* (Wellington, 1957). James Belich, *I Shall Not Die: Titokowaru's War New Zealand, 1868–69* (Wellington, 1989), provides fascinating insights into the last phases of the wars, as does Maurice Shadbolt's novel, *Monday's Warriors* (Auckland, 1990).

On the consequences of the wars see Judith Binney, *Redemption Songs: Te Kooti Arikirangi te Turuki* (Auckland, 1995)—probably the most sophisticated book yet published on New Zealand history, which forces readers to rethink Maori history. Her essays in J. Binney, J. Bassett, and E. Olssen, *The People and the Land Te Tangata me Te Whenua: An Illustrated History of New Zealand 1820–1920* (Wellington, 1990), are equally valuable, as is Ann Parsonson's chapter "The Pursuit of Mana" in *The Oxford History of New Zealand*, ed. W. H. Oliver and B. R. Williams, 140–67 (Wellington, 1981).

The most important books on the 1870s are Rollo Arnold, *The Farthest Promised Land: English Villagers, New Zealand Immigrants of the 1870s* (Wellington, 1981), and Raewyn Dalziel, *Julius Vogel Business Politician* (Auckland, 1986). On the economic side compare J. B. Condliffe, *New Zealand in the Making: A Study of Economic and Social Development*, 2nd ed. (London: Allen & Unwin, 1959), and G. R. Hawke, *The Making of New Zealand: An Economic History* (Cambridge, 1985). Jim McAloon, *No Idle Rich: The Wealthy in Otago and Canterbury 1840–1914* (Dunedin, 2002), suggests that most wealthy colonists came from middle-class rather than gentry backgrounds and made their fortunes from hard work.

Miles Fairburn, *The Ideal Society and Its Enemies: The Foundations of Modern New Zealand Society, 1850–1900* (Auckland University Press, 1989), challenges cozy notions of pioneer community in a most provocative fashion. Rollo Arnold, *New Zealand's Burning: The Settlers' World in the Mid-1880s* (Wellington, 1994), counters many of Fairburn's arguments but concedes that colonial New Zealand was a raw and rather dangerous place.

Geoff Park, *Nga Uru Ora (The Groves of Life): History and Ecology in a New Zealand Landscape* (Wellington, 1995), provides a vivid account of the impact of bush-clearing and swamp-draining on the New Zealand environment, as does his essay in *Environmental Histories of New Zealand*, ed. Pawson and Brooking, 151–68.

On refrigeration and the climb out of depression see Belich, *Paradise Reforged;* Martine E. Cuff, *Totara Estate: Centenary of the Frozen Meat Industry* (Wellington, 1982); Kenneth Cumberland, *Landmarks* (New South Wales, 1981); and Donald Denoon, *Settler Capitalism: The Dynamics of Dependent*

Development in the Southern Hemisphere (Oxford, 1983), for the broader perspective. Mervyn Palmer, "William Soltau Davidson: A Pioneer of New Zealand Estate Management," *New Zealand Journal of History* 7, no. 2 (1973): 148–64, is very useful on the input of big business. Condliffe and Hawke are also helpful, as is Eric Warr, *Bushburn to Butter: A Journey in Words and Pictures* (Butterworths, 1988).

The most important work on sweating and Liberal labor reform remains locked away in the university theses, but these findings are summarized in Erik Olssen, *A History of Otago,* and Julia Millen, *Colonial Tears and Sweat* (Wellington, 1984). Keith Sinclair, *William Pember Reeves: New Zealand Fabian* (Oxford, 1965), is also indispensable as is W. P. Reeves, *State Experiments Australia and New Zealand in Two Volumes* (Melbourne, 1968; first published 1902).

Several books have also appeared on the Liberal era that add much on the ideas, politics, land, labor and welfare reforms, and social history of the period. The most helpful are David Hamer, *The New Zealand Liberals: The Years of Power, 1891–1912* (Auckland, 1989); Margaret Tennant, *Paupers and Providers: Charitable Aid in New Zealand* (Wellington, 1989); Ross Galbreath, *The Reluctant Conservationist: Walter Buller* (Wellington, 1989); Kerry Howe, *Singer in a Songless Land: A Life of Edward Tregear* (Auckland, 1991); Michael Bassett, *Sir Joseph Ward: A Political Biography* (Auckland, 1993); Miles Fairburn, *Nearly Out of Heart and Hope: The Puzzle of a Colonial Labourer's Diary* (Auckland, 1995); Jean Garner, *On His Own Merit: Sir John Hall—Pioneer, Pastoralist and Premier* (Christchurch, 1995); Tom Brooking, *Lands for the People? The Highland Clearances and the Colonization of New Zealand. A Biography of John McKenzie,* (Dunedin, 1996); and David Thomson, *A World without Welfare: New Zealand's Colonial Experiment* (Auckland, 1998).

The most important book on women and the vote remains Patricia Grimshaw, *Woman's Suffrage in New Zealand* (Auckland, 1972). Also useful are R Bunkle and B. Hughes, eds., *Women in New Zealand Society* (Auckland, 1980), Reeves, *State Experiments,* and Andre Siegfried, *Democracy in New Zealand,* trans. by E. V. Burns, with an introduction by William Downie Stewart and David Hamer (Wellington, 1982, first published 1904). Betty Holt, ed., *Women in Council: A History of the National Council of Women of New Zealand* (Wellington, 1980), is helpful for later developments. W. B. Sutch, *Women with a Cause* (Wellington, 1973), adds more detail. Margaret Lovell-Smith, *The Woman Question: Writings by Women Who Won the Vote* (Auckland, 1993), is a useful collection of contemporary opinion, while Charlotte Macdonald, ed., *The Vote, the Pill and the Demon Drink: A History of Feminist Writing in New Zealand, 1869–1993* (Wellington,

1993), and Charlotte Macdonald and Francis Porter, eds., *My Hand Will Write What My Heart Dictates: The Unsettled Lives of Women in Nineteenth Century New Zealand* (Auckland, 1996), constitute rich collections of women's views on a host of subjects. Caroline Daley, *Girls and Women, Men and Boys: Gender in Taradale 1886–1930* (Auckland, 1999), is the best study of gender relations in this period.

Dorothy Page, *The National Council of Women: A Centennial History* (Auckland, 1996), provides an up-to-date and balanced account of this important organization, and Anne Else, ed., *Women Together: A History of Women's Organisations in New Zealand* (Wellington, 1993), is an indispensable source of information on women's organizations. Sandra Coney, *Standing in the Sunshine: A History of Women in New Zealand since They Won the Vote* (Auckland, 1993), is a lively popular history of New Zealand women since 1893. Caroline Daley and Melanie Nolan, *Suffrage and Beyond: International Feminist Perspectives* (Auckland, 1994), provides a less celebratory examination of this intriguing phenomenon.

The most important work on prewar industrial militancy is locked away in articles and papers by Erik Olssen and an MA thesis by P. J. Gibbons. Olssen's *The Red Feds: Revolutionary Industrial Unionism and the New Zealand Federation of Labour, 1908–1913* (Auckland, 1988), made much of this material more accessible. His *Building the New World: Work, Politics, and Society in Caversham, 1880s-1920s* (Auckland, 1995), is indispensable for understanding the broader context in which Labor's challenge emerged. P. J. Gibbons, "The Climate of Opinion," in *The Oxford History of New Zealand*, ed. W. H. Oliver and B. R. Williams, 302–32; Barry Gustafson, *Labour's Path to Political Independence: The Origins and Establishment of the New Zealand Labour Party, 1900–1919* (Auckland, 1980); R.J. O'Farrell, *Harry Holland Militant Socialist* (Canberra, 1964); and Len Richardson, *The Denniston Miners' Union: A Centennial History* (Westport, 1984), are also useful.

The posthumous publication of Jim Holt's study of the IC&A system, *Compulsory Arbitration in New Zealand: The First Forty Years*, edited and completed by Erik Olssen (Auckland, 1986), deepens our understanding of this event. Len Richardson, *Class, Coal and Community: The United Mineworkers of New Zealand, 1880–1960* (Auckland, 1995), and Richard S. Hill, *The Iron Hand in the Velvet Glove: The Modernisation of Policing in New Zealand 1886–1917* (Palmerston North, 1995), add detail on both industrial militancy and the development of the Labor Party.

On New Zealanders at Gallipoli see Ormond Burton, *The Silent Division* (Sydney, 1935); C. E. W. Bean, *The Official History of Australia in the War 1914–18: The Story of Anzac, Vol. I and Vol. 2* (Brisbane, 1981, first published 1921); Kit Denton, *Australians at War: Gallipoli. One Long Grave* (Sydney,

1986); Bill Gammage, *The Broken Years, Australian Soldiers in the Great War* (Canberra, 1974); Christopher Pugsley, *Gallipoli: The New Zealand Story* (Auckland, 1984); and Keith Sinclair, *A Destiny Apart, New Zealand's Search for National Identity* (Wellington, 1986).

Strangely, there is as yet no major study of New Zealand's participation on the western front. Most of this chapter has been based on war diaries of the New Zealand First Division and the First, Second and Third Brigades held in the War Archives series at National Archives, Colonel H. Stewart, *The Official History of New Zealand's Effort in the Great War. The New Zealand Division, Volume 2, France* (Wellington, 1921), and Ian McGibbon, *The Oxford Companion to New Zealand Military History*. Also see N. Boyack and Jane Tolerton, *In the Shadow of War* (Auckland, 1991), for soldiers' recollections. On Passchendaele see Glynn Harper, *Massacre at Passcendaele: The New Zealand Story* (Auckland, 2000). On the spring offensive in general see Martin Middlebrook, *The Kaiser's Battle 21 March 1918: The First Day of the German Offensive* (London, 1983). On New Zealand's part see Paul Enright, "Repelling the Hun," in *Milestones*, Tom Brooking with Paul Enright, 133–39, Glynn Harper, *Spring Offensive: New Zealand and the Second Battle of the Somme* (Auckland, 2003). Christopher Pugsley, *On the Fringe of Hell: New Zealanders and Military Discipline in the First World War* (Auckland, 1991), adds much about the practices and problems of the New Zealand Army. On Maori involvement see Christopher Pugsley, *Hokowhitu a Tu: The Maori Pioneer Battalion in the First World War* (Auckland, 1995).

The four major literary accounts of the First World War also tell us much about both soldier and civilian experience of the war: Burton's powerful and personal account, *The Silent Division;* John A. Lee's novel, *Civilian into Soldier* (Auckland, 1963, first published 1937); Robyn Hyde's novel based on the story of James Douglas Stark, *Passport to Hell*, edited and introduced by D.I.B. Smith (Auckland, 1986, first published 1936); and Archibald Baxter's compelling autobiography of his pacifist protest, *We Will Not Cease*, 2nd ed. (Christchurch, 1968, first published 1938).

On the home front and the conscription debate see Erik Olssen, "Waging War," in *The People and the Land*, ed. Binney, Bassett, and Olssen, 299–318; Paul Baker, *King and Country Call: New Zealanders, Conscription and the Great War* (Auckland, 1988); and Jock Phillips, *A Man's Country? The Image of the Pakeha Male: A History* (Auckland, 1987).

On internal Maori developments during the First World War see Judith Binney, Gillian Chaplin, and Craig Wallace, *Mihaia: The Prophet Rua Kenana and His Community at Maungapohatu* (Wellington, 1979); Judith Binney and Gillian Chaplin, *Nga Morehu: The Survivors* (Auckland, 1986); Peter Webster, *Rua and the Maori Millennium* (Wellington, 1979); Jeff Sissons, *Te*

Wai Mana: The Springs of Mana (Dunedin, 1992); Michael King, *Te Puea: A Biography* (Auckland, 1977); J. McLeod Henderson, *Ratana: The Man, the Church, the Political Movement* (Auckland, 1972); and Ranginui Walker, *He Tipua: The Life and Times of Sir Apirana Ngata* (Auckland, 2001). Walker's recent biography is also indispensable for Maori developments up to 1950.

On the influenza pandemic see Geoffrey Rice, *Black November: The 1918 Influenza Epidemic in New Zealand* (Wellington, 1988). Also see his article in the *New Zealand Journal of History* 13, no. 2 (1979): 109–137. R. M. Burdon, *The New Dominion. A Social and Political History of New Zealand 1918–1939* (Wellington, 1965), contains some useful information as does Linda Bryder, "The 1918 Influenza Epidemic in Auckland," MA (Auckland, 1981), summarized in *New Zealand Journal of History* 16, no. 2 (1982): 97–121.

There is no one detailed study of the 1920s, but Burdon, *The New Dominion*, is a useful introduction, as is R. M. Chapman and E. R Malone, *New Zealand in the Twenties: Social Change and Material Progress* (Auckland, 1969). Several political biographies contain much helpful information, especially Michael Bassett, *Coates of Kaipara* (Auckland, 1995). Part Three of the *Oxford History of New Zealand* is also helpful.

On the Depression the best single book for catching the feel and texture of the time is Tony Simpson, *The Sugarbag Years. An Oral History of the 1930s Depression in New Zealand* (Wellington, 1974). His *The Slump* (Auckland, 1992) adds more detail. Also see Burdon, *The New Dominion;* James Edwards, *Riot 1932* (Christchurch, 1974); Erik Olssen, *A History of Otago* and *John A. Lee* (Dunedin, 1974). Autobiographies are especially helpful, particularly Janet Frame, *To the Is-Land* (Auckland, 1982), and Ruth Park, *Fence around the Cuckoo* (Auckland, 1992).

On the first Labor government and the erection of the welfare state see Elizabeth Hanson, *The Politics of Social Security: The 1938 Act and Some Later Developments* (Auckland, 1980); Burdon, *The New Dominion;* Barry Gustafson, *From the Cradle to the Grave: A Biography of Michael Joseph Savage* (Auckland, 1986); Michael King, *Te Puea;* Erik Olssen, *John A. Lee;* and Keith Sinclair, *Walter Nash* (Auckland, 1976). Ian Carter, *Gadfly: The Life and Times of James Shelley* (Auckland, 1993), adds much on the cultural initiatives and experiments in broadcasting undertaken by Labor, as does Rachel Barrowman, *A Popular Vision: The Arts and the Left in New Zealand, 1930–1950* (Wellington, 1991). Michael Bassett and Michael King's biography of Peter Fraser, *The Song Remains the Same* (Auckland, 2000), untangles the complex politics of this period, along with the other political biographies mentioned above. David Thomson, *Selfish Generations? The Ageing of New*

Zealand's Welfare State (Wellington, 1991), argues somewhat controversially that the welfare state created by the generation covered in this chapter became a nightmare for subsequent generations. Margaret McClure, *A Civilised Community: A History of Social Security in New Zealand 1898–1998* (Auckland, 1998), and Bronwyn Dalley, *Family Matters: Child Welfare in Twentieth Century New Zealand* (Auckland, 1998), both examine the innovations of the 1930s within a longer time frame. Key novels include Robin Hyde, *The Godwits Fly* (London, 1938), and John Mulgan, *Man Alone* (London, 1939).

The best coverage of military involvement in the Second World War is once again provided by Ian McGibbon, ed., *The Oxford Companion to New Zealand Military History.* There is also a useful collection of essays in John Crawford, ed., *Kia Kaha: New Zealand in the Second World War* (Auckland, 2000). For the enthusiast there are numerous official histories of campaigns and battalions written by the War History Branch, such as N. C. Phillips, *Italy, Volume 1, The Sangro to Cassino* (Wellington, 1957), and Robin Kay, *Italy Volume 2, From Casino to Trieste* (Wellington, 1967). John McLeod, *Myth and Reality: The New Zealand Soldier in World War II* (Auckland, 1986), attempts some revision of New Zealand's proud military record, and Dan Davin, *The Salamander and the Fire: Collected War Stories* (Auckland, 1986), catches the feel of the New Zealand experience.

On the home front see Deborah Montgomerie, *The Women's War: New Zealand Women, 1939–45* (Auckland, 2001), Lauris Edmond, ed., *Women in Wartime: New Zealand Women Tell Their Story* (Wellington, 1986), and Nancy M. Taylor, *The Home Front, New Zealand in the Second World War 1939–45*, 2 vols. (Wellington, 1986). David Grant, *Out in the Cold: Pacifists and Conscientious Objectors in New Zealand during World War Two* (Auckland, 1986), tells the story of opponents of the war effort. Gaylene Preston's wonderful film, *War Stories Our Mothers Never Told Us*, evokes the Second World War story as well as anything else, but the Communicado series, New Zealanders at War, is very uneven and frequently inaccurate.

There is no major study of the immediate postwar period, but Keith Sinclair's *Walter Nash*, Erik Olssen's *John A. Lee*, and Michael Bassett's *The Song Remains the Same* cover the politics adequately. The major study of the 1951 waterfront strike is Michael Bassett, *Confrontation 51: The 1951 Waterfront Dispute* (Wellington, 1972). C. K. Stead's novel, *All Visitors Ashore* (Auckland, 1984), catches the feel of the time, as does the second of Janet Frame's autobiographies, *An Angel at My Table.* On postwar New Zealand in general see Part IV of W. H. Oliver and B. R. Williams, eds., *The Oxford History of New Zealand.* On the economy see J. D. Gould, *The Rake's Progress? The New Zealand Economy since 1945* (Auckland, 1982). Margaret

Clarke, ed., *Sir Keith Holyoake: Towards a Political Biography* (Wellington, 1997), helps explain National's dominance of politics in the 1950s and 1960s.

On social change see David Bedggood, *Rich and Poor in New Zealand* (Auckland, 1980), Brian Easton, *Income Distribution in New Zealand* (Wellington, 1983), and Brian Easton, *Wages and the Poor* (Wellington, 1986). Michael King's superb biographies, *Sargeson: A Life* (Auckland, 1995), and *Wrestling with the Angel: A Life of Janet Frame* (Auckland, 2000), make clear the enormous difficulties overcome by our writers, as does W. H. Oliver's biography of a leading poet, *James K. Baxter* (Wellington, 1983). On the Maori Women's Welfare League see Miria Simpson and Anna Rogers, *Early Stories from the Maori Women's Welfare League as told to Mira Szazy* (Wellington, 1993), and Michael King, *Whina* (Auckland, 1983). On Maori struggles in adjusting to urban life see Ranginui Walker, *Nga Tau Tohetohe: Years of Anger* (Auckland, 1987), and *Ka Whawhai Tonu Matou: Struggle without End* (Auckland, 1990). Witi Ihimaera's (author of the story on which the movie *Whale Rider* is based) short stories *Pounmau, Pounamu* (Auckland, 1972), and Patricia Grace's novel *Cousins* (Auckland, 1992), catch the difficulties involved in changing from a rural to an urban people. Erik Schwimmer, ed., *The Maori People in the Nineteen-Sixties* (Auckland, 1968), is a useful collection for learning about the aspirations of both Maori and Pakeha politicians and bureaucrats at that time.

On Muldoonism see Barry Gustafson, *His Way: A Biography of Robert Muldoon* (Auckland, 2000), J. D. Gould, *The Muldoon Years: An Essay on New Zealand's Recent Economic Growth* (Auckland, 1985), and Ian Wards, ed., *Thirteen Facets* (Wellington, 1978).

On second-wave feminism see Sandra Coney, *Standing in the Sunshine*, (Auckland 1993); Christine Dann, *Up from Under: Women and Liberation in New Zealand, 1970–1985* (Wellington, 1985); Sonja Davies' autobiography, *Bread and Roses* (Auckland, 1984); Maude Cahill and Christine Dann, eds., *Changing Our Lives: Women Working in the Women's Liberation Movement, 1970–1990* (Wellington, 1991); and Caroline Daley and Deborah Montgomerie, *The Gendered Kiwi* (Auckland, 1999).

On the causes of the big shifts from 1984 see Colin James, *The Quiet Revolution: Turbulence and Transition in Contemporary New Zealand* (Wellington, 1986), which is sympathetic toward these big shifts. Bruce Jesson, *Behind the Mirror Glass: The Growth of Wealth and Power in New Zealand in the Eighties* (Auckland, 1987), presents a much more critical view. Brian Easton, *In Stormy Seas: The Post War New Zealand Economy* (Dunedin, 1997), provides up-to-date coverage of the radical reforms of the late 1980s and early 1990s. Jane Kelsey questions their worth in *The New Zealand Exper-*

iment: A World Model for Structural Adjustment? (Auckland, 1995). A fascinating insider justification is provided by Richard Prebble in *I've Been Thinking* (Auckland, 1996). Anne Else, *False Economy* (Auckland, 1996), provides a feminist critique of new right policies and argues that there is no economy without community. Bruce Jesson, *Only Their Purpose Is Mad: The Moneymakers Take Over New Zealand* (Palmerston North, 1999), updates his critique of new right policies and their impact, as does Paul Dalziel and Ralph Lattimore, *The New Zealand Macro Economy: A Briefing on the Reforms*, 4th ed. (Auckland, 2002).

On Maori responses to these changes and use of the Waitangi Tribunal to settle grievances see George Asher and David Naulls, *Maori Land* (Wellington, 1987). Donna Awatere, *Maori Sovereignty* (Auckland, 1984), remains a provocative classic statement of radical Maori opinion. Witi Ihimaera and D. S. Long. eds., *Into the World of Light: An Anthology of Maori Writing* (Auckland, 1982), is still the best introduction to Maori writing.

Michael King, *Maori: A Photographic and Social History* (Auckland, 1983, reissued 1997), was controversial when published but still contains striking images of Maori history. His *Being Pakeha* (Auckland, 1988), provides an insight into Pakeha response to Maori cultural assertion. Sidney Moko Mead, ed., *Te Maori: Maori Art from New Zealand Collections* (Auckland, 1984), catches the look and feel of the exhibition. Hiwi Tauroa (former race relations conciliator), *Race against Time* (Wellington, 1982), stresses the urgency of the many race relations problems confronting New Zealand. Ranganui Walker, *The Years of Anger* (Auckland, 1987) and *Ka Whawhai Tonu Matou: The Struggle Is without End* (Auckland, 1990), assert the Maori point of view concerning developments in the 1980s. Andrew Sharp, *Justice and the Maori. Maori Claims in New Zealand Political Arguments in the 1980s* (Auckland, 1990), is very helpful on the setting up and early work of the Waitangi Tribunal. So too is W. H. Oliver, *Claims to the Waitangi Tribunal* (Wellington: Department of Justice, 1991). William Renwick, ed., *Sovereignty and Indigenous Rights: The Treaty of Waitangi in International Context* (Wellington, 1991), places the New Zealand story in a broader global context. To understand how the failure to provide adequate reserves forced marginalization upon the southern section of Ngai Tahu, see Bill Dacker, *Te Maemae me te Aroha: The Pain and the Love: History of Kai Tahu Whanui in Otago* (Dunedin, 1994). Similarly, the reissue of Pei Te Hurunui Jones, *Nga Iwi o Tainui: The Traditional History of the Tainui People*, edited and annotated by Bruce Biggs (Auckland, 1995), provides vital background material on the Tainui claim and explains the bitterness felt over confiscated land *(raupatu)*. Real enthusiasts will find the various reports on the claims, especially those relating to Ngai Tahu, Tainui, and Taranaki, extremely rich sources of information. Two matching books provide an interesting survey of both Pakeha and Maori views on Maori sovereignty and reveal a surprising degree of tolerance on both sides. See Hirini Melbourne, *Maori Sovereignty: The Maori Perspective;* and Carol Archie, *Maori Sovereignty: The Pakeha Perspective* (both Auckland, 1995). This hopeful tone is offset by Stuart C. Scott, *The Travesty of Waitangi* (Dunedin, 1995). This is the most carelessly researched book to be published in New Zealand for a very long time, but reveals much about the pathology and fears of late-twentieth-century Pakeha. Its success (it sold over 12,000 copies) suggests that much fear and ignorance has to be overcome before the process of reconciliation and reparation is complete.

For useful updates on recent happenings in Maoridom, especially in relation to treaty matters, see Mason Durie, *Te Mana, Te Kawanatanga: The Politics of Maori Self-Determination* (Auckland, 1998), and Alan Ward, *An Unsettled History: Treaty Claims in New Zealand Today* (Wellington, 1999).

Index

About the Author

TOM BROOKING is Associate Professor of History at the University of Otago in Dunedin, New Zealand. He specializes in New Zealand and comparative rural and environmental history and has published five books and numerous book chapters, essays, and articles.

Other Titles in the Greenwood Histories of the Modern Nations
Frank W. Thackeray and John E. Findling, Series Editors

The History of Argentina
Daniel K. Lewis

The History of Australia
Frank G. Clarke

The History of Brazil
Robert M. Levine

The History of the Baltic States
Kevin O'Connor

The History of Canada
Scott W. See

The History of Chile
John L. Rector

The History of China
David C. Wright

The History of Congo
Didier Gondola

The History of Cuba
Clifford L. Staten

The History of France
W. Scott Haine

The History of Germany
Eleanor L. Turk

The History of Holland
Mark T. Hooker

The History of India
John McLeod

The History of Iran
Elton L. Daniel

The History of Ireland
Daniel Webster Hollis III

The History of Israel
Arnold Blumberg

The History of Italy
Charles L. Killinger

The History of Japan
Louis G. Perez

The History of Mexico
Burton Kirkwood

The History of Nigeria
Toyin Falola

The History of Poland
M. B. Biskupski

The History of Portugal
James M. Anderson

The History of Russia
Charles E. Ziegler

The History of Serbia
John K. Cox

The History of South Africa
Roger B. Beck

The History of Spain
Peter Pierson

The History of Sweden
Byron J. Nordstrom

The History of Turkey
Douglas A. Howard